surrender
or
starve

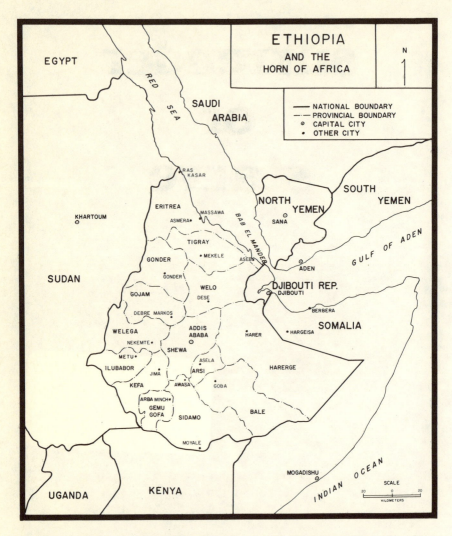

Reprinted by permission from Mulatu Wubneh and Yohannis Abate, *Ethiopia: Transition and Development in the Horn of Africa* (Boulder, Colo., Westview Press, and London, England, Avebury, 1988), p. 4.

surrender
or
starve

THE WARS BEHIND THE FAMINE

Robert D. Kaplan

Westview Press
BOULDER AND LONDON

Portions of the author's material previously published in the *New Republic,* the *Atlantic,* the *American Spectator,* and the *Wall Street Journal* have been incorporated into this book with the kind permission of the publishers.

Published in 1988 in the United States of America by Westview Press, Inc., 5500 Central Avenue, Boulder, Colorado 80301

Library of Congress Cataloging-in-Publication Data
Kaplan, Robert D.
  Surrender or starve : the wars behind the famine / Robert D.
Kaplan.
    p. cm.
  Bibliography: p.
  Includes index.
  ISBN 0-8133-0754-6
  1. Ethiopia—Politics and government—1974– . 2. Famines—Ethiopia.
3. Food supply—Ethiopia. I. Title.
DT387.95.K37 1988
963'.07—dc19   88-14363
                                                                        CIP

Printed and bound in the United States of America

The paper used in this publication meets the requirements of the American National Standard for Permanence of Paper for Printed Library Materials Z39.48-1984.

10   9   8   7   6   5   4   3   2   1

To Maria

contents

preface

Before moving to Greece in 1982, I bought several books about modern Greek politics, all but one of which were balanced, objective, and devoid of any emotion. They left me unmoved, and now are useful only as reference books to check a date or the spelling of a name. One of the books, however, was passionate, opinionated, and far more subjective than the others. The book, *Greece Without Columns* by the late British journalist David Holden, was a debunking of modern Greece as the birthplace of Western civilization. Although the book was pilloried by philhellenes, in a strange way I found it pro-Greek. It did something that none of the other, dull, predictable tomes did: it fired my imagination and made me want to know more, not less, about Greece. The following pages attempt to do the same for the Horn of Africa.

I had no intention of writing a dispassionate rehash of yesterday's headlines. Famine in the Horn is both a tool and an aspect of ethnic conflict, with the Ethiopian Amharas of the central highlands pitted against the Eritreans and Tigreans of the north. The overwhelming majority of U.S. journalists have reported on Ethiopia from one side only—that of the Amharas in Addis Ababa. I wanted to show the story from the other side, in order to redress a grievous imbalance in news coverage. If the reader finds this book polemical, be advised that I meant it that way. To get people excited, you sometimes have to light a fire, and that was my intention.

This book covers the period from late 1984 to the early part of 1987. In late 1987, the famine returned, mainly for the very reasons cited inside. The section on the media is not exhaustive. I'm sure that there were both good and bad examples of reporting that escaped my attention. However, I seriously doubt whether they would have affected the overall thrust of coverage in the 1984–1987 period.

A journalist often does little more than articulate the concepts of others. Countless diplomats, government officials, and relief workers in

Ethiopia, Sudan, Somalia, Uganda, North Yemen, and Washington, D.C., provoked my interest with what they had to say. A few, however, did more: they helped me to think about Africa and the famine in a bold, unpopular, but more realistic way, judging Africa by the same standards of moral conduct that would apply to any other part of the globe. Because many of these analysts and diplomats are in sensitive, official positions, it is better that they go unnamed. They all have one thing in common, however: they know Africa from personal experience, not from artificial notions constructed from thousands of miles away.

The title of this book is taken from a Western diplomat's remarks to Robert J. Rosenthal of the *Philadelphia Inquirer.* Sections of the book appeared as works in progress in a number of publications. I therefore wish to thank editors at the *Atlantic,* the *New Republic,* the *Wall Street Journal,* and the *American Spectator* for their encouragement. The impetus for the book arose out of reporting trips to the Horn, financed by the radio division of *ABC News,* the *Atlantic,* the *Atlanta Journal-Constitution,* and the *Toronto Globe and Mail.* A grant from the Institute for Educational Affairs of Washington, D.C., enabled me to take a year off in order to write and research the book. Whatever merit there is on the following pages is partly due to all these organizations.

Robert D. Kaplan
Athens, Greece

ONE

imperial tempest

*Usually it is said that periodic droughts cause bad crops and therefore starvation.
But it is the elites of starving countries that propagate this idea. It is a false idea.
The unjust or mistaken allocation of funds or national property is the most frequent
source of hunger.*

—Ryszard Kapuscinski, *The Emperor*

*Sand has various qualities relevant to this discussion, but two of these are especially
important. The first is the smallness and sameness of its parts. . . . The second is
the endlessness of sand. It is boundless. . . . Where it appears in small heaps it is
disregarded. It is only really striking when the number of grains is infinite, as on
the sea-shore or in the desert.*

*Sand is continually shifting, and it is because of this that, as a crowd symbol,
it stands midway between the fluid and the solid symbols. It forms waves like the
sea and rises in clouds; dust is refined sand.*

—Elias Canetti, *Crowds and Power*

If the earth were really flat, northwestern Somalia would approximate
the edge. A landscape more bleak and disorienting is hard to imagine.
Not a tree looms in the distance; there are only anthills. Curtains of
dust weld desert and sky into one dun-drab pigment. The clumps of
short grass have a freeze-dried, glacial aspect, even though the equator
is only six hundred miles to the south.

As the Land Cruiser in which I am riding moves closer to the
Ethiopian border, swarms of canvas huts zoom into focus, without
warning, through the swirling dirt. The vehicle halts. The lips and
noses of refugees, who live in these huts, press against the windows.
The expressions I see through the glass are opaque; there is a particle-
like uniformity to the faces. They lack the angular, Semitic beauty and
globular eyes that television viewers normally associate with the people
of Ethiopia. The shreds of material on their backs are characterless
synthetics; not the traditional *shamma*s that make the Ethiopians of
the famine-stricken north resemble extras in a biblical epic.

1

Nor were these people, whom I had come to interview, starving. They were not Auschwitz-like sacks of bones. Had they been, the skill of television cameramen could have at least endowed them with an individuality. They were only normally malnourished and suffered from the usual roll of African diseases. Not beautiful, and not starving, these people made no impression. They were just a large mass, significant only because of their numbers. Television could do nothing with them. By the sensational standards of evening news coverage in the United States, they offered no visual drama. The only thing these people had to offer were their stories.

*   *   *

Ethiopia, as a historical and romantic concept, is a loose and wondrous fragment of the Middle East, and this group of humanity on the Somali frontier represents the more mundane African reality that always has threatened Ethiopia's romantic image. The late twentieth century in Ethiopia is little different than the late nineteenth. While Semitic Christian warlords in the northern highlands—today fighting as communists—battle for control of an ancient kingdom, the lowland underbelly of Ethiopia is teeming with Africanized Moslems, called Oromos. As opposed to the highland northerners, who, like the Jews and Arabs, are said to descend from Shem, the eldest of the sons of Noah, the Oromos, linguistically at least, trace their roots back to Ham, the youngest of Noah's progeny. Although the Oromos are the most numerous of Ethiopia's peoples, they have never really mattered, and at least until recently, they suffered less than those who did. Unlike the lives of the Amharas, Tigreans, and Eritreans of the north, the lives of the Oromos were not a continual cycle of war and drought. In fact, the Oromos of the Hararghe region, near to the border with Somalia, were relatively prosperous farmers. Joseph Stalin would have classified them as kulaks. On account of their numbers, and the food they produce, they have the capacity to support *and* to undermine the Ethiopian regime in the capital of Addis Ababa. To judge by his actions, Ethiopian leader Mengistu Haile Mariam, whose preeminent title is General Secretary of the Workers' Party of Ethiopia, evidently agrees with Stalin.

Formerly, the Oromos could be exploited, but every aspect of their daily lives could not be controlled. But now that situation has changed dramatically. Supported by the Soviet Union and the rest of the Eastern bloc to a degree unprecedented in Africa, the present leaders in Addis Ababa—Christian Amharas all—have invigorated Ethiopia's age-old despotism with modern, totalitarian techniques.

Through one of these techniques, the waves of Moslems crashing against the Christian mountain fortress has now been dammed up. The process is called "villagization," an awkward translation from Amharic that means something strikingly similar to collectivization, as originated by the Soviets after the Bolshevik Revolution. As we will later discover, the famine holocaust in Ethiopia—although resembling what transpired in Biafra in the 1960s and Cambodia in the 1970s—actually is derivative of the Stalinist experiment in the Ukraine in the 1930s, when, according to Hoover Institution scholar Robert Conquest, more people perished than had in all of World War I.

During the mid-1980s, the declared intent of the Ethiopian government was to move all the Oromos into village clusters, where Oromo labor could be better organized and the authorities more easily could provide the Oromos with essential services. Eyewitness accounts of what really happened during villagization were provided by many of the fifty thousand Oromo refugees who stampeded over the Somali border in 1986, fleeing the program's horrors. "In my life I never saw drought," exclaimed Zahara Dawit Kore, a mother of two children. "It's not from drought that we ran; we ran because of the soldiers. . . . They made us bare-handed," she told me during an interview I conducted in late October 1986. What the soldiers did to these Oromos was apparently terrible enough to spark an exodus to northwestern Somalia.

All the eyewitness accounts were basically the same; all the Oromos apparently were brutalized in a similar way. Sexual violation and religious persecution were the tools used to destroy local village culture. But listen closely and long enough—several hours for each refugee— and one discovers that despite the shared experience, each man and woman suffered in a particular way. Each account had its own characteristics. Tens of thousands of Oromos, perhaps more, suffered, but each differently.

Fatma Abdullah Ahmed, the mother of four children, had buck teeth. The top of her head was covered with a cheap orange shawl, and in her hand she held a string of prayer beads. The trouble for Mrs. Ahmed began in late 1984, when U.S. citizens began a massive outpouring of aid to famine victims in another part of Ethiopia, in response to dramatic television pictures and pleas for help from the Mengistu government. Flies buzzed around Mrs. Ahmed's lips as she spoke.

I am from the village of Bakallan, near Babile, where there was no *abar* [drought], only oppression. When the Amhara soldiers first came to our village they destroyed the school and took all the children—about a thousand—to another school, twelve hours east by foot in Abdur Kader, near Arrir. The soldiers said it was a better school. On Saturdays and Sundays the children were allowed to walk home.

Later the soldiers came again. My family had four goats and eight oxes. The soldiers slaughtered the big oxes and ate them. We had to pay the soldiers 12 birr every week to guard the smaller ones. Some of our neighbors had cows. There were several Christians in our area. The soldiers made the Christians slaughter the cows of the Moslems, and the Moslems those of the Christians. This was against our tradition.

The soldiers explained that socialism meant that everything had to be shared equally. They ordered every wife in the village to sleep with another husband, not her own. We were afraid. We told them we accepted, but we didn't do it. So the soldiers made intercourse compulsory. Then went into every *gambisa* [mud hut] to watch. They said, "Do it, do it." Those who did not were beaten with fists. The prettiest girls were taken by the soldiers. Our own soldiers [Oromos recruited into the national army] were just as bad as the Amharas: you see, these Oromos were not from our area.

The soldiers said no one could read the Koran, because it is Arab politics. The mosque was turned into an office for the soldiers. Seventeen sheikhs in the area were shot; each was the leader of a farmers' group. Their hands and feet were bound and they were buried in one long trench. The soldiers used a *dozer* [bulldozer] to fill in the dirt.

Then [in late 1985, a year after the school was destroyed] our maize was collected by the soldiers and taken for storage. We never saw it again. Party cadres destroyed our *gambisata* [mud huts]. The smaller oxes and the goats were killed. The soldiers had cameras. Like white people, the Amharas are always taking pictures.

We were marched three hours by foot eastward where we were made to build new *gambisata* in a straight line. The new town was called Gamaju [Oromo for gladness]. Unlike Bakallan, there was no water nearby. We had to walk a long way for water. We worked from dawn till dusk planting yams and maize. The men were taken every day to work in a place called Unity farm. We were hungry and complained to the soldiers. They said, "Eat your flesh." Vehicles came daily to bring food to the soldiers. Occasionally, they would give biscuits to the women they had raped. . . .

[In late February 1986] we escaped after midnight. It was raining and there were no stars. We ran from the few soldiers who were not sleeping. There were many of us. The men carried the children. After walking through the night we spent the day at Dakata, a place the Ethiopian soldiers were afraid to go because it was frequented by the WSLF [Western Somali Liberation Front]. . . . The second afternoon the Ethiopian soldiers found us at the end of a forest. We all ran. Nine were caught. . . . The eighth night [in March 1986] we crossed the border. We are afraid to go back. It is better to die here.

Mrs. Ahmed's new home was a tent in the Oromo refugee camp of Tug Wajale B, which was due west of the Somali town of Hargeisa and five miles from the Ethiopian border. At the end of 1986, the camp was a breeding ground for scurvy, hepatitis, relapsing fever, tuberculosis, cholera, pneumonia, diarrhea, and conjunctivitis. Only malaria, usually the most common illness in black Africa, was surprisingly rare. International relief officials were embarrassed about the sanitation situation at the camp. The smell of ordure was all around; wherever one looked, people were defecating. But the refugees at Tug Wajale B complained less than had those at better equipped camps I visited. Indeed, explained Halima Muhumed Abdi, another mother of four, "all this is nothing compared to the disaster that we've suffered."

The fifty thousand Oromo refugees were among the 3 million "villagized," according to the Ethiopian government's own reckoning. But the collectivization of the Oromos never registered on the U.S. consciousness. Although the major U.S. newspapers all published at least one article about the Oromos' situation, the people at Tug Wajale B never made the news on any of the three major networks in the United States. Not only didn't Tug Wajale have good visual possibilities for television, but its story unfolded too late, occurring in 1986, after the famine had peaked and interest in the Oromos' situation had gone into remission. The few U.S. journalists who did make the journey to the Somali-Ethiopian border tended to emphasize the awful conditions of the camp, rather than what had driven the refugees there in the first place.

The U.S. Embassy in Addis Ababa was roused into action not by anything the media uncovered, but as a result of interviews with the refugees, conducted several months before I visited Tug Wajale, by Jason W. Clay, the research director of Cultural Survival, an independent human rights organization based at Harvard University. The embassy investigated the matter of human rights violation against the Oromos to the greatest degree possible, given the restrictive conditions in a country that, more than any other in Africa, approximated the Soviet model. The investigation drew a blank; it could neither confirm nor confute the refugees' horror stories. "We will never really know the truth about villagization," the administrator of the U.S. Agency for International Development (USAID), M. Peter McPherson, admitted to me. The issue died before it was ever raised, lost in a heap of other cruelties for which the West had no independent confirmation.

In the final analysis, the accounts given by the refugees made little impact. The road to the edge of the earth never became well trodden. Eventually, many of the Oromos were moved out of Tug Wajale and dispersed to other camps strung out along the Ethiopian border. Sand covered their tracks.

*   *   *

"There is an air of nightmarish fantasy about affairs in Ethiopia," wrote Alan Moorehead in *The Blue Nile,* referring to events of the late eighteenth century. But as the refugees' stories indicate, the "medieval melodrama" has been heightened by a chilling, twentieth century thoroughness and precision. Progress, as so often happens, has been inverted by ideology; the passions that stir the rulers of present-day Ethiopia are perhaps even more difficult for a middle class, Western mind to grasp than those of tyrants from previous epochs. It is doubtful whether the U.S. public understands Ethiopia, Sudan, or the rest of Africa much better now than it did before the famine emergency started in October 1984. Beginning then and continuing through the middle of 1985, the public was bombarded with images of people starving in an exotic land, images that gripped viewers by the throat and elicited a more emotional audience response than had occurred in relation to any other foreign news story of recent years. The result was that U.S. citizens and their government flooded Ethiopia and neighboring Sudan with aid, the procurement, use, and misuse of which provided the media with most of their story. It was, in short, a U.S. story, about U.S. involvement in Africa.

But that was only the external side of the drama. The internal dimension—famine as a manipulated consequence of war and ethnic strife—was passed over. Newspapers and television left unwritten and unfilmed what both media initially were designed to capture: history in the making. A country in Africa, the first to do so, was in the long, bloody process of converting to communism—as completely as had Cuba and Vietnam. The architects of this transformation, as we shall discover, were encountering stiff resistance from guerrillas who were better trained and inflicted more damage in bigger battles than did similar groups in southern Africa and Central America. This was not, in the parlance of old Africa hands, just another "*bongo* war." The technical and organizational abilities of the combatants, who were beneficiaries of the only culture in black Africa with a written language that went back two thousand years, resulted in masterfully fought, albeit ignored, set-piece battles involving tanks and fighter jets. War and the mass population movements it engendered were the main features of the Ethiopian landscape. Ethiopia was reenacting the experience of Soviet Russia in the years following the overthrow of the czar, when the new communist rulers battled a host of rebel armies in order to maintain a reactionary nineteenth century empire. Famine, as in USSR, was a partial consequence of this historic struggle. But almost none of this got through to the U.S. audience. The media were more interested in the politics of relief agencies than in the politics of Ethiopia.

The U.S. public was left only with images: of charming, suffering people, whose awesome physical beauty was being graphically savaged by what appeared to be an act of God. Drought, according to those first, memorable media reports, was the villain, and if anyone was to blame, it was the overfed West. Predictably, the Reagan administration caught more flak in the early stages of the emergency than did Ethiopia's own government. Giving food, for individual U.S. citizens as well as for the administration, thus became a convenient means to expunge guilt. As the weeks wore on, however, the media began to paint a more complicated picture. Famine, it emerged, was not just an act of God, but an act of humans too. As more and more revelations came out about Ethiopian government misconduct, the U.S. public began to feel cheated; its penitent offerings of food were not really all that was required. By this time, however, the story was slipping away. The novelty value was gone. Other people and events were crowding in and competing for the sympathy and understanding of the U.S. television audience: hostages taken from a TWA plane in Beirut, blacks fighting for their freedom in South Africa, Nicaraguans reeling from the blows of repression and civil war. Just as the famine emergency was changing gears—moving from a charity issue to a deeply political issue—it began to fade. A fog of bewilderment remained.

The images on the television screen shocked, but they didn't clarify. For all their horror, the images did not reveal to the U.S. public the intrigues and bloody conquests that were behind this suffering. Nor did the images reveal themselves as the result of Marxism and Amhara misanthropy. (Donald L. Levine, in his landmark study of Ethiopian culture, *Wax and Gold,* wrote that the Amhara "suffers from no illusions about homo sapiens at his best—unless they are dark illusions. . . . The generic word for 'man' in Amharic, *saw,* is the subject of a number of negative associations. . . . One may say that the Amhara's view of human nature is dominated by his perception of man's inherent aggressiveness and unworthiness.") Thus, the U.S. public, sitting in front of television screens, was ignorant of the world from which the strange and disturbing images had sprung.

* * *

The Oromos stranded on the Somali plateau were but a symptom of their times. In the mid-1980s, Ethiopia evoked a scene out of Boris Pasternak; millions were displaced, often caught between rival armies, and on the move. They crossed a landscape of jagged mountain peaks and flaming sulfur deserts. In the extreme north, more than one hundred fifty thousand Ethiopian army troops were battling thirty-five thousand Eritrean guerrillas in a war that has witnessed the largest infusion of Soviet arms in all of Africa and—a few other cases aside—all of the Third World. In the neighboring province of Tigre, fifteen thousand self-declared Marxist rebels were fighting an insurgency against the government, which responded by burning crops and bombing village markets from the air. Other, smaller rebel outfits in Gondar, Wollo, and elsewhere also were tearing away at Mengistu's army. According to Western diplomats, as quoted in a January 6, 1985, article in the *New York Times* by correspondent Clifford D. May, approximately twenty-five rebel organizations were active in Ethiopia. As a means to clear strategic swaths of the northern countryside of supposedly hostile concentrations of civilians, hundreds of thousands of highlanders were resettled in mosquito-infested swamps of the jungly southwest, where these highlanders were placed under the brutal supervision of Marxist cadres. Rather than risk being taken for resettlement at government feeding centers, hundreds of thousands of other famine-stricken people, mostly Tigreans, trekked westward for weeks on foot to refugee camps inside the Sudanese border. In southern Ethiopia, the Oromo Liberation Front (OLF) was active, which was one of several, obvious motives the government had for villagizing the Oromos. The fifty thousand Oromos in Somalia were a fragment of that particular convulsion.

Ethiopia, when the U.S. television audience discovered it in late October 1984, was not so much a country as an empire in the throes of dismemberment. It had startling similarities with contemporary El Salvador and Afghanistan, not to mention Pol Pot's Cambodia and the Soviet Union under V. I. Lenin and Joseph Stalin. Nevertheless, this age-old Christian-dominated state on the Horn of Africa had its own, grim method of dealing with its subjects: "surrender or starve."

*   *   *

The spectacle of blood and starvation—a spectacle that is unprecedented, even by the inhuman standards of Ethiopia's own past—continues to present the United States with one of its most compelling foreign policy challenges in the Third World since the start of the cold war. Yet U.S. policy toward Ethiopia—massive grain deliveries notwithstanding—is as calcified as ever. The nationalist aspirations of the Eritreans are ignored, even though this is an underlying cause of hunger in the north of the country. The media, despite a surfeit of famine coverage, much of it repetitive, rarely reported in depth on official

U.S. attitudes toward the nationalist aspirations of the Eritreans and other insurgent groups.

A hungry child may know no politics, as the U.S. government slogan proclaims, but politics—in Ethiopia and in the world at large—is really why that child is hungry. Every day, the gap widens between the number of people in Ethiopia and the amount of food produced there. Experts foresee a much greater famine in the 1990s. Aid is simply not effective in the face of regimes that do not have to ensure the well-being of their subjects in order to stay in power.

Less proximate than Nicaragua, less crucial than Iran (although just as populous), Ethiopia still remains one of the few big pieces that the USSR has managed to knock off the U.S. side of the board. Located at the entrance to the Red Sea through which more and more of the free world's oil must pass, Ethiopia is truly strategic. Like Nicaragua and Iran, Ethiopia was lost while Jimmy Carter was president. The Carter State Department counseled restraint. After all, Moscow's clumsy and brazen gambit to grab Ethiopia was certain to fail; unlike Iran, Ethiopia's revolution was not anti-U.S. The Ethiopians, who never had been colonized, had a habit of ejecting foreigners and surely would want to do so again, so the logic of the liberals went. In a sense, they were right: Soviet influence is universally despised by the Ethiopian people. But even more so than in other places in the Third World, Ethiopia is a *thugocracy:* thugs run it, and only what they think and feel counts. The Soviets, therefore, were not ejected. To ever believe that they would have been was incredibly naive.

Thugs get overthrown in Africa. Ethiopia, however, is different. Here the Soviets have implanted not only their influence, but their entire system and security apparatus as well. In the midst of the famine, with the media preoccupied with relief politics, Ethiopia converted its "provisional military" government to a "socialist democracy." Socialist democracies are less easily dismantled. Cuba and Vietnam prove the point.

With grain alone, "you're not going to charm a Stalinist oriented government out of its dependence on the Soviet Union," the assistant secretary of state for African affairs, Chester Crocker, said to me. Although the Reagan administration was more realistic about Ethiopia than was the Carter administration, the former did precious little with its realism. If ever a Third World country were a candidate for the Reagan Doctrine, it is Ethiopia.

*   *   *

But Ethiopian politics plays to an empty house in the United States. There is no personality to capture the crowd's attention. Lieutenant

Colonel Mengistu Haile Mariam has proved himself to be more ruthless and more cunning than either Muammar Gaddafi or Ayatollah Khomeini. By the standards of several human rights reports, Mengistu is the world's cruelest leader. But like many communist rulers, he is a faceless bureaucrat. The vast majority of the U.S. populace wouldn't even recognize him.

Mengistu had a predecessor whose face was known throughout the world—Haile Selassie. To many, Ethiopia—a Greek word meaning the land of the "burned faces"—still brings to mind that other image in addition to the one of the starving child: Haile Selassie, the little dark man with the beard, as small as he was larger than life. To understand the world of the starving child, one must first flesh out the quaint image of the storybook emperor.

He is like some figure out of a dream. Clad in cape and pith helmet, or bedecked with medals, Emperor Haile Selassie I, *Negus Negusti* (King of Kings), Conquering Lion of Judah, Elect of God, appears in our minds in a series of flashes, each only a few seconds long, separated not only by years but also by decades. On June 30, 1936, at the League of Nations in Geneva, he wore a black cape over a white tunic and pleaded from the rostrum for help against Benito Mussolini, whose fascist Italian army had invaded the primitive land of Ethiopia with tanks and poison gas. No help ever came. Henceforth, the emperor always would be enshrouded in sympathy, part of the West's guilty conscience, the face of a people whom the democracies had failed. In January 1941, he is back again. This time the face is half buried under an oversized pith helmet, the beard jutting out from beneath, more prominent than ever. The emperor has crossed the border from Sudan to regain his kingdom; here he is quixotic, yet on the verge of real triumph. At his side, increasing the aura of romance, is Orde Wingate, the British major and savant of the Old Testament. Wingate is himself a man of near-legend, who later will die in the jungles of Burma fighting the Japanese, but not before he has trained the Jewish army in Palestine, giving Moshe Dayan his most valuable lessons in the art of warfare. Finally, there is November 25, 1963, the first memory I and many of my generation have of Haile Selassie. President John Kennedy's coffin is passing through the streets of Washington, D.C., and dignitaries from around the world are escorting the caisson. The emperor, in full military regalia, is there. He marches near Charles de Gaulle, the tallness of one highlighting the shortness of the other. What a sight! So small and seemingly vulnerable, yet so proud and full of authority. Millions of Americans, glued to their television sets that weekend, always will remember the marching emperor. Haile Selassie signified not only a distant, fairy-tale kingdom, but the very world beyond the United States and Europe in all its diversity. Had the turbaned wise men from the East come to pay homage to the dead young president, it would have been only slightly more impressive.

The truth about Haile Selassie is that, like the little, medal-bedecked man on the television screen, he really was an emperor, and like any absolute monarch, he required a large dose of cruelty to keep his throne and the empire that went with it. The images on television and in the newsreels didn't lie. The deception was the viewer's. The U.S. public was so dazzled with the spectacle that no one thought to look beyond it, or even closely at it. Why bother? After all, he was pro-U.S. He was seeking to modernize his country. Ethiopia was so far away that it barely seemed real. Haile Selassie's last appearance in our collective memories was almost a quarter century ago. Communications satellites didn't yet exist. Whatever sins the emperor did commit were years away from being effectively brought into Western living rooms.

The official U.S. attitude toward Ethiopia was similarly indulgent. The emperor welcomed the United States, granting permission for a military communications complex near Asmara, the capital of Eritrea, so naturally the United States supported him. The evils of his rule certainly were well known to U.S. policymakers, and generous economic aid from Washington was designed to mitigate the suffering of the Ethiopian masses. But beyond that, U.S. officials, as with most everybody else, preferred not to criticize. Pushing for reform would have been like tinkering with the divine order. We all stood in awe of Haile Selassie. C. L. Sulzberger, chief foreign correspondent of the *New York Times,* related in his memoirs that he bowed three times when meeting the emperor in 1952. Unlike other African leaders, Haile Selassie was not looked down on by Westerners, either in cultural or racial terms.

As strange and primitive as Ethiopia was, it had a distinctly Middle Eastern flavor, with vague bridges to the West. Although the faces of the people were black, their sharp features were not altogether African. The emperor claimed descent from the Hebrew King Solomon and the Yemeni Queen of Sheba, and like the old imam of Yemen, the emperor kept lions as pets. Ethiopian names had a Hebraic ring, and there were a significant number of Jews, known disparagingly as *falasha*s (strangers), among the northern rural population. The Christian religion of Ethiopia, like the written language, went back to antiquity and was heavily grounded in the Pentateuch. During the five-year Italian occupation of Addis Ababa (1936–1941), several members of the royal family spent their exile in Jerusalem. There was a biblical dimension to Ethiopia that not even modern Israel could claim. Ethiopia's roots as an empire were deep and reached back to Roman times when it was forged by tribespeople from southern Arabia. Ethiopia was not some artificially created African state, whose boundaries had been drawn up on the spur of the moment by a group of European powers. The emperor had been in a position of power since 1916. Coup watching was not a pastime of the diplomatic circuit in Addis Ababa the way it was elsewhere on the continent.

Blinded by the armor of tradition, few noticed that the portrait of power was flawed, and that cracks were opening up on the canvas. The noble bearing and the stern, impassive gaze were not a result of high birth, but of race. Haile Selassie was an Amhara. Rich or poor to the point of starving, Amharas see themselves as born to the purple: millions have the emperor's piercing eyes. "Being an Amhara is . . . belonging to a superior category of human beings. This is not simple ethnocentrism; it reflects rather a basically aristocratic orientation," wrote Levine in *Wax and Gold*. Amharas account for only about one-fourth of Ethiopia's 42 million people, yet have imposed their rule over the whole population. To the world, Haile Selassie represented Ethiopia. But to the large majority of Ethiopians, Haile Selassie was an Amhara imperialist, with no more, nor less, popular legitimacy than that given to the British viceroy in India during the last phase of the Raj. The borders of this Amhara empire had been drawn in the late nineteenth century by Haile Selassie's predecessor, Emperor Menelik II, whose armies swept out of their home province of Shoa to subjugate the more populous Oromo kingdoms in the south and southeast. In the north, Menelik stopped the advance of the Italian army—the best-equipped colonial force in Africa—which had marched out of Eritrea to conquer all Ethiopia. The Battle of Adowa, which took place on a Sunday, March 1, 1896, marked the first time that an African army ever had defeated a European one. The empire that Menelik bequeathed to his descendants—modern-day Ethiopia—was larger than Texas, Oklahoma, and New Mexico combined.

Along with the Thais, the North Yemenis, and the Afghans, the Ethiopian Amharas never have been truly colonized. Their national institutions and cultural patterns have been subverted only twice—by the Italian fascists, from 1936 till 1941, and by the Soviet communists, from the late 1970s until the present.

Ethiopians who are not Amharas, especially Eritreans, interpret this history differently. In a sense, not only were the Italians defeated at Adowa in 1896, but the Eritreans were, too. Eritreans made up a significant part of Italy's sixteen-thousand-troop invasion force, and one thousand Eritreans were taken prisoner by Menelik, who ordered that their right hands and left feet be cut off. For Menelik, the Eritreans were traitors. For the Eritreans, Menelik was a colonialist, more dangerous than the Italians because he was on Eritrea's border. Almost forty years later, when another Italian army, a fascist one, advanced into Ethiopia, scimitar-wielding Eritrean irregulars were in the front lines; the world may have sympathized with Haile Selassie against Mussolini, but much of Ethiopia's own population did not. The 1935 Italian invasion, coming as it did during the rise of fascism in Europe and as a prelude to World War II, is remembered for the sickening newsreel images of a white European army, equipped with the most lethal modern weaponry, brutalizing a primitive black African nation. But the images were partly false. Many of the white soldiers not shown on the screen were black; they were Eritreans and others for whom the Amharas of Haile Selassie were the true enemy.

Likewise, the emperor's triumphant return from exile in 1941, which was applauded by the Allies, sparked fear and bitterness in much of his own country. As historian Anthony Mockler related in *Haile Selassie's War: The Italian-Ethiopian Campaign, 1935–1941,* the British actually debated whether it was wise to let the emperor return at all. According to Mockler, the Foreign Office in London "always questioned the wisdom of restoring Haile Selassie" to the throne because many in Ethiopia "wished to be free of Amhara rule" and might not rally around the emperor to throw out Mussolini's forces. Haile Selassie's eventual role in the liberation was as a figurehead really; British officers planned and led the assault on the Italian army in Ethiopia. In Mockler's book, there is a photograph of Selassie and Wingate hunched over a map "in a symbolically accurate pose—with Orde Wingate laying down the law . . . and Haile Selassie looking neat and impressive."

Once he was back on the throne after the war, the emperor tried moving the clock forward and backward at the same time. The country was opened to foreign investment, and thousands of students were sent abroad for an education. But the style of rule remained anchored in another era. When the students returned, armed with new ideas and insights from their stays in the United States and Europe, they didn't like what they saw. One of them, Germame Neway, a graduate of Columbia University in New York City, influenced his brother in the imperial bodyguard to attempt a coup on December 14, 1960. The coup failed, but the grumbling, especially among the students, no longer could be suppressed, and a decade of protest set in.

In late 1961, Eritrea rose in revolt. By the time Haile Selassie came to Washington in 1963 to pay his respects to a slain U.S. president, he was a monarch at war, whose power was in steep decline. On the day that President Kennedy was buried, the majestic figure of the marching emperor was more appropriate to the United States than to Ethiopia.

Haile Selassie's psychological isolation from the forces of upheaval gathering outside the palace was documented by Polish journalist Ryszard Kapuscinski in *The Emperor*. Critics saw *The Emperor,* which was first published in 1978 and was loaded with the piercing irony common to the best dissident writing, as an allegory for the situation in Kapuscinski's native Poland prior to the eruption of the Solidarity trade union movement. An Eastern European writer was at an advantage in Ethiopia during the 1970s: the revolutionary process that toppled and killed Haile Selassie was a story more familiar to a Pole or a Russian than to an African. Kapuscinski was able to paint a portrait of an emperor who was not simply at war with one segment of the population but was a monarch at war with reality.

The Emperor, however, listened to neither the aristocratic grumbling nor the university whispers, believing as he did that all extremes are harmful and unnatural. Demonstrating innate concern and foresight, the Emperor widened the scope of his power and involved himself in new domains, manifesting these new interests by introducing the Hour of Development, the International Hour, and the Army-Police Hour, between four and seven in the afternoon. With the same goals in mind, the Emperor created appropriate ministries and bureaus, branch offices, and commissions, into which he introduced hosts of new people, well-behaved, loyal, devoted. A new generation filled the Palace, energetically carving out careers.

*   *   *

The story began with the 1973–1974 famine in Tigre and Wollo. Except for its severity—an estimated two hundred thousand peasants starved to death—there was little that was unusual about this famine. Like the five previous ones that had devastated Ethiopia since Haile Selassie assumed power in 1916, this famine took place in the north; an area that the Amhara emperor had a strategic interest in keeping underdeveloped, on account of Amhara historical conflicts with the Eritreans and Tigreans. A feudal landowning system, an absence of investment, crippling taxation, and drought were the causes of the famine. As far as the palace was concerned, there was nothing to be alarmed about. According to Kapuscinski,

Death from hunger had existed in our Empire for hundreds of years, an everyday natural thing, and it never occurred to anyone to make any noise about it. Drought would come and the earth would dry up, the cattle would drop dead, the peasants would starve. Ordinary, in accordance with the laws of nature and the eternal order of things . . . none of the dignitaries would dare to bother His Most Exalted Highness with the news that in such and such a province a given person had died of hunger.

In late 1973 there was one difference, however. Between the 1960s famine and the one in the 1970s, television coverage of overseas events finally had come into its own—encouraged no doubt by the intervening Vietnam War. British reporter Jonathan Dimbleby's film on the famine, *The Unknown Famine,* of course was not broadcast in Ethiopia, but information about the film filtered back to radicals in Addis Ababa, thereby fostering a strong empathy on their part for the starving peasants up north. A similar bond had eluded Russian revolutionaries until the beginning of this century. In Poland, the convergence of workers and intellectuals into one movement was crucial to Solidarity's initial success. But in Africa, where radicals tend to come from an urban elite that knows, cares, and thinks little about the countryside and the peasants in it, such a development is unusual.

As news of the famine, conveyed by other journalists who followed Dimbleby's trail, reached the streets and campus in Addis Ababa, it had the same effect as the 1905 shooting of marching workers in front of the Winter Palace had on Czar Nicholas II—the news broke the emperor's spell. The edifice of legitimacy, erected by history and tradition, was smashed. What followed was a series of events as drawn out, bloody, and intellectually insane as the Russian and French revolutions, but even more complex. Scholar Bertram D. Wolfe's depiction of revolutionaries in Russia in *Three Who Made a Revolution* could easily apply to Ethiopia: "With fiercer passion than ever, they fell to engaging in controversies of a minuteness, stubbornness, sweep, and fury unheard of in all the history of politics."

The first phase of the uprising in Ethiopia was known as the "creeping coup." At the beginning of 1974, taxi drivers in Addis Ababa, protesting a rise in gasoline prices, went out on strike. A general strike of all workers followed in March. At the same time, an army mutiny, sparked by a government defeat in Eritrea, was taking place. In Negelle, in the far south of Ethiopia, junior officers arrested their superiors, forcing the generals to eat the same miserable food and dirty water as did the enlisted men. Out of this and other barracks' rebellions came the Dergue (Amharic for committee), a coordinating body of educated junior officers, with representatives from units throughout the country. The uprising began as a class struggle. But, as pointed out by Marina and David Ottaway in *Ethiopia: Empire in Revolution,* the ethnic animosities basic to an empire of great diversity quickly became dominant. Almost as soon as it was formed, the Dergue began to fissure along ethnic lines. Because his ancestry was not wholly Amhara, Mengistu's rise to power was aided by his ability to be seen as a unifying figure.

It was a gradual process. The portrait of one ruler, as so often happens in the Third World, was not abruptly taken down one day from the wall and replaced with that of another. It was as if the picture imperceptibly changed, day by day, a line at a time, during a period of months, until the face of Emperor Haile Selassie was completely wiped out and the face of Mengistu Haile Mariam had emerged from out of the dim background, anonymous and impenetrable; the face of the masses at their most brutal. In the void opened by the absence of democratic institutions and the chaos of revolution, the worst national traits came to the surface.

Mengistu's origin is obscure. By one account, he is the son of a night watchman and a palace servant; by another, the illegitimate descendant of a nobleman and his mistress. Mengistu's complexion is extremely dark, and he is assumed to be part Oromo. During the first years of his rule, his official portrait was touched up to lighten his complexion, so he would appear like an Amhara.

In 1974, Mengistu was a thirty-two-year-old army captain, a graduate of the Holeta Military Academy, which was an institution of no prestige designed for prospective officers whose family backgrounds were neither wealthy nor aristocratic. Like Haile Selassie, Mengistu was short: five feet, five inches. But his reputation was always that of a roughneck; he was constantly getting into fist fights. For eight long years, until the outbreak of the "creeping coup," Mengistu sat behind a desk in a cramped, dusty office in Harar, while serving as an ordnance officer for the Third Army Division—a typical dead-end job. From this vantage point, noted Rene Lefort in *Ethiopie: Revolution Heretique,* Mengistu learned how to master the system at its most vicious, petty, and bureaucratic level. Favors, payoffs, and other dirty business regularly crossed his desk. The future author of resettlement and villagization followed Stalin's dictum well: "Paper will put up with anything that is written on it."

The barracks disturbances in early 1974 were perfect opportunities for Mengistu's cunning and thuggishness. Only a true "desperado" could challenge an absolute monarch in a society as violent and secretive as Ethiopia's. At the Dergue's founding meeting in late June 1974, Mengistu was chosen immediately as one of its leaders.

The emperor tried to meet the mutineers' challenge by appointing a new prime minister, who was given a mandate for reform. Meanwhile, Mengistu and the other members of the Dergue worked behind the scenes to unite the faction-ridden armed forces. Haile Selassie was deposed on September 12, 1974; he was driven away from the palace in the back seat of a green Volkswagen and taken to the basement of the Fourth Division headquarters. Two months later, in November, a dispute about the conduct of the war in Eritrea led Mengistu to eliminate his chief rival, General Aman Michael Andom, who was gunned down in his home (see Chapter 3 for details).

In December, students were dispatched to the countryside, ostensibly to revolutionize the masses. But the relocation of the students, many of whom were members of the Ethiopian People's Revolutionary party (EPRP), allowed the Dergue to consolidate its power in the cities by forming its own left-wing party, the All-Ethiopian Socialist Movement, known by its Amharic acronym, MEISON. The Dergue then set MEISON against the EPRP.

On August 28, 1975, the English-language *Ethiopian Herald* announced that Haile Selassie had died the day before of circulatory failure. However, Mengistu is said to have suffocated the eighty-three-year-old deposed emperor with a pillow.

A few weeks later, the Dergue shot contingents of EPRP marchers down in the street. This, as Mengistu no doubt expected, only whetted MEISON's appetite. By early 1976, MEISON cadres were conducting house-to-house searches, killing anyone suspected of belonging to the EPRP.

Within the Dergue, Mengistu continued apace to eliminate rivals. In July 1976, the members of a faction that supported a peaceful solution to the war in Eritrea all were executed. Undeterred, another group, led by General Teferi Banti—this time calling for democratic reforms—demanded that Mengistu's power be circumscribed. Mengistu, uncharacteristically, submitted. A few months went by. Then, on February 2, 1977, General Banti and his colleagues were murdered by Mengistu inside the palace. By now, having destroyed the EPRP with the help of MEISON, the Dergue was turning against MEISON itself.

The Russians were very impressed with Mengistu's performance thus far, and a group of East German security police were dispatched to Addis Ababa to advise the emergent Ethiopian leader on what to do next. What followed was the Red Terror, which began in May 1977. On May Day eve, soldiers that had been brought into town by convoy machine-gunned to death hundreds of demonstrating students, including many children. During the coming months, dozens of new bodies would turn up on the street every morning; most of them were teenagers who were vaguely connected with revolutionary politics at a time when there was no right side to be on. The victims' families had to pay a fee to the government in order to get the bodies back for burial.

The revolution ground to a halt the next year. The death toll was estimated to be thirty thousand, not including tens of thousands of battlefield deaths. (In Tigre, an insurgency had broken out against the new military rulers, and in Eritrea, Mengistu's uncompromising stance toward the guerrillas resulted in intensified fighting.) Of the 120 members of the original Dergue, only a small fraction were still alive. Compared to the hundreds of political prisoners in jail in Haile Selassie's day, tens of thousands were being held in 1978. Torture reportedly was widespread.

The Darwinian process of revolution had proved efficient and had elevated Mengistu in a very short time from the very bottom to the very top, where he both orchestrated and survived four years of the most violent internecine struggles imaginable. Constantly underestimated by his rivals, he never once miscalculated. The standard of treachery he was judged by, given the paranoia engendered by the revolution, was much higher than that ever applied to Haile Selassie. A Marxist revolution once again had brought an outdated despotism up to a modern standard, with a programmed killer installed in the emperor's palace.

Mengistu belonged to the most lethal class of dictator: the kind not distracted by greed. As with Hitler, Stalin, and Pol Pot, Mengistu was not personally corrupt, and corruption never has been a key element in his style of rule. Apologists for the Ethiopian regime—and in Europe, especially, there are many—point out that it is more honest and efficient than the previous one. This is certainly true. Mengistu has none of the all-too-human foibles of other Third World rulers, Ferdinand and Imelda Marcos, for example, whose evil was of a lesser variety, one to which the U.S. public could relate. (Is there a more tangible symbol of conspicuous, nouveau riche, middle-class consumption than Mrs. Marcos's fetish for shoes?) This is one reason why even during the height of the famine, the media never bothered much with Mengistu. As a personality he was too austere and his evil too remote for mass audience appeal.

Whatever his bloodlines, Mengistu had the ascetic discipline required to keep an empire, torn by several wars, from splitting apart. He has proven to be a more aggressive imperialist than Haile Selassie was, and in this endeavor, the USSR has been a better ally for Mengistu than the United States was for the emperor. Massive Soviet arms shipments turned the tide against guerrillas in Eritrea and the Somali army in the Ogaden desert. In the densely populated Ethiopian countryside, Marxism was more efficient than feudalism in controlling the lives and movements of the peasants, not all of whom were loyal to the regime or to the Amhara cause. In place of landlords, whose interests were similar, but not always identical, to those of the emperor, the government has been able to rule more efficiently through its own peasant associations. Eastern bloc advisers influenced the 1979 proclamation on collectivization; the proclamation put additional emphasis on state farms, which were (and are) useful as bases and listening posts for the government because they were not manned by local people. Between 1977 and 1984, state farms expanded threefold in area. Even though production on state farms continued to fall, government plans called for a doubling of the state farm sector, according to Allan Hoben, in the January 21, 1985, issue of *The New Republic.*

Hoben wrote that "to extend its economic control over agriculture, the government has reimposed taxation, established a government marketing agency, fixed prices, experimented with production quotas imposed on peasant associations, and interfered increasingly with private grain trade. Not surprisingly, these measures have reduced the peasants' incentives to produce."

Correspondent Paul Vallely described this policy in progress in an article entitled "How Mengistu Hammers the Peasants" in the March 1, 1985, issue of *The Times* of London.

> The government men were lying in wait for the peasant farmers in the market place of the small town of Areka. The harvest of teff, Ethiopia's staple grain, had not been plentiful in the southern province of Sidamo but at least that meant, the peasants thought, that they would get a good price for what little surplus they had. They were reckoning without the fixed-price marketing strategy of Mengistu's government.
>
> There was almost a riot in Areka that day. The officials from the Agricultural Marketing Corporation waited until most of the peasants had brought their teff into the dusty market place and then made themselves known. They announced the official price they had decided on and told the farmers that the AMC would buy their entire stock.
>
> The price was ludicrously low. The peasants protested. Some even began to gather up their grain saying they would rather not sell at such a price. The AMC men then announced that no one would be allowed to withdraw his produce. The farmers began to shout and drag their grain away. The AMC men were jostled. Then the government heavies moved in and the peasants knew they had no choice but to comply.

The effects of this policy were made clear to Clifford D. May, who observed in the December 1, 1985, issue of the *New York Times Magazine* that while famine ravaged the north of Ethiopia, in the central province of Shoa outside Addis Ababa, grain was going unpicked because farmers didn't want to sell at the official price. But these facts never have been taken into account by the Ethiopian authorities. At the end of the last decade, although every available statistic pointed to the failure of made-in-Moscow agricultural philosophy, the regime pushed ahead with Soviet-modeled policy and went one step further by beginning the resettlement of peasants from the north to the south against their will. In the eyes of the Dergue, incontrovertible data are mere obstacles to be overcome by the force of ideology. While production suffers, a rural power base is built. (Even in the campaign to increase literacy—one of the regime's few undeniable success stories— extending the central government's control over the peasants is a principle theme. Amharic is the language of instruction throughout the country, and the textbooks are a vehicle for Marxist indoctrination.)

In the early 1980s, disastrous agricultural policies, drought, and two major government offensives against guerrillas in Eritrea and Tigre— which devastated the land, the peasant farmers who worked it, and the livestock—resulted in the worst famine since the 1932–1933 famine in the Ukraine. As in the Ukraine, untried, theoretical principles of collectivized agriculture were inflicted on a peasantry burdened by centuries of feudalism, which had been the target of government-inspired ethnic discrimination.

While hundreds of thousands began to die in the northern provinces of Gondar, Wollo, Tigre, and Eritrea, the Dergue spent an estimated $200 million in September 1984 on celebrations marking the tenth anniversary of the revolution. The event was supervised by North Koreans, and dignitaries from all over the Eastern bloc attended. By then, Mengistu was in all but name the new emperor—one of the strongest in the two-thousand-year-long history of the empire. *Time* chief of correspondents Henry Muller and the magazine's Nairobi bureau chief, James Wilde, were perhaps the only U.S. journalists to have ever interviewed the Ethiopian leader. They described their summer 1986 interview in an article in *Time* (August 4, 1986).

[Mengistu] sat at the head of a long U-shaped table in a sparse conference room decorated with portraits of Marx and Lenin. . . . Throughout the four-hour interview, he remained statue-still, his impassive face animated only by an occasionally furrowed brow. Mengistu refused to answer any questions that had not been previously submitted. While he spoke softly, his words carried a tone of icy, uncompromising certitude. Not once did his eyes focus on his guests: at times he appeared to be speaking to an unseen audience, or to the portraits on the wall.

After the tenth anniversary celebrations, the magnitude of the famine finally forced itself on the Dergue's attention. Western television crews were allowed into the country. The Western public's response was dramatic: a Soviet ally was not going to be undermined by a famine the way a U.S. ally was a decade before. U.S. congressmen rushed to Addis Ababa to meet with Ethiopian government officials and to see what could be done to alleviate the suffering. Christopher J. Matthews, an administrative assistant to the U.S. Speaker of the House, was part of a congressional delegation that met with Mengistu. According to Matthews in an article that appeared in *The New Republic* (January 21, 1985), the Ethiopian leader described the famine thus: "The death toll in human and animal lives is really astounding. . . . Hardest hit in the human bracket are children and senior citizens."

At least the Dergue was keeping count. During the famine in the Ukraine, according to scholar Robert Conquest in *The Harvest of Sorrow,* the Kremlin kept figures for livestock mortality, but not for human mortality.

*   *   *

The Dergue's own Relief and Rehabilitation Commission (RRC) had turned its attention to the famine much earlier. (The RRC was another of the handful of solid achievements for which the regime properly received credit.) Mindful of the role the 1973–1974 famine played in toppling the emperor, the Dergue created the RRC soon after the revolution to serve as a separate, governmental authority for dealing with food shortages and related matters. For years, the RRC had been predicting terrible consequences if more help from the West was not forthcoming, and in the RRC's annual aid request issued on March 30, 1984—seven months before television footage from the relief camp at Korem finally galvanized Western governments into action—the commission stated with impressive accuracy the extent of the emerging famine.

The Reagan administration was universally criticized for not responding to these prescient cries for help sooner. After an RRC plea in October 1982, only 8,000 tons of grain were pledged by Washington, compared with 400,000 given in the first six months after the October 1984 plea, when President Reagan was under intense public pressure to do more. It goes without saying that had the administration been more generous in 1982 and in the year following, more lives would have been saved, and in a perfect world, the harsh judgments rendered against the administration would have been fully justified. But to argue, as many have, that President Reagan was prepared to let Ethiopian children die because their government was communist is to miss the point. Had the Dergue, in 1982 and 1983, evinced even the slightest inclination toward flexibility in its agricultural policies, the U.S. government and other donors might have been more compassionate. Stalinist economics and the two largest government offensives against the Eritrean and Tigrean guerrillas in the history of the war were dooming northern Ethiopia to be forever on the brink of famine. The United States obviously did not want to get into the position of subsidizing a regime that was burning crops and dropping cluster bombs in the drought zone with one hand and using its relief agency to beg with the other.

This fear was borne out by subsequent events. Even the deaths of as many as 1 million peasants in the 1984–1985 famine did not cause the Dergue to alter its policies in the slightest. In fact, the famine appeared only to stiffen the regime's resolve. The resettlement of Tigreans and the villagization of Oromos were accelerated, and a July 1985 offensive against guerrillas in Eritrea resulted in the heaviest fighting there of the decade. Consequently, although the drought had ended by mid-1985, the structural food deficit kept growing, according to USAID. With production stagnated, the grain shortfall in 1990 in Ethiopia is expected to be 2.5 million tons, compared with a 1.7 million ton shortfall during the height of the famine. USAID, fed up with the state of affairs in Addis Ababa, phased down its Ethiopia operation in 1986, leaving only one, small feeding program of 20,000 tons in place. The decision was greeted without a murmur of protest from the U.S. public—which already had lost interest in the issue— or from liberal Democrats, such as Senator Edward M. Kennedy, who had tired of extending the olive branch to a regime that refused to learn from experience. The formation of a full-fledged, ruling communist party (the Workers' Party of Ethiopia), the regime's conversion to a "socialist democracy," its continued appetite for war, and a failure to countenance any economic reforms even in the wake of a famine only seemed to vindicate the administration's consistently negative attitude toward the Dergue. USAID administrator M. Peter McPherson—President Reagan's special adviser on the famine emergency—remarked to me that Mengistu's refusal to ever meet with McPherson was like "a badge of honor."

Not only was the Ethiopian government's policy a disincentive to aid, but so was the government's public attitude toward the donors. In *A Year in the Death of Africa,* author Peter Gill accused the RRC commissioner, Dawit Wolde Giorgis, of "a directness of manner that bordered on rudeness." Gill, a British television reporter whose book was devoted to aid agency politics in 1984, wrote that Dawit "produced an unnerving moral equation between rich Governments in the West and the miserable poor in his own country. It was a formula that seemed at times to exclude his own government from further obligation."

Dawit's superiors in the Dergue appeared even more impervious to his warnings of impending disaster than did the Western governments he always was ready to criticize. The louder the RRC's cries for help got, the more preoccupied the Dergue became with the war, the formation of the party, and the coming anniversary celebrations. How were Western governments supposed to get worked up about what the RRC was saying if the RRC's own bosses weren't?

Originally, the RRC might have been created with the intention of forestalling future famines. But by 1984, the RRC had become a mere vestige of the emperor's powerless westernized elite, given the task of collecting relief donations for a regime that spent half its budget on fighting wars in collaboration with the Soviet Union. The famine was good business for the Dergue. A port fee of $12.60 was charged for each ton of donated grain. This replaced coffee as Ethiopia's biggest hard currency earner. The United States paid $5 million just to have its first 400,000 tons pass customs inspection. It appeared far from coincidental that the costliest-ever government offensive against the Eritrean guerrillas was launched in July 1985, on the heels of the massive influx of relief supplies from the West.

In late 1985, RRC commissioner Dawit defected to the very country he had been the most publicly critical of—the United States. Dawit, who had defended Mengistu to the point of justifying the brutal expulsion of fifty thousand people from a relief camp in Gondar the previous April, lost no opportunity once in the United States to criticize the Ethiopian leader. At an East-West Round Table meeting in New York in late 1986, Dawit said, among other things:

> Mengistu's dream and primary objective is to make Ethiopia the first African Communist country, in the fullest sense, by restructuring the national social fabric and creating a regimented, controlled society. . . .
>
> His [Mengistu's] indifference to the emergency aggravated the effects of the drought, leading to mass death, starvation and migration at the earliest stage of the crisis.

After berating the West for years for not giving enough aid, Dawit was quoted in the *Wall Street Journal Europe* (April 1986) as stating that the aid kept an inhuman regime in power: "Without this help there would have been a bloody chaos which would have resulted in the removal of Mengistu and his henchmen."

The Reagan administration's attitude toward Ethiopia thus had been vindicated by the Marxist government's top official for dealing with the famine. Rarely in the Third World was the conservative position so authoritatively proven correct. It's a pity more conservatives weren't paying attention. Few of them wrote about it. Like the liberals, most conservatives were preoccupied with other issues by the time of Dawit's defection.

In early 1986, Dawit's top assistant in the RRC, Berhane Deressa, followed Dawit into exile. Approximately eighty Ethiopian officials had defected by then. In Africa, however, officials flee their own countries all the time, and they never are referred to as "defectors." The media's instinctive use of the word for this high-level exodus was perhaps the most eloquent proof of Ethiopia's transformation into a communist society, a transformation that was completed in the midst of the Western famine relief effort.

*   *   *

Emergency aid meant people, and in late 1984 Ethiopian authorities were forced to allow an influx of Westerners into Addis Ababa—relief workers, government officials, journalists, and celebrities—which in terms of relative size and suddenness was unprecedented in the Eastern bloc. The Hilton Hotel, whose occupancy rate normally hovered around 50 percent, was filled to capacity for the next nine months. An article of faith among many in the Hilton lobby during this period was that the very presence of so many people like themselves from North America, Western Europe, and the rest of the free world would work to moderate the foreign and domestic policies of the regime. Ethiopia, it was said, was being forced by the famine to open itself to Western influence. Seldom have so many people been so wrong in such a naive fashion about what was going on all around them.

"In fact, it is to *Alice in Wonderland* that my thoughts recur in seeking some . . . parallel for life in Addis Ababa," wrote Evelyn Waugh, in his evocation of 1930s Ethiopia, *Remote People.* Waugh might have felt a tinge of déjà vu had he been able to pay a return visit a half century later. The nest of restrictions imposed by a totalitarian system, combined with the insidious effects of local history, placed this throng of unknowing intruders from the West in a politically watertight compartment, with distorting mirrors at every turn.

The physical setting of the Ethiopian capital and the manner in which it was built were elements in this deception. Addis Ababa (Amharic for new flower) was built by Menelik II, starting in 1889. As the first Amhara emperor, Menelik wanted to shift the focal point of the empire southward from Tigre to the highlands of Shoa. The site chosen was the plain beside Mount Entoto. But at an altitude of 8,000 feet, the scarcity of wood presented a problem. It was solved in 1900 by the introduction of the fast-growing eucalyptus tree from Australia. As a result, the first sensation a traveler had upon arriving in Addis Ababa was one of bodily well-being, brought about by the invigorating mountain climate and the shade and ubiquitous fragrance of the eucalyptus trees. Diplomats and aid specialists accustomed to the leaden heat and blinding sunlight of other African and Middle Eastern capitals found "Addis" a godsend. It was like arriving at a hill station in the Himalayas after weeks on the hot, teeming plains of the subcontinent. Gone was the irritability stirred by dusty, clammy skin and a shirt drenched with sweat at ten in the morning. One's mood was vastly improved and thus made a person better disposed toward his or her hosts.

The real hosts in "Addis" went unseen. Addis Ababa was conceived by Menelik as an Amhara fortress, and its most striking architectural detail is its walls, whether of stone, mudbrick, wattle, or corrugated iron. High walls of stone block off the sprawling grounds of the palace from public view, and few members of the Western community ever were allowed to see beyond these walls. Mengistu and the rest of the eleven-person Politburo met rarely with resident nationals of countries outside the Third World or Eastern bloc. Only for Kurt Jansson, a native of neutral Finland and the U.N. assistant secretary general for emergency operations in Ethiopia, was an exception made. (Mengistu was especially shrewd about whom he chose to receive among the temporary visitors from the United States. As I mentioned, he never agreed to meet with USAID administrator McPherson, who was directing the delivery of one-third of all the emergency assistance reaching Ethiopia from the outside world. But the Ethiopian leader did meet with liberal Democratic congressman Howard Wolpe—by Washington standards an apologist for the regime—and with singer Harry Belafonte, whose twenty-minute meeting with Mengistu in June 1985 was partly taken up by a discussion about human rights violations in South Africa.

The policies of the Dergue were invisible, too. Visits to resettlement and villagization sites, with the exception of showcase camps, were prohibited. The chilling reports of large-scale human rights abuses usually filtered into "Addis" by way of refugee stories from Sudan and therefore were treated with deep suspicion; the product merely, it was thought, of exaggerations and interviews with refugees conducted through biased translators sympathetic to the Tigrean guerrillas. Like the regime, many nongovernmental Western aid people in Addis Ababa saw the Tigrean and Eritrean guerrillas as "bandits" who were largely to blame for the regime's failure to get more food to the countryside. The aid community had few ways of knowing that the guerrillas in the north were among the most sophisticated insurgents in the world, enjoying mass popular support, and that the regime often was bombing the places it professed to be feeding. There never were any reports in the official media about the fighting. Many relief officials had no interest in finding out. The vacuum of official information in Addis Ababa, as in other Eastern bloc capitals, was sufficiently formidable for rumors to be far more prevalent than facts about such issues as resettlement, villagization, and the war in the north. In fact, the difference in perceptions between the foreign community in Addis Ababa and the one in Khartoum (which functioned as a rear base for the guerrillas) was almost as profound as that between the foreign communities in Tel Aviv and Damascus.

There were, in fact, two Ethiopias—the one inside the watertight compartment and the one outside. Outside was the war, the Dergue, its East German–advised security service, the thousands of political detainees, and the drive toward collectivization. This world—the world inhabited by Mrs. Ahmed and the Oromos of Hararghe, whose troubles began about the same time that Westerners began pouring into Addis Ababa—constituted a reality that was somewhat vague, suspect, and threatening to the foreigners who didn't want to be ejected all at the same time. It was best not to bring this world any closer by provoking it. In Sudan, the famine-wracked country next door, openly discussing the evil qualities of the pro-U.S. government of Jaafar Nimeiri was one thing, but in Ethiopia, where the evil was of an entirely different magnitude, it was quite another. Criticism of Mengistu by Westerners in Addis Ababa was muted. When a French relief group, Medicins sans Frontieres (Doctors Without Borders, or MSF), was thrown out of Ethiopia for unreservedly criticizing the resettlement program, the Western community in Addis Ababa did not come to the group's defense. Everyone appeared to run for cover.

After all, the world inside the compartment—the world of Dawit, the RRC, and RRC-approved day trips to emergency feeding centers—contradicted much of what was outside and much of what Medicins sans Frontieres was saying. The RRC might have been bureaucratic, as everything in Ethiopia traditionally was, but it was not corrupt. With persistence, the bureaucracy could be circumvented, couldn't it? Was there a more dedicated and efficient African relief organization than the RRC? Didn't the very efficiency of the RRC testify to the positive qualities of the Dergue and to the Dergue's commitment to the relief effort? Wouldn't more Western support for the RRC improve Dawit's bargaining position inside the palace? Wasn't this the very way in which to draw Ethiopia toward the West?

It was true; the RRC was not corrupt. Grain shipments very likely were misappropriated in Ethiopia by the government for strategic reasons, but little of the grain was pilfered for personal gain. Mengistu, his other faults notwithstanding, did not tolerate the level of thievery common to countries such as Zaire and Nigeria. As I've suggested, were he more corrupt, less people might have been murdered and tortured. As to the bureaucracy, it certainly could be managed, but that depended upon who you were. U.S. Embassy officials and others likely to ask critical questions always seemed to have difficulty getting permission to travel outside the capital. General Julius Becton, Jr., director of USAID's Office of Foreign Disaster Assistance, told *Newsweek* (June 3, 1985), "[Ethiopian] officials knew I was going to be there 30 days in advance. But the night before I was supposed to depart I was told, 'We don't have your travel permits.'"

Admittedly, the efficiency of the RRC was impressive. But this was not due to any humanitarian commitment on the Dergue's part. In Ethiopia, administrative finesse was not exclusive to the RRC. Ethiopian Airlines was the best-run national carrier in black Africa; the airlines' record of punctuality was as good as many airlines in the West. The guerrilla-affiliated relief agencies in Tigre and Eritrea were just as effective as the RRC and quite a bit more resourceful considering the more difficult conditions under which they had to work. Just consider: could the government of any other sub-Saharan country—after announcing an intention to collectivize several million people—actually be able to do it, however crudely? Ethiopia's hunger and poverty may have been typically African, but the causes weren't. The underdevelopment of the northern provinces could not be blamed on ignorance and incompetence. Efficiency was a national trait, and while one branch of the bureaucracy was effectively working to save lives, others were operating just as effectively in a different direction.

Rather than draw Ethiopia toward the West, as many in the Western community in Addis Ababa predicted, the relief effort coincided with a further radicalization of the Dergue. At the beginning of 1985, when the Hilton was literally bursting with Western visitors, four Marxist ideologues—Alemu Abebe, Shewandagan Belete, Shimelis Mazengia, and Fassika Sidelel—nicknamed the Gang of Four, emerged as Mengistu's top advisers. On February 9, an austerity program was announced that was aimed at further decimating the urban middle class. Also, government employees earning more than $250 per month were from then on required to wear North Korean–styled tunics in place of Western suits; this was another measure that reinforced Marxist aesthetics. In April, at a meeting of the Workers' Party of Ethiopia, Mengistu praised the Soviet Union and condemned "American imperialism" but made no mention of the massive Western relief effort. In May, the pace of forced collectivization increased. Meanwhile, Dawit and his associates, having succeeded at bringing the famine under control, were becoming more and more isolated. Anyone with any political street-smarts could have predicted Dawit's demise. If there really had been an opportunity for a basically pragmatic, Western-oriented official such as Dawit to increase his influence inside the palace, the regime would have had a different personality than it did.

The truth was that many in the Western community in the Ethiopian capital, who served as the West's eyes and ears during the famine and provided the media with much of its information, did not want to admit the truth. Whatever nightmares the word "Ethiopia" may have conjured up in the United States, "Addis" was a nice place to be. (The same could not be said about capitals elsewhere in Africa, where the suffering in the countryside was far less.) The mountain climate was only partly responsible for the pleasant ambience. As the head-quarters of the Organization of African Unity, the Ethiopian capital was relatively clean, with good roads, a plethora of new public buildings, and well-manicured parks. The Hilton Hotel was one of the best-managed, centrally located Hiltons in the world; the Hilton's heated, outdoor swimming pool served as a magnet for the foreign community on weekend afternoons.

As for the food, millions may have been starving in the adjacent countryside, but for foreigners, "Addis" was one of the better places on the continent to eat: a well-prepared charcoal-broiled steak, Nile perch, and Italian and Chinese cuisines always were available. Not only was the Hilton equipped with several fine restaurants, but around the city there were several more. No nearby, heartrending scenes spoiled the repasts; just as walls of stone blocked off the sinister reality of the Dergue, walls of corrugated iron blocked off the equally unpleasant reality of the slums. Nor were there many beggars in Addis Ababa; far less than in Egypt, for example, where nobody was starving. Christopher J. Matthews, in his article in *The New Republic* (January 21, 1985), made one of the most insightful observations ever about Ethiopia's capital: "In a country where millions were starving, there was no sign of anyone begging or hustling to survive. I began to wonder. The price of coming into town must be higher than the price of staying away. If the price of staying away in the barren, dying parts of the country is near-certain death, the price of coming into the city must be even more terrible, even more certain."

Matthews, perhaps without being aware of it, had stumbled close to the central fact of 1980s Ethiopia, a fact that many foreigners who actually lived there and many of the journalists who interpreted the famine for the public failed utterly to grasp—Ethiopia, in the manner of Syria and Iraq, was a modernizing and controlled, praetorian police state, with a single tribe or ethnic group on top, supported by the most brutal and sophisticated means of repression. For the officers in charge, preserving the integrity of the empire against rebels was a far more uplifting and important goal than fighting a famine was. The Soviets, the only great imperialists of the nineteenth century to have survived the twentieth, understood this. They helped, through massive arms shipments, the Dergue achieve its more important goal; the United States helped in the less important one.

As Matthews perceived, like the walls around the palace and around the slums, there was a wall around the famine, too. Destitute peasants were rounded up and arrested even before reaching the city limits. While Eritreans, Tigreans, and others in the northern provinces died by the hundreds of thousands, the markets of the Amhara fortress of Addis Ababa were brimming with grain. The price of it may have risen dramatically, but at least it was there. In Asmara, too, the government-held, fortified provincial capital of Eritrea, food was abundant because it was strategically necessary for the regime to keep the local population pacified. According to a confidential report by a Western relief agency, the "dedicated and efficient" RRC was virtually starving the worst famine regions in Wollo, while at the same time pouring food into embattled, militarily vital areas of Tigre and Eritrea and stockpiling it outside Addis Ababa. (Although in the first six months of 1985, Ethiopia got, more or less, all of the 750,000 tons of grain it required for that period through foreign donations, in Wollo the RRC distributed only about one-quarter of the grain allocated to that area.)

The sanitized reality of the Ethiopian capital, a condition that only the most chillingly brutal of regimes could create, helped make the place especially attractive for its foreign residents. "Addis" was a plum posting for a relief official. The situation in the country was "absolutely horrifying" and thus "in the news," which translated into prestige and career advancement for those on the scene. Few seemed to want to rock the boat when rocking the boat could get you thrown out. In the Hilton lobby, it was easier to criticize the Reagan administration than it was to criticize the Dergue.

*   *   *

In 1921, the nascent Bolshevik regime in the Soviet Union was shaken by a great famine that its own ruthless policy of crop requisition had caused. Foreign aid was essential, and the U.S. people proved to be the most generous. Herbert Hoover, who seven years later would be elected president of the United States, spearheaded an effort that put food in the mouths of more than 12 million peasants. The regime survived to inflict an even greater famine in the following decade.

But in Ethiopia and in the United States, nobody paid attention to this legacy. In the February 7, 1985, report on the famine, issued by the Senate Subcommittee on Immigration and Refugee Policy and arising out of Senator Kennedy's Christmas 1984 visit to the emergency feeding camps, six previous famines were listed in a table entitled, "Famine in Modern History." The famines in the Ukraine, which were the largest of all, were not included in the list.

The mid-1980s Western relief effort in Ethiopia, like the one more than sixty years earlier in the Soviet Union, was idealistically conceived and succeeded at saving, for the time being, an uncountable number of lives. To some extent, turning the other cheek in the face of an ugly reality was necessary to achieve this. (One also could argue the opposite.) However, it is undeniable that the latter effort was far more critical to the survival of Mengistu than was Hoover's to the survival of Lenin and Stalin. If we are to believe Dawit after his defection, the effort was absolutely crucial to the continued existence of what today has become the People's Democratic Republic of Ethiopia, whose future, foodwise, appears even bleaker than its past.

The problem with a policy based solely on relief was that it ignored so much else of the drama in Ethiopia. What was ignored, although less visually stirring, was, as we shall see, more central to Ethiopia's future. It is time now to explore how and why U.S. attention was kept focused on a thin and exposed stratum of reality. Then we can go on to plumb the depths beneath.

TWO

what the media saw

As the corpse went past the flies left the restaurant table in a cloud and rushed after it, but they came back a few minutes later.
—George Orwell, *Marrakech*

Although there was one famine in Ethiopia, its estimated 8–10 million victims were divided up, in terms of responsibility, among three major armies and other minor ones in the warring north of Ethiopia. Outside of the main towns, most of Eritrea and Tigre were in the hands of antigovernment guerrillas: the Eritrean People's Liberation Front and the Tigre People's Liberation Front (TPLF), each with its own famine relief organization whose declared purpose was the same as the RRC's. With troops constantly on the move, and mass migrations of peasants in progress, it often was impossible to know exactly how many starving people were in the territory of any one army at any particular time. As few as one-third, or as many as two-thirds, of those starving could have been in areas held by the EPLF and the TPLF on a given day. A common assumption was that almost half of the 8–10 million affected peasants were in territory reached only by guerrilla relief agencies. For journalists, this meant that the Ethiopian capital of Addis Ababa was a useful base for covering one side of the famine only. The base for covering the other side was Khartoum and the squalid Sudanese settlements near the border with Eritrea and Tigre.

Organizing transport and travel permits for a trip to the part of Tigre province controlled by the Ethiopian government took one to three days. During this period, the journalist resided at the Hilton Hotel in Addis Ababa. From there, it was a fifteen-minute drive to the airport, where the British Royal Air Force could get a reporter up to the emergency feeding camps at Makelle, in the heart of Tigre, the same morning on one of the air force's relief flights. Having seen the RRC operation at Makelle, in February 1986, I wanted to see how the RRC's rival, the TPLF guerrilla-affiliated Relief Society of Tigre

31

(REST), dealt with hungry peasants in its zone. But getting into the part of Tigre controlled by the TPLF was much more difficult.

The TPLF was recognized by no one in the international community (the weapons the TPLF fought with were captured from the Dergue). Unlike Eritrea, which bordered on the Red Sea, Tigre was a landlocked province that throughout history had little or no contact with the outside world. REST had far fewer resources in terms of money and educated staff than had the RRC. The RRC, headquartered in an internationally recognized capital and run by people like Dawit who had attended university in the United States, was at least somewhat acquainted with the demands of visiting foreigners whose time in the country was limited. REST was even less so. Moreover, REST was at the mercy of the Sudanese authorities, who were far less efficient than their Ethiopian counterparts.

As with the RRC, it usually took one to three days for REST to arrange a field visit for a journalist. But instead of the Hilton Hotel in Addis Ababa, a journalist had to wait at the REST guesthouse in Gedaref, a refugee center in the wastes of eastern Sudan, several hours by bus from Khartoum.

The guesthouse was a small compound on a garbage-strewn street crowded with beggars and all types of vehicles whose drivers never stopped beeping their horns. The baking sunlight, the absence of shade, and the deafening cacophony kept most journalists inside the enclosure, where I waited three days with a British colleague for a truck convoy into TPLF territory. While we waited, we sat in uncomfortable chairs, staring at windows boarded up against the desert sun. Unboiled, unfiltered lemonade was brought in an old plastic pitcher every few hours and placed on a broken metal table covered with an oilcloth. The overhead fan didn't work, and the room was ridden with flies. There was no running water, and the toilet facilities were unspeakable. Coarse blankets were provided for sleeping out in the courtyard. As it was late February, there were thankfully few mosquitos, and therefore the risk of contracting malaria was slight.

After the first day, no more meals were provided at the guesthouse. REST, which was strapped for funds much more than was the RRC, had a rule that thereafter visiting journalists and aid workers had to fend for themselves. As no restaurant in town served even reasonably edible food by Western standards, we ate in the main market of Gedaref, sipping heavily sugared tea and eating fried bread and grapefruits on a buckled bench amid flies and garbage, with blaring music all around. The third day, a relief worker living in Gedaref took pity on us. He gave us the keys to his house prior to leaving for Khartoum. We took hot showers and raided the kitchen cupboard, which was filled with cans of Heinz soup. The three days at the guesthouse had depleted our reading material, but all we saw on the shelves were a copy of Albert Schweitzer's *Out of My Life and Thought* and an old issue of *Penthouse*. Those few hours passed at the relief worker's house proved to be the most comfortable of our journey. Once inside the TPLF zone in Tigre, physical conditions were even worse than at the guesthouse.

Nevertheless, the physical discomforts I experienced were bad but not unusual by the standards of Africa-based correspondents. Others suffered worse hardships. *Time* correspondent James Wilde's two-week trip along the Zaire River was far more harrowing than mine in Tigre. Gary Strieker of Cable News Network (CNN) and Blaine Harden of the *Washington Post* went several days without any food at all while traveling in southern Sudan with African rebels who were at war with the Arab government in Khartoum. Yet I recount the details of my stay at the guesthouse in Gedaref because they are central to an understanding of how and why the famine got reported as it did.

Journalism is competitive enough for reporters to willingly suffer the inconveniences that I did if it means getting a story that is going to greatly impress their editors. But most editors in the United States would not have been greatly impressed by the results of a trip into Tigre, where Tigrean Marxists were fighting an Amhara-dominated government that also was Marxist. Tigre held out fascinating insights into the relationship among war, hunger, and ethnic hatred. But visually it often was not exciting. Unlike the situation at the feeding camps on the government side, starving people were not always gathered together in large multitudes. The primary concern of editors was to have their reporters "in there" among starving people as soon as possible and then out again just as quickly to where there were telex and satellite facilities to transmit the story back to the United States. If a reporter could accomplish this task on a day trip by airplane from the Hilton Hotel in Addis Ababa, why wait in a hovel in eastern Sudan and then ride around in a truck convoy for two weeks in Tigre under awful, illness-producing conditions? With such a comfortable alternative, was this really necessary? People were starving everywhere. Did it matter from which side of the battle lines the famine was covered?

If famine alone were the issue, it wouldn't have mattered much at all. But the famine was part of something larger and even more important—something that was not merely a story but an unprecedented historical process, which could be better understood from the guerrilla side because the authorities in Addis Ababa had no interest in bringing this process to light.

*   *   *

No other foreign news story of the decade highlighted the media's role as public servant to the extent that the Ethiopian famine did. Television pictures and news articles brought the pain of starvation into U.S. living rooms, thereby eliciting a flood of relief aid that saved countless lives. But while the technical wizardry of television was able to make the U.S. public *feel* starvation, the media, by and large, failed to make the public understand it. Even newspapers, which should have been less visually oriented, became fixated with the drama of mass starvation, while the historical and political context in which the famine belonged went largely unexplored. The famine exposed a disturbing trend: television's increasing ability to control the direction of a story and, by this very power, to intimidate the print media into following television's lead.

With few exceptions, U.S. journalists came into the story after it started and left in the middle. While they were there, their perspective was incredibly narrow and self-absorbed. U.S. journalists displayed a far greater interest in the Western relief effort than in Ethiopia itself. Ethiopia was never really covered; the famine was. Because the effects of Africa's longest-running war could not be seen well from the government side, the cause of the famine was mainly ascribed to drought. Thus, in the public mind, the famine became another disaster story, like the Mexican earthquake. As public service journalism this was fine. But as straight foreign news coverage—whose purpose was to make the public more sophisticated about a certain area of the world— the U.S. media failed miserably to live up to the standards it had set for itself in the Middle East, Southeast Asia, and other parts of the Third World. Because television footage was required to focus public attention on Ethiopia's plight, and because television thus set the pace, media coverage in general was both unusually powerful and superficial.

On February 22, 1987, more than a year after Ethiopia had faded from the news, a momentous world event took place that was little written about: Ethiopia formally became a Marxist state, the People's Democratic Republic of Ethiopia, with a Marxist party as the "guiding force." This was no mere window dressing. Ethiopia, black Africa's most strategically located and second most populous country, had in almost every conceivable way adopted the Soviet model, the first country on the continent ever to do so. The Coptic Orthodox church had been suppressed and coopted, in the manner of other orthodox churches in communist states in the Balkans and in the USSR itself. A great mass of peasants had been forcibly collectivized; the Soviet Union had been provided with major military bases; and the wheels of the state machinery, including the party, the security apparatus, and the crucial ministries, had been integrated into the Eastern bloc network. The other African states that were pro-Soviet, Angola and Mozambique, had gone through no such experience, nor even—to such an intense degree—had Nicaragua.

It was a thirteen-year process, beginning with the overthrow of Emperor Haile Selassie in 1974. But the revolution that brought a Marxist-inclined regime to power didn't end until 1978, and only in late 1984, on the eve of the famine emergency, was a communist party, the Workers' Party of Ethiopia, officially formed. The brief period in 1984 and 1985 during which the U.S. media maintained an intense interest in Ethiopia corresponded with the most critical phase of this operation.

Outside of the Warsaw Pact, only a handful of countries in the world have ever implemented Soviet-style communism. It is a rare, strategically pivotal event anywhere, and in Africa it is unprecedented. In every place where Soviet communism has been instituted, the cost in human suffering has been immense, with famine often the result— whether it be in the Ukraine, Cambodia, or northern Ethiopia. But this was the first time that the U.S. media were there in such force when the conversion to communism actually was taking place. Yet this history was not recorded in the pages of U.S. newspapers to nearly the extent that it should have been.

*　　*　　*

David Ottaway of the *Washington Post* and Judith Miller of the *New York Times* were the first U.S. journalists on the scene when both the famine and the formation of a ruling communist party became visible realities in the first days of September 1984. In his diplomatic memoir, *Ethiopia, the United States and the Soviet Union,* the former chargé d'affaires at the U.S. Embassy in Addis Ababa, David A. Korn, was highly critical of both journalists, especially Ottaway—an expert on Ethiopia—for placing more emphasis on the implementation of communism than on the famine. Admittedly, both correspondents had erred in not realizing the extent of the suffering in the provinces of Wollo, Tigre, and Eritrea, which seven weeks later would be the major foreign news story in the United States. However, both Miller and Ottaway, whatever their other faults on this particular assignment, were percipient enough to recognize that the building of real, Soviet-style communism by an African regime was a benchmark historical event, in the context of which the famine and all other developments in Ethiopia would have to be seen. At least in Miller's case, this did not mean that the famine was buried. She did write a story about it, but there was no public response.

The hundreds of U.S. media personnel who descended on Addis Ababa in the wake of those first graphic images for the most part were neither interested in nor very much aware of the momentous cataclysms of the previous decade in Ethiopia. In *The Quality of Mercy,* a book about the world's reaction to the tragedy in Cambodia in the late 1970s, author William Shawcross wrote that "some areas of the world are bathed in the glare of publicity, from some there are only glimmers of light, and others are in total darkness." How this light gets distributed is a rather arbitrary process, according to Shawcross. The media searchlight is forever scanning the globe, stopping for awhile in one place, before moving on to the next. Although the story rolls on, the media are unable to focus simultaneously on more than a few areas of the world on a continuing basis; thus, the media are forced constantly to decide when public awareness of a certain country or region will stop, even if events don't. This cannot be helped. Nevertheless, I think it should be clear that when the searchlight comes back to a place, the press and television have a responsibility to fill the gaps in the intervening darkness. In the case of Ethiopia, this was not done. As a result, historical amnesia set in. The U.S. media's overall performance in the Horn of Africa, when examined closely, is an object lesson in the general failure of modern memory.

*   *   *

In the middle and late 1970s, Ethiopia was a big story around the world. Haile Selassie was overthrown, a bloody revolution ensued, the USSR moved in, the United States moved out, Somalia invaded, the province of Tigre rose in revolt, and the guerrilla movement in Eritrea mushroomed overnight. Journalists poured into the region. One of them, Philip Caputo of the *Chicago Tribune,* even wrote a bestselling novel, *Horn of Africa,* about a mythical African country that obviously was modeled on Eritrea. Eventually, the media tired of the story. Then the Iranian revolution and the Soviet invasion of Afghanistan completely wiped Ethiopia off the world news map. But the fighting in northern Ethiopia continued unabated. Almost every year in the early 1980s, the Addis Ababa government launched a fresh offensive against the guerrillas; two of those offensives were even bigger than the late 1970s offensives the media had covered in force. War was destroying the land and the peasants on it, and the drought and Marxist agricultural policies were only making the situation worse. A famine resulted in 1984, bringing droves of journalists back to Ethiopia for the first time in six years. The famine and the drought were reported in depth. The rest was largely forgotten. The linkage between the headlines in the 1970s and those of the 1980s was never made. It was almost as if the former headlines had occurred in another country, in another part of the world.

The U.S. media actually was quite slow in responding to the famine. Intermittently, in 1983 and 1984, area-based correspondents tried to arouse their editors' interest in reports of widespread hunger in northern Ethiopia, usually to little avail. One network crew even managed to obtain hard-to-come-by Ethiopian visas, but was told by its editors to proceed to Lebanon instead. Moreover, in the spring and summer of 1984, as starvation increased, a surfeit of other major international stories occupied the news space: the fortieth anniversary celebrations of D-Day, deadlocked Israeli elections, and the Los Angeles Olympics, which included the media buildup to the games and the Eastern bloc boycott. It was a BBC correspondent, Michael Buerk, and a Kenyan television cameraman, Mohammed Amin, working for the European agency Visnews, who really broke the Ethiopian famine story in the United States.

A *New York Times* article by Sally Bedell Smith, appearing a month later on November 22, 1984, chronicled what happened. Under an arrangement whereby the BBC and NBC each get exclusive use of the other's material, NBC's London-based European news director, Joseph Angotti, reviewed Buerk's report the afternoon of October 23, 1984. Angotti alerted NBC editors in New York, who told him only that "they would consider it, possibly for the next day or day after." Angotti saw the film again a few hours later on the BBC's 9 P.M. newscast. It was only 2 P.M. in New York. Angotti then decided to do something, the significance of which would be incalculable. He decided on a direct approach to Paul Greenberg, executive producer of *The NBC Nightly News.* Greenberg watched Buerk's film when it arrived by satellite at 5 P.M. New York time and immediately decided to cut the film into two segments, for use that night and the next. The Dachau-like images from the Ethiopian desert had a shattering audience impact and were enhanced by Buerk's measured and poignant commentary, which permitted a generous use of natural sound. Courtenay Tordoff, the BBC-TV foreign news editor, indicated to the *New York Times* that the British style of delivery (correspondents speaking slowly, with large pauses between words, to let the images speak for themselves), almost as much as the actual footage, was responsible for the film's effect on U.S. viewers.

It may have been no accident that a British journalist broke the story. Having invaded Ethiopia in the nineteenth century, and having administered neighboring Sudan and colonized neighboring Kenya,

Britain traditionally paid closer attention to this part of the world than did the United States. British coverage of the Horn of Africa throughout the 1980s always evinced a full-bodied, historical continuity that U.S. coverage lacked. British journalists always came to cover the war and politics as well as to cover the famine. For example, Jonathan Steele, one of *The Guardian's* senior London-based correspondents, remarked to me in Khartoum that he was interested mainly in writing about the political situation in Sudan because a freelancer, Ed Hooper, was adequately covering the relief side of the story for the paper. It was an attitude untypical of U.S. journalists, who in many cases were predominantly interested in the famine to the exclusion of the attending political and military factors that would have helped explain it.

Buerk's report, broadcast October 23 and October 24 on *The NBC Nightly News with Tom Brokaw,* ignited several weeks of nonstop, intensive coverage of the famine. Between October 23 and late January 1985, the famine was the dominant international story in the United States. The revelation of Israel's dramatic rescue of starving black Jews in eastern Sudan in late 1984 further intensified the public's interest in Ethiopia and the Sudan. Also, there was a lack of news elsewhere in the world. By late October 1984, both the media and the public in the United States were exceedingly bored with the marathon, lackluster presidential campaign whose results already appeared cut and dried. Buerk's report had arrived at the perfect moment. Had U.S. Marines still been in Lebanon; had Konstantin Chernenko died a few months sooner, bringing the fascinating Mikhail Gorbachev to power in the Soviet Union in late 1984 instead of in 1985; or, had South Africa exploded a bit earlier, those unforgettable images of starving Ethiopian children might have had much less impact than they subsequently did.

The window in the news stayed open for a surprisingly long time. The Middle East in the early months of 1985 was relatively quiet. Israel, for the first time in its history, was taking painful, bipartisan steps to shore up its domestic economy, and Israelis were more preoccupied with their own internal problems than ever before. Iran was virtually closed off to Western journalists. Iraq was not always easy to enter. Although U.S. correspondents still reported from Lebanon, the factional fighting there during this period seemed to have exclusively Lebanese implications, thus giving the story reduced appeal. The kidnapping of the Associated Press Beirut bureau chief, Terry Anderson, and the evacuation of U.S. Embassy personnel from Beirut in mid-March certainly were important events, but they only led the news for a few days. The paucity of really good stories in the region was illustrated by the unusually large number of distinguished journalists who chose to cover the Greek parliamentary elections the first week of June. Ethiopia and Sudan thus had an eight-month run on the front pages.

Afterwards—until the famine returned in late 1987—the story didn't totally die. As recently as autumn 1986, the famine in southern Sudan was on the front pages of some newspapers and made the evening news on the networks. However, public attention was most concentrated between the autumn of 1984 and the summer of 1985, and, therefore, this was the time when indelible impressions were made.

* * *

There was no gradual buildup of U.S. journalists in the region prior to the broadcast of Buerk's report. Few correspondents covered Ethiopia and Sudan on a constant basis. Both countries were peripheral to the Middle East, thus placing them within the bailiwick of the Nairobi press corp, whose members often had more than forty-five countries in Africa to monitor. Moreover, the U.S. media were not as well represented in Nairobi as they were elsewhere. Not all of the major dailies had bureaus there, and of the four networks, only CNN had a fulltime correspondent for black Africa. Buerk's report, therefore, caught the U.S. media offguard. *Newsday* was an exception: because the paper's top editors had the foresight to watch Ethiopia in 1983 and 1984, the Long Island, New York, daily already had a special three-person reporting team in place in Addis Ababa when the story broke.

Otherwise, when the U.S. press corp rushed into the Horn of Africa at the tail end of 1984, it did so with less preparation and less expert knowledge to draw from than had been the case on any previous foreign story of comparable size. As one correspondent for a major U.S. daily explained, "In Ethiopia we learned as we went along, just like everybody else. And by the time we realized the importance of the war, our stories were not being read as fervently." The *Washington Post*'s David Ottaway, who along with his wife Marina had authored a book on the Ethiopian revolution, was perhaps the only U.S. journalist with much experience in the country. Predictably, his periodic reports from Washington covered aspects of the Ethiopian reality that almost nobody else's reports did—such as an April 25, 1986, account (co-written with Patrick Tyler) about how Ethiopian security police seized and tortured a CIA agent who had been operating under official diplomatic cover as a commercial attaché at the U.S. Embassy in Addis Ababa. Ottaway took an approach toward Ethiopia that was desperately needed and in rather short supply.

The media didn't normally approach African countries the way the media did other places in the Third World. Unlike Latin America, black Africa was not geographically close, nor did it have the strategic importance of the Middle East or the economic impact of Asia. Black Africa was a "human interest" story; a place tailormade for good feature writers, preferably unmarried ones, who could live out of a suitcase, writing colorful pieces on subjects that were more intrinsically interesting than they were relevant to a U.S. audience. Most U.S. journalists, I strongly believe, were not psychologically prepared to interpret Ethiopia through the same sharp, analytical filter as was used for a place such as Syria; even though Ethiopia was one African country that, at this stage in its history, often did warrant such an approach. After all, there was more than a famine occurring in Ethiopia. As President Reagan himself indicated, in his October 24, 1985, address to the United Nations General Assembly, Ethiopia was one of five countries in the world where the Soviet Union was actively involved in a war to spread its influences. But the media did not sufficiently flesh out their coverage of the famine to work in this other reality. By and large, Ethiopia was packaged for the public as a feature story about hunger and relief assistance.

Of course, many journalists did not always see Ethiopia in these narrow terms. Nevertheless, media coverage was constricted by the personnel and logistical considerations peculiar to Africa. Both Clifford D. May and Blaine Harden were responsible for many other countries on the continent in addition to Ethiopia and were for long stretches the only representatives of their news organizations in Addis Ababa and Khartoum. Neither could afford to avoid breaking news. As Harden pointed out, the televised scenes at the emergency feeding centers on the government side were "so unprecedented" that these stories had to be covered, and May added, "We couldn't ignore starving babies because TV had made it compelling."

The Ethiopian government always tried to deny that there was a war and severely discouraged journalists from writing about anything except starvation and the country's need for grain. Also, the visual character of the story did not foster a desire among journalists to seek out the nonvisual "process" of famine, which often meant long visits to war-stricken regions where there were no starving people. For those journalists who were willing to visit such areas, the Eritrean and Tigrean guerrillas were not always helpful.

The guerrillas—who were products of cultures and national movements that traditionally held out little regard for foreigners—were as ambivalent toward Western journalists as the Ethiopian government was hostile. In December 1984 through February 1985, there was usually a crowd of reporters in Khartoum trying to get into Eritrea or Tigre. But their time was limited, and neither of the two guerrilla relief agencies, particularly REST, properly understood that most reporters could not devote three weeks to a trip into the war zone, which is what traveling from Khartoum to Gedaref to Tigre and back again to Gedaref and Khartoum entailed. (A year later, when I inquired about interviewing prisoners who had been broken out of an Ethiopian jail by the TPLF, Samuel Mariam, a REST official in Gedaref, told me it was possible if I had "a month to spare.") Clifford May had wanted to observe the famine and war from the guerrilla side, but the *New York Times* foreign desk understandably could not afford to have him out of phone or telex contact for several weeks, in case he was needed urgently elsewhere in Africa. Similar constraints prevented Blaine Harden from making the same trip. (At the very end of 1987, Harden finally paid a visit to the guerrilla side in Eritrea. Had he done this two years earlier, it might have had a much greater impact.)

Even when a reporter was willing to invest the time, it wasn't always possible to get into rebel areas. Paul Vallely tried on and off for six months in 1985 to get into Tigre. He was even hoping to write a book about his journey. But the fighting, which the press corp in Addis Ababa barely mentioned, was so heavy and the government's advances so swift during parts of the spring that the TPLF did not want Western reporters or aid workers in Tigre. When, on rare occasions, the guerrillas made a special effort to get a team of journalists quickly into their territory and back out again, the results were worth it. The Eritrean People's Liberation Front (EPLF) arranged for the ABC News U.N. correspondent, Lou Cioffi, to be inside Eritrea within a few days of his arrival in Sudan direct from New York. Although Cioffi's report did not make *World News Tonight,* ABC's prime-time evening news program, the report did appear on *Good Morning America.*

A whole new, and truer, perspective of Ethiopia was achieved by those few representatives of the major media who either spent a long period with the guerrillas or, because they lacked the time, who pushed like crazy to quickly get in and out of Eritrea or Tigre in order to see the reality of the war. After a trip to Eritrea in the first weeks of 1985, Robert J. Rosenthal wrote in the *Philadelphia Inquirer* (February 24, 1985):

> Occasionally there was a burst of automatic rifle fire from the army's trenches less than 500 yards away. The rebels of the Eritrean People's Liberation Front checked their weapons before heading into the no man's land between their trench lines and those of the government. Another night of warfare was about to begin.
>
> This is not the Ethiopia made familiar to the world on television, not the Ethiopia where images of starvation prompted urgent efforts to

feed several million people, not the Ethiopia where cameras now record
the arrival of relief workers and bulging grain sacks.

This is an Ethiopia that is largely isolated, under siege—and famished."

Allen Pizzey of CBS News spent close to a month on the Tigre story
and was able to report March 22, 1985, on the *CBS Evening News
with Dan Rather* that the Ethiopian government's "only contribution
to hunger is bombs. Village paintings record memories of government
attacks. One day last month, two MIG fighters strafed this town [Abbi
Adi] fifteen times. Almost all the 200 dead and wounded were civilians."

Still, these reports constituted the rare exceptions. Their impact was
severely depleted by the deluge of coverage from the government side.
Although Rosenthal's series of articles on Eritrea was certainly gripping,
one must keep in mind that nobody in Washington or New York, or
many other cities for that matter, saw them. Neither the *New York
Times,* the *Washington Post,* nor the *Los Angeles Times*—perhaps the
three most influential general news dailies in the United States—ever
had a reporter in guerrilla-held Eritrea or Tigre during the entire
period of the famine, from 1984 through 1986, even though from one-
third to two-thirds of the 8–10 million starving in Ethiopia were in
those areas.

It was a television reporter, Bonnie Anderson of NBC News, who
gave the U.S. people their first, and maybe only, lasting impression of
a war rooted in ethnic conflict and exacerbated by Soviet involvement
that was central to the process of hunger. The NBC crew lugged their
cameras and other gear into TPLF territory in the very first weeks
of the famine emergency, before the flight of Eritrean and Tigrean
refugees into Sudan alerted the world to the fact of starvation in areas
not under government control. Anderson and her colleagues were extremely demanding. One British relief worker on the scene said the
TPLF people just couldn't understand why she always seemed to be
in a rush. But given the dilatory nature of the TPLF in its dealings
with journalists, a bold and occasionally brazen manner was absolutely
essential. The first of her reports appeared on the *NBC Nightly News
with Tom Brokaw* on November 29, 1984. This was when public interest
in the famine was at its peak—three months before Rosenthal and
Pizzey produced their pieces on Eritrea and Tigre, which appeared at
a time when interest already had begun to wane. Anderson reported
allegations that "the Marxist government in the capital city is inten-
tionally blocking relief efforts here [in Tigre], to starve the people and
weaken their ten-year-old struggle for independence . . . yet uses its
Soviet-supplied fighter planes to strafe and bomb the refugees." On
November 30, she reported that "while dozens of international agencies

work with the Ethiopian government, there are only a handful in rebel Tigre," where "3 million people are starving." On December 5, she told the viewing audience that "9 million people in northern Ethiopia are receiving virtually none of the food being sent to that country from around the world. . . . But little is being done. . . . Ethiopian officials . . . don't even admit there's a civil war going on." (The figure of 9 million referred to the total combined populations of Eritrea and Tigre, not specifically to those affected by the famine.)

Too few correspondents were willing, or able, to strike out on their own, away from the herd, the way Anderson did. For the most part, the barrage of screen images revealed nothing of one of the Third World's biggest wars, in which approximately twenty thousand soldiers were engaged in the heart of the famine zone. ABC television's record was typical of the media as a whole. Of thirty-four famine reports appearing on *World News Tonight with Peter Jennings* between October 29, 1984, and September 20, 1985, the war never really was discussed. There were only two brief mentions of it. In a November 29, 1984, report about military expenditures in drought-affected African countries, correspondent Barrie Dunsmore said only that "Ethiopia has been fighting its civil war for two decades. This year the bill is estimated to be about $440 million." On March 8, 1985, Tom Jarriel reported that "in northern Ethiopia today armed rebels kidnapped two French doctors, two French nurses and a five-man crew of a French air force transport plane delivering food to famine victims. And they were seized at gunpoint after their plane landed at Wollo province. The whereabouts of the hostages is unknown." Otherwise, ABC's prime-time coverage included four individual reports on a less-than-honest relief charity; scenes of Charlton Heston, Harry Belafonte, and Michael Jackson's brother Marlon Jackson with famine victims; a story about deaf children in New York City dancing to raise money for Ethiopia; the fundraising activities of British and U.S. pop stars; and a piece about President Reagan donating the proceeds from an autographed Stetson hat to the relief effort. The only substantive treatment of area politics was during the April 1985 coup in Sudan, when pro-U.S. president Jaafar Nimeiri was overthrown. The internal political situation in Ethiopia, whose regime had one of the worst human rights records in the world, never was given more than a passing reference on *World News Tonight*.

Even when war and politics were at the very heart of the issue at hand, they not only weren't discussed, but on one occasion weren't even mentioned. In a January 30, 1985, report lasting more than two minutes about the relief camp at Wad Kowli on the Sudanese border, ABC's chief foreign correspondent, Pierre Salinger, completely failed to explain why eighty thousand ethnic Tigreans had to come to Sudan for food in the first place. Identifying the refugees only as "Ethiopians," Salinger said they came because "there was nothing to eat in their own country." This was both false and misleading. Almost all of those people chose to walk for weeks on foot to Sudan, rather than risk being captured or turned away at feeding centers only a few miles from where they lived in Tigre by soldiers of a government that was prosecuting a war against the province. The famine camps in Sudan (as I shall explain more fully in the next chapter) were a political phenomenon that existed only because the civil war had forced tens of thousands of people to run from the internationally recognized regime in Addis Ababa, rather than to seek succor from it. But anybody watching Salinger's report would have merely gotten the impression that there was drought in the land that caused starving people to flee their country for someplace else—an act of God really.

The coverage on the other networks was somewhat better. NBC's record was helped by the decision to air Buerk's report and by Anderson's trip into Tigre. CBS, in addition to sending Pizzey into Tigre, had correspondent John Blackstone on the guerrilla side in Eritrea in mid-December 1984. Moreover, Blackstone's reporting from the government side frequently demonstrated an awareness of political and military issues, although that awareness did not always result in the situation being put in its proper perspective. For example, in a November 20, 1984, report on the *CBS Evening News with Dan Rather,* Blackstone noted that "Ethiopia is not only starving; it is also torn by civil war." He went on to describe how the war was interfering with the relief effort and how the government was using the famine as a tool in the war. This was all too true and should have been discussed by the media much more than it was. But Blackstone, as well as other journalists conscientious enough to raise the issue of the war, created the distinct impression that the war, rather than being an integral cause of the famine, was yet another calamity afflicting this unlucky country.

Unlike the other networks, CNN broadcast news continuously and therefore was able to give its audience many more hours of famine coverage. It is questionable, however, whether those extra hours provided viewers with a clearer understanding of what was happening in the region. For instance, CNN used its extra time to show a thirteen-part report entitled, "Africa's Crisis: The 11th Hour," in which the emphasis was almost exclusively on environmental and relief issues. Even when, in late 1985, war and politics finally became important themes in famine coverage, the overwhelming majority of CNN's reports dealt with the relief effort; little time was devoted to other aspects of the Ethiopian reality.

A problem for all the networks was that they couldn't cover what they couldn't film. The war was off limits, unless one was willing to enter Ethiopia from a place like Gedaref. Although tens of thousands of people later were reported to have died as a consequence of the Ethiopian government's resettlement policies, television barely investigated the issue because, with the exception of rare visits to "showcase" camps, cameras were not allowed into the resettlement area. The famine aside, the Ethiopian government probably was responsible for fifty times more deaths of black Africans in the 1984–1985 period than were South African security forces. But the media were much less aggressive toward the regime in Addis Ababa than toward the regime in Pretoria. This may not have been so had the media been nearly as restricted in South Africa as it was in Marxist Ethiopia (however, stringent press regulations were put into effect in South Africa in 1986). Another factor was that Mengistu, far more so than South African president P. W. Botha, made himself practically inaccessible to Western television cameras. Botha, with his bluff, ox-like visage bespeaking all the insufferable, uncompromising qualities of the Afrikaner burgher, offered a perfect target for U.S. political cartoonists. But, because the crimes of the Ethiopian regime could not be identified closely enough with any particular face or personality, in the minds of U.S. viewers the evil became abstract and outside the realm of human accountability. In every facet of policy, Mengistu, unlike the embattled South African leader, really was uncompromising; the high stone wall around the palace in Addis Ababa was literal as well as figurative and constituted a barrier too formidable for the media to scale.

A survey of *New York Times* articles indicates the degree to which the U.S. media narrowly interpreted its mandate in Ethiopia during the period of the famine emergency. From January through October 1984, before the United States "discovered" the Horn of Africa, more than half of the articles appearing in the country's most influential daily newspaper dealt with the various civil wars ravaging Ethiopia and the role of Marxism and the Soviet Union in Ethiopian affairs. But following the broadcast of Buerk's report on *The NBC Nightly News,* all this seemed forgotten. From October 24 through December 31, 1984, almost 90 percent of the sixty-odd articles on Ethiopia in the *New York Times* didn't touch on the war or anything else except hunger and relief. This slant on coverage barely altered in the first months of 1985. By mid-August 1985, the *New York Times* had published close to two hundred articles on Ethiopia and Sudan since the famine began; only about thirty dealt with political and military causes.

Finally, in a December 1, 1985, *New York Times Magazine* article about the famine by correspondent Clifford D. May, "war" was highlighted in the headline, but it never actually was explored in the piece, which concentrated mainly on the experiences of Western relief workers in Africa.

The thrust of coverage in the *Washington Post* was little different. However, in late 1985 and early 1986, correspondent Blaine Harden wrote several articles on subjects such as the Eritrean war, resettlement, and the forced collectivization of ethnic Oromos, which were either so complete or so tellingly written that they couldn't fail to have a lingering effect on Washington policymakers, even if the general public had by that time become distracted with other issues.

Newsday won a Pulitzer Prize for its famine coverage. Therefore, to criticize its reporting in Ethiopia would be tantamount to heresy, or even worse, such criticism might appear petty. Nevertheless, I believe that *Newsday*'s coverage exemplified not only the best, but also the most unsettling, aspects of the media's basic approach to Ethiopia. *Newsday*'s reporting of the famine was anything if not serious. The Long Island daily spent a lot of money getting its special team of two reporters and a photographer to the most remote corners of famine-stricken Africa, and *Newsday* spent this money before the story became hot news and without any assurance that it would.

Newsday reporters Dennis Bell and Josh Friedman, and photographer Ozier Muhammad, were the only U.S. journalists in Ethiopia when Buerk's film was broadcast by NBC. The planning showed: the stories, although long and packed with detail, made effortless reading. The writing was extremely polished, as Bell and Friedman were the only U.S. reporters who didn't have to rush to catch up with the news. In a piece appearing in *Newsday* November 4, 1984, Bell picked his way through a morass of statistics and allegations to give a perfectly objective record of why there wasn't enough grain in the country when the famine hit. Muhammad's photographs were heart wrenching but never sensational. In a text accompanying his pictures, he observed that in the midst of famine, "women in the camps were still having babies, little girls were preoccupied with their appearance, little boys were up to familiar hijinks, and the men were involved in being role models." Because he concentrated on their ability to be normal in abnormal conditions, Muhammad's subjects never lost their dignity.

Newsday did not use its advantage to play to the bleachers the way television did. There were no cute features on the activities of individual U.S. workers in the relief effort. Bell and Friedman focused more on the Ethiopians than on the foreigners who were trying to help them. *Newsday*'s coverage of starvation, relief assistance, and the role of the

RRC was complete. It was *Newsday's* predilection to disregard the other layers of the local reality that I find deeply disturbing.

Newsday covered what everyone else covered better than everyone else did, but it also ignored what everyone else ignored, in some respects to an even greater degree. In more than twelve thousand words of copy about Ethiopia included in a special supplement of reprinted articles about the famine, the name of Mengistu Haile Mariam never appeared once. To read Bell's and Friedman's copy, "the government," as it often was referred to, its self-destructive agricultural policies, and the war it was waging against its own people in the middle of the famine zone seemed vague, distant realities in a world dominated by Dawit's RRC. The war was mentioned exactly five times, for a total of less than four hundred words. On all occasions, the war was buried deep down in the story; as in a December 2, 1984, piece by Bell, where in the next-to-last paragraph, he confused the Tigrean guerrillas with the Eritreans.

The famine's causes, according to Friedman, in a December 23, 1984, *Newsday* article, were both natural and manmade. Among the manmade ones he listed the unstable world economy, the rise in the price of oil, and bad agricultural policies (which were not discussed). Many, many paragraphs later he wrote that "the ravages of drought are made worse by civil strife," adding that "some people . . . cannot receive aid because of active rebellions against central governments"—as if it were the guerrillas, not the government, who were refusing to negotiate. (On the other hand, in a rare reference to the famine's political background, *Newsday* noted in a January 4, 1985, editorial that "food must be funneled secretly into rebel areas that the callous government of Ethiopia wants to punish by starvation.")

Freidman's December 9, 1984, account of a visit to a resettlement camp at Asosa was the first, and one of the few, on-scene reports about resettlement, which later studies would conclude had remarkable similarities with the brutal relocation of Cambodian city dwellers to the countryside by the Khmer Rouge. Entitled "New Start for Chosen Few" in the special supplement, Friedman's twenty-five-hundred-word piece, one of the longest in the series, served to put the best possible light on a program that, at least, was extremely controversial and, at worst, constituted one of the most massive violations of human rights in the history of the postcolonial Third World. The *Newsday* reporter dutifully catalogued the litany of abuses, especially the separation of families, the forced removal of people from their ancestral homes, and the lack of supplies at the new sites. He also stated that although these abuses were now ending, U.S. and other Western officials still were suspicious. Therefore, Friedman went on, "of all the countries that have stationed more than 50 aircraft in Ethiopia temporarily to ferry food and supplies, only the Soviet Union and Libya have allowed their planes to carry refugees to resettlement camps." He failed to note that although all the aircraft of Western countries in Ethiopia were there for relief purposes only, all but a handful of the hundreds of Soviet aircraft—including MIGs and helicopter gunships—were there exclusively for the war. He also didn't mention that the Antonovs designated for use in the resettlement program were not pressurized and thus caused several people to die in the cargo bays on each flight. Investigations by the Harvard-based Cultural Survival and Berliner Missionswerk, not to mention a 1986 article by Blaine Harden (*Washington Post, International Herald Tribune,* March 11, 1986), would later reveal that rather than having ended, the worst phase of resettlement-generated human rights abuses did not even begin until early 1985 (see Chapter 4). Friedman's impressions were obviously those of a reporter who visited only the government side.

It was more than that, however. Just consider what had happened: a black African government in the process of building the first Marxist-Leninist state on the continent had, through crop requisitions, the fixing of market prices, the forced collectivization of peasants, and the unwillingness to halt a war in which fields were burned and livestock decimated, brought its people to a point of such unprecedented, graphic deprivation that human suffering was all the media cared to focus on. This allowed the perpetrators of the catastrophe to go largely uncensured and, in some cases, unremarked. In the pages of the *Newsday* supplement—the centerpiece of the paper's Pulitzer Prize–winning effort—the man more responsible than any other for the famine was completely forgotten. Mengistu had accomplished the ultimate disappearing act of a Marxist functionary: in addition to being faceless, he had become nameless. (In fact, the only Ethiopian official that the *Newsday* supplement directly linked to deaths through starvation was the pro-U.S. emperor Haile Selassie, whom reporter Bell, in his November 4, 1984, article, noted was overthrown because of the two hundred thousand deaths in the 1973–1974 famine in Wollo and Tigre.)

The media's incredibly indulgent attitude toward a black, Soviet-style regime in the first, most intensive weeks of famine coverage was too much for even *The Nation*—a journal as feisty as it is left-wing—to abide. In a January 19, 1985, front-page article by a Boston-based writer, Jonathan B. Tucker, *The Nation* gave its small audience a better insight into Ethiopia than that provided by all of the prize-winning articles in *Newsday*. Tucker, and the people he quoted, explained that Ethiopia was a country spending half of its annual budget on one of Africa's best-equipped armies; that the government was conducting a war against civilians in famine-stricken areas with parallels to "U.S. counterinsurgency methods in Vietnam"; and that although half the famine victims were in guerrilla-held areas, international aid was running twenty to one in favor of the government side.

Rarely before have periodicals, news magazines, and a paper such as the *Wall Street Journal*—which, although a daily, does not have a typical daily newspaper approach to news—been quite so valuable to public awareness as in the matter of the Ethiopian famine. All of these publications, whether on the left, like *The Nation,* or on the right, like the *Wall Street Journal;* whether normally frivolous, like the rock magazine *Spin,* or sententious, like *U.S. News & World Report,* offered their readers basic and necessary insights into a unique and tormented African country that should have been, but hardly ever were, in the pages of the daily newspapers or on television screens. Perhaps because these organs were less close than the daily media were to breaking news about the famine, they were less blinded by the emotional intensity of the public reaction.

At the same time as *The Nation,* the January 21, 1985, issue of *The New Republic* had the famine on its cover. *The New Republic,* which often defies ideological categorization, offered its readers a package of three articles. As I intimated in the previous chapter, Christopher J. Matthews' piece on the visit of a congressional delegation to Ethiopia held insights about the atmosphere on the government side that many journalists in Addis Ababa never cared to make. Allan Hoben's article on Ethiopian agriculture explained how Stalinist tactics toward the peasantry had helped cause the famine. The third article, which I wrote, dealt with the strategic impact of Eritrean and Tigrean refugees pouring into Sudan from the guerrilla side.

In his December 1, 1985, article in the *New York Times Magazine,* Clifford May wrote that the famine was an aspect of the African reality that has "long existed outside the pages of *National Geographic.*" Whether or not May realized it, it was an astonishing statement for a *Times* reporter to make, considering that three months earlier, in its September 1985 issue, *National Geographic* highlighted an important, harrowing aspect of the famine (the war in Eritrea) that to a large extent had existed outside the pages of the *New York Times.* When the famine story broke the year before, *National Geographic* sent Pulitzer Prize–winning Black Star photojournalist Anthony Suau to Eritrea. Suau's text was too short to do much more than introduce the issue to readers, but his photos made a startling visual report about the relationship between war and starvation. Were *National Geographic* able to get its pieces into print as quickly as could the *New York Times Magazine,* the latter's readers would have had to buy the so-called noncontroversial geographic journal for some of their hard news.

But it took a rock magazine, *Spin,* edited by *Penthouse* publisher Bob Guccione's son, Bob Jr., to fill in the massive holes in coverage left vacant by the elite daily media. In a series of articles that appeared in the latter half of 1986, Robert Keating threw a penetrating light on the resettlement program and the alleged culpability of the Live Aid charity in indirectly keeping the system of human rights abuse going. Keating also investigated the personality of a regime that, as he pointed out, received the lowest human rights rating of any other government in the world in a comprehensive book published by *The Economist.* The *Spin* articles may have fallen short of the standard of objectivity required by a paper such as the *New York Times,* but in terms of the themes that Keating chose to deal with, *Spin*'s approach was weightier.

The *Spin* articles were praised in a mid-1986 editorial in the conservative *Wall Street Journal,* which also was devoting significant attention to the revelations about resettlement. Writing about the war and the regime's abuses was more a matter of seriousness than of ideology. In Europe, for example, the unilateral disarmers of the British Labor party were among the Ethiopian government's biggest critics. Some of the most trenchant analyses of the war in northern Ethiopia came from *The Guardian,* a left-leaning British daily whose sympathies for the neutralist, Soviet-leaning attitudes of the Third World were well known.

In addition to *Spin,* the periodicals *Time, Newsweek, Commentary, Reader's Digest,* and *U.S. News & World Report* all published, at one point or another, a major story about resettlement and Ethiopia's drift toward orthodox communism. Indeed, because of the individual initiative of a New York–based staffer, Edward W. Desmond—who donated his vacation time to go to Eritrea—*Time* had a correspondent on the guerrilla side in late 1985. But all of these pieces, it must be strongly emphasized, like those in *Spin* and *National Geographic,* did not appear until the middle of 1985 at the very earliest. By then, the impact of famine-related stories had been reduced because of a series of terrorist incidents in the eastern Mediterranean that riveted U.S. attention back on the Middle East. (A noteworthy exception was a three-page spread in the January 21, 1985, edition of *Time* entitled, "Flight from Fear: Behind the Famine, the Grim Outlines of a Strategy to Win a Civil War." The story resulted from a trip to the Sudanese border by James Wilde. If the Tigrean guerrillas had a system for getting people like Wilde in and out of Tigre in only a few days, *Time* would have been able to do an even better job at covering the other half of the famine.)

*   *   *

At the close of 1986, *Los Angeles Times* correspondent Scott Kraft wrote a piece on Ethiopia, that in the December 13–14, 1986, edition of the *International Herald Tribune* carried the headline, "New Famine Seen as Ethiopia Relief Fades." Kraft reported the opinion of analysts that despite the massive 1984–1985 Western aid effort, "another famine is inevitable." (As it turned out, another famine did break out in 1987.) He wrote that despite the $1.5 billion of foreign assistance in 1985 alone, "things have pretty much returned to normal, which is to say that more than two million people still face the danger of starvation." Kraft also reported that "average income is about 30 cents a day and falling." As was so often the case in the media's coverage of the famine, the key point was buried near the very bottom of a very long piece: in the next-to-last paragraph, Kraft quoted an international financial expert in Addis Ababa as saying that the problem was "the dedication to a controlled economy. . . . If the world at large had confidence that Ethiopia was following a strategy that would prevent famine in the future, then the government would get more aid."

Kraft's article implied a note of surprise. Clearly, the fact that the *Tribune* editors saw fit to play the story on the front page at the time of the "Irangate" scandal meant that in the editors' view Kraft's findings might very well startle the paper's readers, who mainly depended on the *New York Times,* the *Washington Post,* and the *Los Angeles Times* wires for news. Of course, had one not read any of those daily news-papers as well as others, but *had* read just one of the articles in *Spin* or the *Wall Street Journal,* or the piece by Robin Knight in *U.S. News & World Report* that—appearing as it did in the summer of 1985—was obscured by coverage of the TWA hijack in Beirut, one wouldn't have been startled by Kraft's thesis at all. In fact, it wouldn't have even been news. The fact is, that any of those articles have stood the test of time better than any of the stories that won *Newsday* a Pulitzer Prize.

*   *   *

Like the public at large, U.S. journalists rushed into Ethiopia in the autumn of 1984 wearing their hearts on their sleeves. Because the media were crucial to the process of raising aid money, they didn't distance themselves enough to see the role of the famine and the relief effort in the overarching movement toward a fully developed communist society in which hunger would remain endemic. In 1987, Addis Ababa, according to a U.S. State Department official, had the political at-mosphere of Ulan Bator, the capital of the Soviet satellite state of

Mongolia. During the eight months when the Horn of Africa gripped the minds of the U.S. public, there were just too few articles and too few broadcasts to prepare the public for this easily forseeable reality.

I was in Ethiopia when the media rushed out. As when the media rushed in, there was nothing gradual about the withdrawal. In fact, it could be tied to a specific day, June 14, 1985, the day a TWA flight en route to Rome was hijacked after takeoff from Athens airport. I was in my room at the Hilton in Addis Ababa, writing a story, when I first heard about the hijack on the BBC hourly news broadcast. I decided to stop writing and go down to the hotel restaurant for dinner. There was no longer any point to finishing the story that night. I didn't need any clairvoyance to realize that editors back in the United States were going to be preoccupied with the hijack for days to come. Radical Shiites had finally got a large group of U.S. passport holders at their mercy: the evil of Beirut, which for months had been lurking in the background of the news, once again had reached out and sucked us all back in. As I suspected, when I got back to Athens, my home base, my radio editors—even before asking about the trip to Ethiopia— inquired if I could get to Cyprus to help out in covering the hijack. It was weeks before my stories from Ethiopia were used. I was merely part of a trend. The hijack had triggered a renewed media obsession with the Middle East. The blanket, and controversial reporting of the hostages' ordeal in Beirut kept the public focused on the area throughout the entire summer. Momentum in coverage of the Middle East was kept up in the fall by more terrorist exploits: the capture of an Italian cruise ship, the *Achille Lauro,* and the hijack of an Egyptian plane to Malta. By and large, until late 1987, the famine was wiped off the news map. The big herd of U.S. journalists in Addis Ababa accompanying Harry Belafonte and the USA for Africa entourage at the time of the hijack was the last. Of course, many journalists, including prestigious ones such as Bill Moyers of CBS News, still would continue to stream into the region, and periodically, into 1987, there would be blips of prime-time, front-page coverage about Ethiopia and Sudan. However, from the day the TWA plane was hijacked, the famine was no longer "*the* story," and from that moment on, anything written about it was bound to have less of an impact.

*   *   *

As the network crews were leaving Addis Ababa in June 1985, the Ethiopian regime was gearing up for the biggest offensive against the guerrillas since the late 1970s. Battalions of T-54 and T-55 tanks and squadrons of MIG-23 fighter bombers were about to engage in a five-month-long carnage in which thousands of soldiers and civilian peasants would be killed, wounded, and displaced. The billion-dollar infusion of Soviet weaponry, which paralleled the billion-plus infusion of Western relief aid, was about to take effect. Large tracts of guerrilla territory would be mopped up, thereby significantly shifting the battle lines for the first time in years and improving the Soviet position in a strategic corner of the world in the months and weeks prior to the Geneva summit. But the U.S. public was to know almost nothing.

THREE _____

the world's biggest
forgotten war

Millions of people are being psychologically traumatized, starved and killed in conflicts that are virtually ignored by the media, Congress and the U.S. administration.
—F. Andy Messing, Jr., executive director
of the National Defense Council Foundation,
writing in the *Los Angeles Times*

For years now there had been no country here but the war.
—Michael Herr, *Dispatches*

ERITREA: SELF-RELIANCE, LIBERATION, AND WAR

South of the Sudanese border, the Red Sea hills erupt into a chain of sandstone and granite peaks whose eroded, sun-blistered faces, ocher and black, suggest the forbidding surface of a distant planet. It is a natural environment of near-total hostility. Plagues of locusts, grasshoppers, and army worms follow drought. The soil has no absorptive capacity, and within minutes of any rainfall, bucketfuls of water streak in dendritic patterns down the canyon walls and flood the valleys. Later, the mud at the bottom dries and cracks and is filtered back into the air as dust. Anything that might pass for a road is blocked by boulders, torn away from the scarps in the deluge. Mostly acacias grow here, and their scrawny roots and branches do little to anchor the soil or shield against the sun's glare. The trees are of better value to the yellow weaverbirds who nest in them and to the camels who munch on the inch-long thorns. As one might expect, an aerial reconnaissance of this region would reveal few signs of human habitation. It is only as dusk approaches, when the sky becomes too dark for Ethiopian pilots to maneuver their Soviet-made MIG-23 fighter jets, that these seemingly inhospitable vastnesses come to life.

In the enveloping darkness, the defiles become crowded with people scurrying forth from daytime hiding places. Captured East German water tankers trundle out of acacia patches, and bulldozers begin clearing rocks from the road. The light of the rising moon catches the glint of metal rods, as many of the inhabitants are amputees equipped with crutches and artificial limbs. Fluorescent lights and gas lamps flick on in slate rock bunkers dug into the cliff sides, where workshops begin to operate. Tables, chairs, and other bits of furniture are being forged from ammunition boxes, while the snaps of the boxes are removed to make clasps for machines that wash lumps of black plastic, molded afterward into sandals for guerrilla fighters. Parts of Soviet-made cluster bombs are being converted into truck flywheels. The tips of spent tank shells are punctured to produce rain gauges for desert agricultural stations to the southwest. Wash basins are made out of exploded MIG shells, and the trip wires are cut into strings for *kirars*, a guitar-like instrument played by the soldiers.

In one bunker, whose roof is camouflaged by dark blankets and acacia branches, people don white lab suits and warm up British, Belgian, and West German machines trucked in pieces from Sudan and then reassembled. This is a tablet factory. In 1986, 40 million pills were produced, according to pharmacist Sennay Kifleyesus, including 3 million aspirin tablets and 5 million doses of chloroquin to fight malaria. Chloroquin is composed of four raw materials: talc, starch, cab-o-sil, and magnesium sterrate. Kifleyesus hopes to start production of some of these items soon. "We have to be more self-sufficient; we can't depend on anyone," he says. Kifleyesus is just one of many university-educated people smuggled into these canyons where no carbonated drinks are available and where the meals offered usually consist of only *wot* and *enjerra,* a lentil gruel served on a soggy, bread-like substance made from sorghum. The tablet factory is merely part of a large hidden medical complex, which includes an 800-bed hospital, where men and women trained in Ethiopia, Italy, Greece, Israel, the Soviet Union, the United States, and elsewhere are at work. In another bunker, four kinds of intravenous solutions are manufactured in reused plastic containers affixed with locally printed labels in the squiggly script of the Tigrinya and Tigre languages. Blood is stored in refrigerators powered by wind and solar energy. Skin grafting is accomplished in an operating room with boarded-up windows, a rough cement floor, and flies buzzing around a dirty fluorescent light.

A few miles away from the medical complex, in a mountainside hut, crippled people operate an Italian-made machine that produces 10,000 sanitary towels per hour for women soldiers at the front. In other workshops, radios and VHS video units are repaired, and architects are designing roads and irrigation systems fed by the floor runoff. While everywhere else in famine-stricken Africa the scientific know-how and initiative are provided by U.S. and European technicians, here it is different: undernourished children are being fed with a dietary supplement invented in 1984 by a local nutritionist, Dr. Azieb Fessahaye, consisting of 55 percent wheat or durra, 20 percent finely ground chick peas, 10 percent sugar, 10 percent milk powder, and 5 percent egg powder. For feeding purposes, one part of the dry mixture is added to three parts of water; 4,400 pounds a month are being produced for 5,000 children.

It is fully dark now, and at an altitude of 5,000 feet the close starscape seems to breathe. In a place where the daily routine is determined by the flight patterns of MIG jets and the lack of an effective antiaircraft cover—where even reservoirs must be concealed beneath camouflage nets—the workday has just begun for black Africa's most ingenious society.

*   *   *

Welcome to Orotta, the base camp of what U.S. intelligence experts consider the world's most sophisticated guerrilla fighters, the Eritrean People's Liberation Front (known in Tigrinya as the Hizbawi Ginbar Harnet Etra), whose civilian offshoot, the Eritrean Relief Association (ERA), is considered the most effective locally based famine relief agency in Africa. If one thinks of Orotta as the administrative capital of a sovereign polity, which in reality it is, then by Western standards of efficiency, Orotta is one of the few black African capitals that actually "works." Orotta also is the only capital not recognized by any Western power, even though the EPLF is doing more to bleed the resources of a Soviet-backed regime than are the contras in Nicaragua or the Angolan rebels led by Jonas Savimbi.

Orotta does not appear on any international map. Even Eritrea, for that matter, appears only as the delta-shaped, northernmost province of Ethiopia, capped at the top by a range of mountains that flattens out to form the Barka plain in the west; with the protruding arm of the Danakil depression—one of the hottest regions on earth—jutting in a southeasterly direction along the Red Sea. It is from the Greek word for the Red Sea, Erythra Thalassa, that Eritrea derives its name. Although only about fifty thousand square miles in area (the size of Pennsylvania or Mississippi or, perhaps more to the point, Nicaragua), Eritrea holds the key to Ethopia's political stability and territorial integrity. Eritrea also forms the basis of Ethiopia's strategic value: without Eritrea, Ethiopia would be a landlocked nation. The late emperor Haile Selassie, who prosecuted a war against the Eritreans for the last twelve years of his rule, was keenly aware of this. So, too, is the new communist potentate, Lieutenant Colonel Mengistu Haile Mariam. At the core of all the mass executions, cabinet-level shootouts, and opaque conspiracies that helped Mengistu consolidate power in the late 1970s were differences about the war in Eritrea. To this day, the fate of the Marxist regime and its close relationship with the Soviet Union is dictated by the progress of the war. The war has been responsible for the majority of logistical boondoggles plaguing the famine relief effort—weapons consignments receive priority at the port of Assab; half of Ethiopia's trucking fleet is utilized by the military; C-130 cargo planes transporting grain have been delayed at local airports because fuel often is siphoned off for patrols over Eritrea and neighboring Tigre province by MIGs and Mi-24 HIND helicopter gunships. If U.S. influence in Addis Ababa is marginal despite the generous outpouring of food aid, it is because of Washington's refusal to get involved in the war.

This is Africa's longest running and most competently fought war. Facing off against the world's best guerrilla fighters are upward of one hundred fifty thousand Ethiopian government soldiers—half of the total troop strength of black Africa's largest and best-trained standing army. (The EPLF, with an estimated thirty-five thousand fighters, is outnumbered by almost five to one.) The war, which has gone on since September 1961, when the government of Haile Selassie abrogated a U.N.-sponsored autonomy agreement with Eritrea, is literally a way without end, by whose interminable standards the Iraq-Iran conflict pales in comparison. More than a quarter million people have died so far on the battlefield, and about three-quarter million Eritreans have been exiled or internally displaced. But these figures are deceptive because the fighting of recent years has been the most bloody.

By 1986, Kidane Ghebermedhin, thirty-five, already had been at the front for nine years. His situation was not unusual. With no fixed period of service, many in Eritrea have fought as guerrillas for a decade or more. Their khaki shirts and shorts, canvas anklets, black plastic sandals, and Kalashnikov assault rifles are often all these guerrillas own. Many have gray hair by their early thirties. Never have I seen people who age as quickly as do these Eritreans. When I asked Ghebermedhin in October 1986 if he were discouraged after being a soldier for so long, he closed his eyes and shook his head. He didn't seem to understand the question. "I'm happy just being a fighter; I never think any more about town life."

A quarter century of conflict in Eritrea has engendered a monastic approach to existence, whereby absolute self-reliance, coupled with deprivation, has become a form of worship. In place of religion, which has been deemphasized in recent years, there has developed an intense form of national and social cohesiveness born of isolation and historical entrapment.

*   *   *

From as far back as 3000 B.C., when, according to Egyptian hieroglyphs, pharaonic galleys journeyed to the farthest reaches of the Red Sea coast in search of myrrh, Eritrea has been pivotal to the overall destiny of Ethiopia, while at the same time evolving separately from it. However clear this pattern may be to the inhabitants of the region, the complexity of this relationship has kept Eritrea from achieving a distinct identity in the minds of foreigners. This failure of comprehension by the outside world has been partly responsible for the almost palpable sense of "aloneness" that permeates the Eritrean psyche.

The first great Ethiopian empire—the Roman-era kingdom of Axum— was centered in neighboring Tigre, thus making Eritrea practically a home province. Axum's maritime trade was conducted through the ancient Eritrean port of Adulis, near modern-day Massawa. Internal dissension, the migration of Beja nomads from Sudan, and the rise of Islam eventually led to the kingdom's demise in the ninth century A.D. From the tenth century onward, according to Colin Legum in the Minority Rights Group report on Eritrea, "the locus of [Eritrean] power moved steadily southwards" and caused Eritrea to drift apart from the rest of the empire, while still retaining its central importance due to the outlet it afforded to the sea. It wasn't until five hundred years later, in the fifteenth century, that the ruling Ethiopian Amharas (who came to be known as Abyssinians) were able to reestablish a tenuous hold over Eritrea. As the Eritrean academic Bereket Habte Selassie noted in his book *Conflict and Intervention in the Horn of Africa,* Amhara rule was "tenuous because the people, geographically isolated and (by then) unaccustomed to outside rule, were fiercely nationalistic and stubbornly resisted Abyssinian attempts" at domination. Yet foreigners could not be kept out. During this period, the Eritrean coastline was frequented by Egyptians, Greeks, Persians, Arabs, and, lastly, Ottoman Turks, who occupied Massawa in 1557. As a result of these influences, among others, Eritreans grew to be more sophisticated and less xenophobic than were the Amharas and Tigreans of the interior, whose cultures and political traditions were to evolve completely on their own. This is why present-day Ethiopian politics (especially during the 1970s) remains very much an enigma to outsiders.

The Turks held sway over the coast for three centuries until they were displaced by the Egyptians, who were aided by the British, in 1875. The Suez Canal had opened six years earlier, in 1869, and with the increased strategic importance of the Red Sea, the British needed the assistance of a proxy in order to exclude the French, who already were ensconced in neighboring Djibouti. But the Egyptians, like the Turks before them, were unsuccessful in penetrating the Eritrean interior due to stiff local resistance. This failure, among other factors, forced the British to use Italian imperial ambitions in the area as a means to keep the French out. With British help, the Italians occupied Massawa in 1885 and began their invasion of the highlands. "The trail was coated with the blood of thousands of Italian soldiers," wrote Selassie. "Nevertheless, by 1889 all of Eritrea had been occupied, and Menelik [the Amhara king] had signed the Treaty of Ucciali, under which he recognized Italian rule over Eritrea." The treaty demarcated the regional boundaries as they exist today. Selassie indicated that "two different imperial territories now existed side by side," the one, Eritrea, governed by a white European colonial power; the other, Ethiopia, governed by a black African colonial power—the Amharas under Menelik—whose subjugation of the Tigreans to the north and of the Oromo people to the south was viewed by the indigenous inhabitants as no more preferable than any European-imposed tyranny.

The fact that Eritreans, Tigreans, and Oromos viewed the black Amharas no differently than these three groups viewed the white European intruders is a truth that many in the liberal West may find hard to accept, but whose implications are crucial to a proper understanding of the present conflict. When the Eritreans say they are fighting Amhara (Ethiopian) colonialism, they mean it in the same way as did other Africans when they struggled against French and British colonialism. The generally darker skinned Amharas of the central highlands, speaking a different Semitic tongue and perpetually insulated from the cosmopolitan influences of foreign cultures, were considered alien by the Eritreans. Although Italian occupation spelled all the evils inherent in colonialism—land expropriation, exploitation of cheap local labor, and delimitation of educational opportunities to serve the needs of an emerging subsecretarial class—in Eritrean eyes, Amhara domination would have been no less intolerable. Eritreans fought in large numbers for Mussolini against Haile Selassie in the 1935 Italian invasion of Ethiopia, and in traveling through Eritrea today, one encounters many an old man, fluent in Italian, who is proud of his part in that war.

From the very beginning, the Italians saw Eritrea as a potential staging post for a future invasion. With this in mind, a road and railway network was constructed and a settler population installed that brought new technological skills along with it. All this development led to urbanization, as Eritreans left their ancestral villages to seek work on these massive projects. A modern capital rose up in Asmara, which, with its yellow stone houses adorned with bougainvillea, is still one of the loveliest cities in Africa. The coming of fascism in Italy led to further investment in Eritrea. In order to convey military and other supplies from the port of Massawa up to Asmara, located 7,000 feet above sea level, the world's longest aerial ropeway was built. The new transport system allowed Eritreans to visit parts of their own country they had never seen before, thus facilitating the growth of a modern national consciousness. Trade unions were established, and local political culture came to be more advanced than was the case anywhere on the continent with the exceptions of Egypt and South Africa. Whatever its sins, Italian capitalism, even under Mussolini, proved to be a liberating social force in comparison to Amhara feudalism. Consequently, Eritrea surged ahead of its Amhara-dominated neighbors.

The fifty-two years of Italian rule were surely the most intensely experienced chapter in Eritrean history and served to crystallize Eritrea's separate identity. By the time the Italians were defeated by the British on the battlefields northwest of Asmara in 1941, Eritrea was a very different place from the rest of Ethiopia, whose experience of the Italians was restricted to the brief and brutal military occupation of Addis Ababa and other garrison towns between 1936 and 1941. Thus, in the aftermath of the war, when the world failed to adequately recognize this distinction, the Eritreans felt utterly deserted. The shattering effects of what, in their eyes, was a gross betrayal by outside powers are apparent in the EPLF's obsession with self-reliance, which is comparable only with the austere individualism of the Albanians— another people who have historically felt themselves to be completely alone.

The British military occupied Eritrea until September 1952, when the Western powers imposed a U.N. mandate on the local inhabitants that made Eritrea a semiautonomous territory under the sovereignty of Ethiopia and Haile Selassie. The rationale for this action was articulated by the U.S. secretary of state, John Foster Dulles, in a Security Council debate: "From the point of view of justice, the opinions of the Eritrean people must receive consideration. Nevertheless, the strategic interests of the United States in the Red Sea basin and considerations of security and world peace make it necessary that the country has to be linked with our ally, Ethiopia." Significantly, in 1953, the United States started work on the Kagnew communications and intelligence-gathering complex outside Asmara and on naval access facilities at Massawa. The Eastern bloc, which had no influence in the region at the time and thus had no strategic interests to look after, sided with the Eritreans, although in later years, hostile Soviet actions quickly would dissipate any feelings of gratitude among Eritreans.

The emperor never respected the U.N. autonomy agreement. The territory's independent institutions gradually were subverted, political parties were banned, and Tigrinya, the official language of Eritrea, was suppressed and replaced by Amharic. In 1961, the Eritrean Liberation Front, or ELF (not to be confused with the EPLF, which emerged later), was formed. The war broke out in September when the guerrillas mounted hit-and-run attacks with antiquated Italian weapons the guerrillas had been able to purchase. The following year, without the slightest protest from the U.N., Eritrea was formally annexed to Ethiopia as its fourteenth province, an action no more natural than the 1975 Moroccan annexation of the Spanish Sahara.

The Eritrean guerrilla struggle began in the 1960s as very much a Moslem-oriented affair. Tom J. Farer, in *War Clouds on the Horn of Africa: The Widening Storm,* wrote:

> Its launching was facilitated by the 1950s recession-bred migration from Asmara and the port cities to Saudi Arabia and the Sudan. The workers, plus young [Eritrean] Muslims who went to Cairo for a university education, formed a pool of latent militants who could be organized beyond the Emperor's reach. A second early asset was the 1962 eruption of civil war in the Yemen. Weapons from patrons poured into and overflowed the arsenals of the Yemeni belligerents. Some of these weapons filtered into the hands of the ELF.

Not surprisingly, the ELF's early supporters included the likes of Syria and the leftist Egyptian regime of Gamal Abdel Nasser. The domination of the ELF by Moslems and outside Arab radicals was a dubious, rather artificial arrangement. The orthodox Coptic Christian highlanders, who always accounted for about half of Eritrea's population, felt immediately estranged. As Farer suggested, after Israel's dramatic success in the 1967 Six Day War, the ELF's Arab patrons became more than ever preoccupied with their own problems and consequently lost interest in peripheral areas such as Eritrea. But with the 1969 coups in Sudan and Libya, which brought two radical regimes to power that supported the ELF, the organization got a new lease on life. The spate of ELF hijackings of Ethiopian Airlines planes constituted the beginning of Muammar Gaddafi's career as the Daddy Warbucks of terrorism. Like all radical organizations, the ELF soon divided into factions, with rival bands aligning themselves in the usual places—Baghdad and Damascus. By this time, of course, the Soviet Union, Cuba, and other Eastern bloc nations had signed on by helping the ELF in order to win prestige in the Arab-Islamic world and to help destabilize the pro-U.S. emperor in Addis Ababa.

However, radicalism did not cause the ELF's eventual decline. The ELF's Arab-Islamic outlook did because Eritrea was not Arab and was only partly Islamic. The population of 4 million was equally split between the Tigrinya-speaking Christians of the highlands and the Tigre-speaking Moslems of the coast and western plains. (Tigrinya and Tigre are closely related Semitic languages, but are almost mutually unintelligible. The language of Tigre should not be confused with the province of Tigre, where Tigrinya is spoken.) Welding these two population groups together psychologically—at which the Italians inadvertently succeeded—was not an easy task. Rather than build on this unity, the ELF, with its Arab cohorts, almost destroyed it.

The EPLF was formed in 1970. It had a strong Christian element, and, as its name implies, had a distinctly Marxist tinge at the beginning. Isaias Aferworki, a Christian, commanded the ELF field forces, while foreign relations were in the hands of Osman Salih Sabbe, a Moslem renegade from the original ELF, whose job it was to keep money flowing in from Arab capitals. Nonetheless, a civil war motivated by religious animosities broke out between the ELF and the EPLF in 1972; six thousand men were killed in this struggle waged in the shadows of the greater Ethiopian-Eritrean conflict. By the time the civil war ended in 1975 with no clearcut victor, Emperor Haile Selassie had been deposed in a coup in Addis Ababa, and a new government, headed by the Dergue, had come to power. The Dergue's initial egalitarian posture and talk of "reform" had raised hopes that the new government would seek to end the bloodshed in the north by compromising with the Eritrean resistance. These expectations were dashed on Bloody Saturday, November 23, 1974, when General Aman Michael Andom, an "Ethiopianized" Eritrean who had been negotiating with the Eritrean guerrillas on the Dergue's behalf, was ordered killed by Mengistu in Andom's Asmara villa precisely because he was believed to be close to achieving a historic peace settlement.

The effects of Andom's death were quick and devastating. Whole units of locally recruited government police in Eritrea deserted to the guerrillas. Students returned to their villages to join the ELF and the EPLF. As Farer revealed, "Having at last converted the great mass of Eritreans into the enemy, the masters of Addis could now pursue the logic of counterinsurgency to its murderous end." The same famine that in the mid-1970s had ravaged Wollo and Tigre and sparked the overthrow of the emperor "now tightened its grip on Eritrea." However, the Dergue did not allow its newly created relief agency to distribute food or foreign donor organizations to work in the area. Farer reported "that the government of Ethiopia tried, with careful premeditation, to orchestrate the starvation of Eritrea's rural population." The Dergue was barely a year old and had only just begun to emerge from the obscurity of the barracks, but already famine had become one of its main tools against a recalcitrant ethnic group: a fact that the world would still find difficult to accept a decade later when the same tactic was used again by the same government against the same group.

The drought and internal divisions notwithstanding, the dramatic, almost overnight growth of the Eritrean guerrilla movement following Andom's death led to the encirclement of Dergue troops in the main towns of Eritrea. Arab and Eastern bloc aid to Eritrea poured in, while the Soviet Union, assisted by Cuba, continued its blackmail of the Dergue by arming the Eritreans in order to get Mengistu to completely sever his links with the United States. The famine, the demise of Haile Selassie, and the possibility of an age-old empire splitting asunder attracted the world media to the Horn of Africa. Eritrea, in 1976, was suddenly a front-page news story.

In a last ditch effort to save its skin, the Dergue conscripted forty thousand Christian peasants in May 1976 for an assault on Eritrean guerrilla positions. The peasants were told they would be fighting "a holy crusade against the Arab infidels." But the new army was cut down by the guerrillas before it had the chance to attack. Jon Swain, the correspondent for the London *Sunday Times,* wrote:

As the bombs and bullets fell among them, the peasants rose in an angry swarm and taking up their weapons—for many only staves—swept forward shouting as they ran. Waves of them fell before they could discharge their guns. The remnants turned and ran away. But they were trapped between the guerrilla lines and the Ethiopian army, which . . . now opened fire in a callous attempt to drive the rabble forward. . . . By four in the afternoon the plain was still. "You could not see the ground. You could only see dead bodies," was how one who participated described the scene.

On the heels of this disaster came the most successful Eritrean offensive in the history of the war. The ELF and the EPLF, each able to field roughly sixteen thousand soldiers, together rolled up the countryside. Nakfa, the district capital of Sahel in the north, was captured by the EPLF, who have held it ever since. The Dergue was driven out of every main town except Asmara and the ports of Massawa and Assab. The road linking Asmara and Massawa was blocked, Asmara was under siege, and street battles raged in Massawa. Between 80 and 90 percent of Eritrea was in guerrilla hands in late 1977. The Dergue was on its knees, not only in Eritrea, but in the southeast of the country as well, where the Somali army was seventy-five miles inside Ethiopia on the road to Harar and Addis Ababa. The empire, forged at Axum in the century of Christ, was about to crumble. Then the Soviets rewrote the script by turning their guns on their former Eritrean allies.

In the midst of the guerrilla offensive, the incoming Carter administration had suspended all military aid to the Dergue because of its poor human rights record. Mengistu thus had nowhere to go except Moscow; because the USSR had armed the Eritreans in the first place, the Kremlin held the key to the war's outcome. "In Ethiopia, the Soviets created opportunities for themselves by causing the problems," observed Alan L. Keyes, a former assistant secretary of state for international organizations. Mengistu arrived in Moscow in May 1977 for a week-long state visit. Soviet arms began arriving in large quantities in Ethiopia later in the year, along with the same Cuban advisers who had been assisting the Eritreans. The obvious ensued: the guerrilla offensive ground to a halt. Soviet navy shelling from offshore battleships prevented the EPLF from taking Massawa. By May of the next year, the Dergue had accumulated enough new weaponry to launch an offensive of its own. The Cubans ran the logistical backup. Throughout late 1978 and into 1979, war swept across the Eritrean landscape. Thousands of civilians were killed, crops were burned, and tens of thousands were forced across the Sudanese border into refugee camps that still exist. Nerve gas and antipersonnel bombs disguised as children's toys reportedly were used. This was a form of warfare that the world would come to know better in coming months when the Soviet army invaded Afghanistan.

As the U.S. media spotlight drifted away from the Horn of Africa in 1979, the Eritrean guerrillas were in retreat, divided among themselves, and only beginning their transformation from a pro-Soviet, Marxist movement to an anti-Soviet, ideologically nebulous one. But the impressions U.S. journalists took with them as they moved on to Iran and Afghanistan at the end of the decade remained, even after they returned to Ethiopia in 1984. In the late 1970s, both war and famine had ravaged Ethiopia, but at that time, the media were predominantly interested in the war. By 1984, however, Third World conflicts with heavy Soviet involvement in Angola, Cambodia, El Salvador, and Nicaragua—not to mention Afghanistan—took the sting out of the Eritrean story. So even though Ethiopia's situation was again a matter of war and famine, this time only the famine got reported because the unprecedented images of masses of people dying of hunger gave the famine story much greater novelty value. Because few journalists bothered to cover the war, most observers still thought of it as just a case of "Marxists fighting Marxists." Neither Congress nor the Reagan administration had any real way of knowing that the situation had changed because U.S. officials could not enter guerrilla-held areas due to a continued U.S. State Department policy of only recognizing Ethiopian sovereignty in Eritrea.

Nevertheless, although the media had consigned Eritrea to obscurity, major fighting continued in the 1980s, and the nature of the guerrilla movement was significantly altered. The EPLF decided on a "strategic withdrawal" in 1979 and deliberately gave up territory in southern Eritrea, including the town of Keren near Asmara, in order to consolidate a base area in the northern Sahel district around Nakfa. In the meantime, troops were deserting regularly from the Arab-backed ELF, which by mid-1980 boasted only six thousand five hundred troops, while EPLF ranks had swelled to almost thirty thousand. The same year, fighting broke out between the two organizations, and in 1981, following an EPLF offensive against ELF concentrations in the Barka region of western Eritrea, the ELF was defeated and its remaining troops were driven over the border into Sudan, where they were disarmed. The ELF, although it still has a small following among Eritrean refugees in Sudan, has been irrelevant ever since.

From then on, possessing a secure base area and faced with no other credible enemy except the Dergue, the EPLF strengthened itself in every way. A network of trenches and underground corridors several hundred miles long was constructed. Thousands of educated ethnic-Eritreans came over to the EPLF side after going into exile abroad because of increased repression in Ethiopia. These new recruits, who were brought in by way of Sudan, staffed the hospital and ran the workshops that were being set up in the Orotta area. Many of the recruits were from middle-class, Christian families around Asmara, and their presence further encouraged the Western-oriented drift in EPLF ideology away from its Marxist bearings, which the 1977 Soviet sellout had precipitated.

The last vestige of Eritrean good will toward the Soviet Union was wiped out by the Soviet buildup of the Ethiopian army, which was expanded from sixty-five thousand to nearly three hundred thousand troops, thus making it the largest in black Africa. Using figures from a Central Intelligence Agency report, James A. Phillips, a senior policy analyst for the Heritage Foundation, noted that "Moscow supplied Ethiopia, a state which had only 62 tanks and 27 jet fighters, with over 350 tanks and 70 jet fighters." "Volunteer" pilots from Cuba, North Korea, and other Soviet bloc states joined the ranks of the Ethiopian air force. More than two thousand Soviet advisers arrived in the country. In return, the Dergue made the Dahlak archipelago, which was off Eritrea's Red Sea coast, available to the Soviet navy, and Soviet planes began making long-range reconnaissance flights over the Indian Ocean from the Asmara airbase that the United States had deserted.

This massive assistance program allowed the Ethiopian government to launch its largest offensive ever against the Eritrean guerrillas in February 1982. Called Operation Red Star, it involved fifteen divisions with an estimated one hundred thousand troops and featured the introduction of Soviet-manufactured Mi-24 HIND helicopter gunships into the region for the first time. The offensive was a total failure. The EPLF held all its major positions, and as many as forty thousand Ethiopian soldiers—close to half the invasion force—may have been killed or wounded. Thousands were taken prisoner by the guerrillas, and large quantities of weapons were captured. Another offensive of the same magnitude was launched in 1983, but the results were just as disastrous. While the U.S. public was preoccupied during this period with fighting in Lebanon and Central America, blood was flowing in larger quantities in the Horn of Africa, in a war that featured a guerrilla resistance—backed by virtually no one—withstanding one of the largest Soviet arms onslaughts in history. There was only one precedent: the struggle of the Viet Cong against the United States. No other resistance group, particularly not the ones well known to the public, were in the same category. Not even the Viet Cong, who were armed and supported by the Chinese and North Vietnamese and who rarely engaged in set-piece battles like the EPLF did, had chalked up such an impressive record.

Nevertheless, Eritrea was in every respect a friendless nation. The transformation of the Soviet Union from ally to oppressor, the continued hostility of the West, and the ambivalence of the Arabs and the rest of the Third World only reinforced the EPLF's obsession with "self-reliance" and its relative disdain for other Middle Eastern and African liberation groups. A mania developed in the EPLF around repairing captured equipment and converting it for other uses. Comparisons between the EPLF and other insurgent organizations were treated with contempt. "Has the PLO ever captured an Israeli tank?" asked an EPLF official scornfully, when the question was raised about similarities with the Palestinians.

In early 1984, the EPLF captured the town of Tessenei on Eritrea's western border with Sudan and overran all government positions eastward up to the Red Sea, thereby gaining the port of Mersa Teklai. War was taking its toll on the land, however. Much of the heavy fighting of the previous years had occurred during harvest season, and to make matters worse, the Ethiopian army was employing the same scorched-earth tactics in Eritrea as the Soviet army was using in Afghanistan. War had restricted the seasonal migration of nomads, which led to the loss of livestock. On account of the security situation, fertile areas of the coast and the Barka plain could not be cultivated. The agricultural balance, always fragile in this corner of Africa where nature is particularly cruel, was destroyed. But when a resultant famine woke the media from its five-year-long sleep, the images that television cameras beamed back into U.S. homes were of a drought-scarred landscape, not a war-scarred one.

*   *   *

Yet from every perspective, Eritrea presents a picture of modern war. The EPLF front line at Nakfa, sixty miles as the crow flies south of Orotta, is a bleak, deforested region brutally cut by landslides and the color of mud. Captured from the Dergue in 1977, Nakfa has been the scene of heavy fighting many times since, leaving the town, which once had a population of seven thousand, a checkerwork of ruins punctuated by a single minaret. Nakfa is sort of a modern-day, African equivalent of Pompeii. The trenches, a few miles further south are perched along the twisting spur of Denden Mountain. Soviet T-55 tanks and five different kinds of artillery lie hidden in manmade recesses. Across the defile, on a similar ridge, are the Ethiopian lines. In some places, the two armies are as close as sixty yards apart, and a pair of low-powered binoculars are all that is necessary to see the individual faces of Dergue soldiers peering through the slits of their own fortifications. In between is a no-man's-land of minefields, defoliated olive trees whose barks are corroded by napalm, and scores of Ethiopian bodies lying like broken toy soldiers, and the uncollected remnants of the November 1985 Dergue attack on Nakfa, in which six thousand government troops were killed or wounded in repeated predawn attempts to scale the Denden escarpment (the same number of casualties attended the successful 1941 British assault on a similar scarp at Keren, which led to Mussolini's withdrawal from Eritrea).

The Dergue threw twenty-five thousand soldiers against the EPLF at Nakfa in November 1985 in the gory, hellbent conclusion to an offensive that lasted from July through November 1985, involved two hundred thousand troops and $1 billion worth of Soviet weaponry, and resulted in an estimated fourteen thousand dead and wounded. It had to be one of the biggest unreported stories of the decade. Not more than a handful of articles were written about it in the U.S. press.

The prelude to the 1985 offensive came in the first week of July, when the EPLF captured the strategic hilltop settlement of Barentu in western Eritrea, a major weapons store for the Dergue. During the next seven weeks, the EPLF took more equipment back to its base area than had been captured in many years. The catch reportedly included fifteen T-55 tanks and dozens of trucks and artillery pieces. The government moved an estimated thirty thousand troops into the area as part of a redeployment of two divisions from the Ogaden desert in the south. According to diplomatic and other sources in Khartoum, there were as many as thirteen attempts to retake the town, and two thousand Ethiopian soldiers were killed or wounded in the process. The EPLF deliberately left open an escape route that it subsequently ambushed; hundreds of bodies littered the field. Finally, the government resorted to bombing from the air. The EPLF withdrew on August 25.

A few days after reoccupying Barentu, Ethiopian troops captured Tessenei, between Barentu and the Sudanese border. Having chopped off the EPLF's western territorial flank, the Dergue struck eastward and rolled up the Red Sea plain. A guerrilla commander told the London-based *Financial Times* (December 13, 1985) that one of the tank battles "was like Rommel confronting the British at Tobruk." The guerrillas now were in control of only an oval-shaped tract the size of Belgium that jutted southward from the Sudanese border and covered Eritrea's central mountain region in the Sahel district. Near the southern tip of this oval was Nakfa, where the EPLF had its largest concentration of heavy weaponry. The Dergue used napalm, cluster bombs, T-55 tanks, and MIG-23s to support its ground attack on Denden Mountain. But after several weeks of fighting, there still was no breakthrough. The offensive ended inconclusively, and by summer 1986, the EPLF had regained the coastal strip.

The biggest victim of the fighting was the famine relief effort. Daily overflights by MIGs and Antonov bombers forced relief convoys coming from Sudan to travel only at night, according to Chris Cartter, Africa program coordinator for Grassroots International. *The Economist,* a British weekly magazine, reported that five of the twenty-three relief camps inside EPLF territory were bombed. During a visit to the camp at Salumna, *Financial Times* correspondent John Murray Brown saw (and reported on December 13, 1985) a "large number of empty cluster bombshells." Eritrean officials claimed that "upon entering the towns of Barentu and Tessenei . . . the Dergue's forces . . . raided a storeroom, seized food, and burned agricultural tools." The most significant loss was the destruction of the Ali Ghidir agricultural scheme near Tessenei, a 12,355-acre ex-Italian farm, mechanized and irrigated by the EPLF. In one of the few articles written about the offensive in the U.S. press, Clifford D. May reported in the *New York Times* (September 29, 1985) that "war, rather than drought, is increasingly becoming the main cause of hunger and homelessness on the Horn of Africa." Unfortunately, the realization came a bit late: the eighth major government offensive in as many years was ravaging Eritrea. In the United States, news coverage of the famine already had peaked several months before, and the public was losing interest in the subject. The last horde of journalists was leaving Sudan and Ethiopia, yet the war in Eritrea still was obscure.

*   *   *

In the warren of slate and sandbagged passageways, noisy with field mice, on Denden Mountain, the war is the only reality. Few existences can be more rugged. Even the strong, sugary tea, which in the austere dietary conditions of the Third World functions as an elixir, rarely is available. Water is usually the only drink, aside from an occasional pitcher of homemade sorghum beer, called *suwa*. Extremes of heat and cold are the norm. Teeth are brushed with the peeled branch of a tree. Soap is nonexistent. The crucible of toil and suffering has broken down sexual and religious barriers. In a society where clitorectomy and infibulation used to be widespread, the exigencies of war have liberated women, who account for almost a third of all EPLF soldiers. But unlike other armies where women make up a large portion of the recruits, such as Israel's, in Eritrea they are in front-line combat units, drive tanks and aim artillery, and perform tasks such as repairing automobile motors (30 percent of the wounded reportedly were women).

After years of living and performing in the field exactly as the men, women have come to physically resemble them. Women's hair is short, their hands and feet calloused, their legs sinewy. As *The Guardian* correspondent David Hirst put it in a February 19, 1985, article: "The integration seems to be so complete and natural, so devoid of competition or coquetry, that it has subtly moulded their physical appearance and demeanour. It often takes more than a glance to tell the difference between the women and the younger men." In the cramped, front-line quarters, although men and women sleep side by side, sex is said to be rare; and pregnancies are unusual despite the unavailability of any means of birth control. The EPLF evidently has a puritanical streak. Except for the few fighters who marry or form intimate liaisons, celibacy seems to be the rule. Still, the atmosphere of pentup emotional tension, so prevalent in almost every Middle Eastern country, is notably absent. Eritrean males also evince little interest in the few Western women they encounter.

Of the few sexually intimate relationships that are established among the guerrillas, many are between Moslems and Christians, who always serve in the same units. The EPLF emerged, in part, as a nonsectarian alternative to the Moslem-dominated ELF, and this history has left its mark in terms of the deliberate unimportance attached to religion by the fighters. In Eritrea, mostly older peasants wear Coptic crosses or Moslem skullcaps, and only a few peasants bear a dirt spot on their foreheads, indicating constant bowing to the ground in the direction of the Moslem holy city of Mecca.

Elsewhere in the world, the breaking down of social barriers often has led to a form of tyranny over the individual, as in communist societies, for instance. But in Eritrea, the reverse is true. There exists a degree of caring for the individual that is extremely rare in Third World armies. Every platoon is equipped with basic medical supplies. Stretchers abound. Makeshift operating rooms are located in the field. One soldier I met, whose eardrums were damaged in a bomb blast, actually was provided with a hearing aid, something I found astounding considering that there isn't even tea in the trenches. Western intelligence sources say that even with satellite photographs, they have no figures on EPLF battle losses, owing to the guerrillas' ability to get their dead and wounded off the field quicker than all but the most sophisticated Western armies. It makes for a striking contrast with the Ethiopians, who leave many of their dead behind. (The Dergue, moreover, refuses to admit the existence of the eight thousand prisoners of war being held by the EPLF; this lack of acknowledgment abandons these prisoners to an almost stateless existence, with little hope of ever returning home.) The guerrilla wounded that cannot be treated at battlefield medical stations are transported by trucks and Land Cruisers to the hospital at Orotta, eight hours away from the closest front-line point. Whenever asked what type of military equipment they are in need of most (in addition to shoulder-fired antiaircraft guns), EPLF officials always mention helicopters to get their wounded to Orotta quicker.

As the Israelis have demonstrated, bravery derives from self-assurance, from the knowledge that whatever the risks, in the event of danger your superiors will go to the limit to save you. The Eritrean guerrillas have proved more than once their ability to take well-calculated risks, such as the January 14, 1986, attack, behind enemy lines, on the airbase at Asmara, in which the estimates of the number of MIGs and other planes damaged or destroyed went as high as forty. Again, by contrast, it is hard to imagine an army with a worse morale than the Dergue's. Many of its soldiers are ethnic Oromos, Moslems from the southern lowlands of Ethiopia, themselves persecuted by the Christian Amharas, who were conscripted forcibly and given minimal training before being dispatched to the mountainous north of the country to fight the Eritreans, a people the Oromos have no interest in fighting. Nor are the Amharas in Mengistu's army enthusiastic. Many of the officers were trained in the West during the reign of the emperor and resent the present government's Marxist ideology and reliance on Soviet military assistance. The Amhara recruits, meanwhile, especially the educated ones, often desert or escape over the border before being drafted. The Ethiopian refugee camps in Somalia and Sudan are filled not just with peasants from the famine-wracked countryside, but with educated Amharas from Addis Ababa as well.

Concerning the EPLF, the comparison with the Israelis is by no means farfetched; it is useful to make this comparison, as it strikes at the heart of what makes the Eritrean guerrilla movement unique in the Third World and, by extension, explains why the ERA is so much more effective than is any other African relief group. Israel has long been noted for boldness in guarding the welfare of its citizens and, in some cases, of Jews outside the country. This was powerfully demonstrated during the rescue of seven thousand five hundred black Ethiopian Jews from the provinces of Gondar, Tigre, and Wollo in December 1984 and January 1985. For Leon Wieseltier, writing in *The New Republic* (February 11, 1985), the rescue was an example of the Israeli "belief in action . . . the idea of getting things done promoted to the status of a principle." In other words, as Wieseltier explained, "make the protestations, and make them again; but also arrange the border crossings, establish the transit stations, obtain the food."

Unlike the Jews, the Eritreans come from a more backward part of Afro-Asia, nor have they had the cultural experience afforded the Jews by centuries of exile in the West. On the contrary, Eritreans always have lived in one of the most brutal, nasty corners of the world and can count even fewer friends on their fingers than can the Israelis. But, by the standards of their own plight and the region they inhabit, the Eritreans have put this principle of moral action into practice. While the U.S. public was awed by the Israeli deliverance of the Ethiopian Jews, at the same time and practically side by side, the EPLF was delivering its people—more than one hundred thousand of them—to the relative succor of emergency feeding centers on the Sudanese border; the EPLF provided these people with whatever water and food it could muster at transit stations set up along the way.

Of the approximately 8 million peasants threatened with starvation by the Ethiopian famine, about 2 million were in EPLF-controlled areas. Yet despite the fact that in late 1984 and early 1985 ERA was the recipient, by some estimates, of less than 5 percent of all the international aid coming into Ethiopia, the efficiency of ERA, coupled with support from Eritrean expatriates in the West and in Saudi Arabia, kept the number of deaths in Eritrea in the tens of thousands; whereas in Dergue-held areas, as many as 1 million people are thought to have perished. Jack Shepherd, a food aid specialist at the Carnegie Endowment for International Peace, wrote in the Africanist journal *Issue* (14 [1985]) that the Eritrean guerrillas (along with those in Tigre) have "reversed the classical guerrilla warfare pattern: Instead of peasants supporting and feeding an army, the guerrillas are feeding and sheltering themselves and the peasants."

"They are just like the Viet Cong," remarked one visitor to Eritrea, "except unlike the Viet Cong, these people like each other." The ERA clinic is a poignant illustration of this point. On a continent where people do the most horrible things to each other, the clinic is a rare institution. It was opened in May 1979 in an unfinished cement building on the outskirts of Port Sudan near the airport. There is not a tree in sight. The goats and stray dogs in the area escape the blazing sunlight of one of the hottest cities in the world by hiding under the rusted carcass of a school bus. Except for making the building available at a monthly rent, no help of any kind is provided by the Sudanese authorities. (Until ERA constructed a small dormitory structure for foreign relief workers and journalists, they had to stay in the clinic itself while waiting for transport into Eritrea.) The rooms teemed with flies by day and mosquitoes by night. In adjacent beds, on soiled mattresses, were close to one hundred amputees and paraplegics, children among them; they were victims of a war about which few people knew.

The clinic functions as both a school and a hospital. It is self-administered: even the teachers are amputees. The wheelchairs and artificial limbs are made and repaired by the patients themselves. Bedside classes are taught up to grade eight. The curriculum includes English, science, mathematics, ceramics, and music. The patients are kept constantly busy. During several days at the clinic in March 1985, and again in October 1986, I detected few signs of depression among the patients. "We have no psychological problems here," said one of the teachers. "Our people accept everything."

The clinic is part of an ERA health care network that includes six regional hospitals and an extension service with several hundred paramedics reaching villages and nomadic encampments throughout the EPLF zone. "I know of no other system, which, given the same conditions and resources available, operates as efficiently," said Dr. Sam Richard Toussie, a Columbia University epidemiologist and rural health specialist, who has worked in insurgent areas of Africa, Asia, and Central America. The EPLF's biggest success has come in the area of infant care. Since 1982, the number of nomads within the EPLF base area giving birth in hospitals has risen 50 percent. Dr. Abrehet Kidan, a Syracuse University–trained gynecologist, said that in 1986 a project was begun to burn all nonsterilized bottles in Eritrea in order to cut down on infections and to encourage mothers to breast-feed longer. Still, 56 percent of Eritrean children are malnourished (compared with 80 percent in mid-1985), according to Dr. Assefaw Tekeste, head of the Orotta hospital, and the general population suffers from all the usual tropical diseases. In large part, this is due to the war-wrought isolation of Eritrea, a constant shortage of supplies filtering into the base area, and the difficulty of reaching people in EPLF territory behind Dergue lines.

ERA's primary function is as an agricultural development and famine relief organization; the ERA is responsible for farms, displaced persons camps, and resettlement schemes. Even in Nakfa, amid the ruins of the town, cabbage, cauliflower, eggplants, sunflowers, and eleven different kinds of tomato are being raised with the help of a motorized water pump captured in 1977 from the Dergue. At Himer, further west in the direction of the Barka plain, 150 irrigated acres of millet and sorghum are under cultivation on a sandy desert so parched that there is not a tree or a bush in sight. The number of displaced persons camps doubled in late 1984 to more than twenty, with an average population of five thousand for each camp. The reason for the increase again was war, not drought, as stepped-up MIG bombing raids on villages drove many Eritrean peasants out of their homes.

ERA's ultimate aim is to resettle all one hundred thousand of these refugees, in addition to several hundred thousand more by the end of the decade, at a cost to foreign donors of $25 million. But, from the looks of the plans and the way ERA officials talk, about the only similarity between this resettlement scheme and the one organized by the Ethiopian government is the name. In Ethiopia, resettlement has sparked an international outcry, with several studies indicating that up to one hundred thousand people have died in the program due to poor planning and brutal treatment of the peasants at the hands of Marxist cadres. Moreover, no food, drinking water, or tools of any kind reportedly were available when peasants arrived at the new sites. In Eritrea, on the other hand, officials always emphasize that resettlement will be carried out only "as conditions permit." ERA documents list not only the exact amounts and kinds of seed, tool, insecticide and other equipment needed at each site before it can be occupied, but the cost of each item, too.

Yet, despite the surfeit of pronouncements by relief experts, politicians, and journalists about the "need for Africans to help themselves," and despite public disgust about the misuse of aid by the Ethiopian government, it wasn't until mid-1985, when the food situation in government-held areas already was being brought under control, that do-

nations to ERA—a group that was doing nothing if not helping itself
and efficiently utilizing available resources—began to proportionately
catch up with donations earmarked for Ethiopia. At the end of March
1985, in Orotta, Tekie Beyene, the ERA information officer, complained
to me that "we have publicized our food situation for five years but
only now does the international community begin to listen. Compared
to what is happening in Ethiopia, we have saved our own people."

A look at the military map in mid-1985 revealed that nearly half
of the areas affected by famine were in the hands of some guerrilla
group, be it the Eritreans, the Tigreans, or one of the smaller bands
operating in Gondar or Wollo. The so-called Ethiopian famine was in
part a misnomer in the sense that the Ethiopian capital was not the
address for many of the victims. By all neutral estimates, several
million of the 8–10 million peasants facing starvation lived in areas
that could be reached only by ERA or REST. As Dan Connell, a
former Reuters correspondent and executive director of the Cambridge,
Massachussetts–based relief information service, Grassroots International, told *The Nation* (January 19, 1985): "Because of the fighting,
very little of the food contributed by the United States and other
donor countries is reaching the starving in the rebel-controlled areas."
But few of the politicians, entertainers, journalists, and donor agency
officials who beat a path to Addis Ababa in the autumn of 1984 were
aware of this. The only Ethiopian group they had any knowledge of
was the Dergue's RRC, whose two top officials, Dawit Wolde Giorgis
and Berhane Deressa, were later to defect and seek political asylum
in the United States, where they would attack the regime they once
had defended before all these foreign visitors.

It took the ghastly spectacle of three hundred thousand starving and
shell-shocked Eritrean and Tigrean refugees, brought safely out of Ethiopia by guerrilla armies and assembled at emergency feeding centers
on the Sudanese border in late December 1984, to make the international community aware of the famine's *other half.* Subsequently, it
became de rigueur for people such as Senator Edward Kennedy and
singer Harry Belafonte to make a stopover at the Sudanese border on
their way home from Ethiopia. But the aid imbalance was slow to be
rectified. Although in the first six months of 1985, Ethiopia received
almost all of the estimated 750,000 tons of grain required for that
period, according to Western relief officials, ERA got only half of the
67,500 tons it requested. By 1986, however, most of the main donor
groups active in Ethiopia also had pledged money for some project or
other in Eritrea. Belafonte's organization for instance, USA for Africa,
whose representatives had been criticized for appearing too respectful

of the Ethiopian government, gave $80,000 for a new medical laboratory at Orotta hospital.

Drawing attention to the situation in Eritrea and Tigre always was hard going, for reasons that seldom were mentioned. Reporting from areas controlled by the guerrillas was not easy: food and lodging conditions were awful, and no phones or telex machines existed for journalists to maintain contact with their home offices in the event of a breaking story elsewhere in Africa. Not many journalists made the trip. As a result, the public was not sufficiently sensitized to the situation behind guerrilla lines. In addition, Addis Ababa offered a far more comfortable atmosphere for foreign visitors than did Khartoum and the refugee camps on Sudan's eastern border. The Sudanese capital is a torpid, dusty city, plagued by temperatures that often rise above 100 degrees. The Khartoum Hilton is far out of town, and the center of the action for relief officials was always a Greek-run hotel on a depressing downtown street that despite its helpful management did not offer the kind of creature comforts ordinarily expected by Western visitors. The border towns of Kassala and Gedaref, close to the refugee camps, were even worse off. Given that relief flights didn't operate daily from Khartoum, as they did from Addis Ababa to camps in government-held areas, it was impossible for visitors who could not charter their own plane to get to the eastern border and back in one day. Not surprisingly, everybody liked "Addis," while few liked Khartoum. Partly as a consequence of this attitude, Sudan, the rear base for ERA and REST, attracted smaller numbers of "fact finders" than did Ethiopia, where the RRC was within walking distance of the Hilton.

It was the Reagan administration, so often criticized in the early days of the famine for its seeming slowness in responding to that emergency in Ethiopia, that was among the first to begin helping Eritrea and Tigre. By early December 1984, Washington already was shipping food directly to the camps on the Sudanese border and funneling cash into the hands of a few private charities, which used the money to bring grain into areas controlled by the EPLF and the TPLF. Publicity about this relatively modest program was kept to a minimum because it appeared to violate Ethiopian sovereignty in Eritrea and Tigre, which the U.S. State Department still officially recognized. It wasn't until a year later, near the end of 1985, that a cross-border feeding program, which more satisfactorily met the needs of ERA and REST, was in place; close to two hundred Mercedes and Fiat trucks operated by Eritrean and Tigrean drivers transported approximately six thousand tons of grain a month into guerrilla territory.

The delay was a matter of both logistics and politics. Tens of thousands of tons of wheat and dried milk powder were piling up in

Port Sudan warehouses in the early weeks of spring 1985, because there were insufficient trucks to bring the food over the border. When the trucks did arrive, it already was summer, and the first substantial rains in several years made the unpaved roads into Eritrea and Tigre impassable until late September. Then the Sudanese government got nervous about the entire project because it was bound to anger the Ethiopians at a time when Sudan was trying to get Mengistu to reduce his support for the African southerners fighting a secessionist war against Moslem Arab Khartoum. Moreover, in the wake of the overthrow of pro-U.S. president Jaafar Nimeiri in April, anti-U.S. feeling was stronger than usual in the capital, as the public of this Arab League state became increasingly aware of the U.S. role in helping black Ethiopian Jews escape to Israel via Sudan in the final months of Nimeiri's rule. The Transitional Military Council, which succeeded Nimeiri, eventually gave its approval for the project, provided that publicity about it be kept to an absolute minimum and that the U.S. role in the actual transport of the grain over the border be as indirect as possible. Among other things, this resulted in many of the responsibilities of Mercy Corps, an Oregon-based charity handling the Tigre side of the operation, being transferred to the International Committee of the Red Cross. Also, although the United States was paying for most of the grain and the trucks, the day-to-day operation on the eastern border was placed in the hands of citizens from other Western countries. Negotiating these provisions took some time, and it wasn't until the end of 1985 that Eritrea and Tigre were getting the kind of massive assistance that Dergue-controlled areas already had been receiving for twelve months.

But the politics weren't only of a Sudanese making. There was stalling by Washington, too. Officials in the State Department and in USAID knew that even the most ambitious cross-border project could not get food into many contested areas of southern Eritrea and central and eastern Tigre as easily as a Dergue-approved initiative operating from Addis Ababa could, mainly because the distances were shorter and the roads better. Also, the Reagan administration, hoping that the famine would provide an opportunity to wean Ethiopia away from the Soviet Union, did not want to alienate Mengistu before at least giving him a chance to approve a feeding program across guerrilla lines from his side of the trenches. Although only food was to be transported by ERA and REST, food could be a strategic weapon in guerrilla societies where there is little distinction between fighters and civilians. So the cross-border program was organized in no particular hurry, on the premise that just the threat of it actually being implemented would force Mengistu to cooperate on a similar program run from Addis Ababa.

The strategy bore mixed results. Following a midwinter meeting in Geneva between Vice President George Bush and representatives of the Ethiopian government, approval for a so-called northern initiative was given. The New York–based Catholic Relief Services was to move 25,000 tons of grain a month into Eritrea, while World Vision, a California-based Protestant charity, was to transport a similar amount of food into Tigre. The RRC pledged to do nutritional surveys in order to identify the needy in front-line areas. But as one donor agency official told me, the surveys were done "either incompletely or not at all." It took several months of further negotiations with the Dergue before the trucks began rolling out of Addis Ababa and the ports of Assab and Massawa. The attitude of the Marxist TPLF constituted another hindrance. Not long after the operation finally got under way, the Tigre side of it ground to a halt in early March 1986 after the TPLF killed two Ethiopian employees of World Vision in the town of Alamata in southern Tigre. The Tigrean guerrillas did not want any people from the government side coming into their area. Although the dead Ethiopians, both women, worked for a Western relief agency and not for the Dergue, the TPLF made no distinctions. According to an account written by Blaine Harden (*Washington Post; International Herald Tribune,* March 29–30, 1986), both USAID and World Vision officials stated that the killings were deliberate, as the two women were shot in the dining room of a relief compound after they had identified themselves as World Vision employees.

The hostile attitude of the TPLF, the purloining of grain by Dergue soldiers in both Tigre and Eritrea, and the Dergue's prohibition against U.S. nationals monitoring grain deliveries in contested areas made the task of World Vision and Catholic Relief Services arguably the most difficult and politically sensitive of the entire emergency effort in Sudan and Ethiopia. If the two charities didn't succeed, it wasn't because they lacked the will. It is questionable just how much of this food, if any, actually made it to needy areas on the guerrilla side of the trenches. USAID obviously assumed that not much would because at about the same time that the northern initiative became operational, the final go ahead also was given for the cross-border program operating from Sudan in cooperation with ERA and REST. From a humanitarian standpoint, it is hard to find fault with the Reagan administration. Faced with a war situation in a barely accessible region of Africa, the administration did the only thing that could possibly be done—bring food up from both sides of the battle lines in the hope of reaching as many hungry peasants as possible.

Where the administration failed was in its political strategy. As the emergency drew to a close in 1986, the Dergue was as hostile toward the United States as in 1984; some would say even more so. U.S. officials didn't seem to understand that it was not the famine but the war in Eritrea—and to a lesser extent in Tigre—that held the key to a political shift in Addis Ababa. But because Washington was operating on the basis of outdated assumptions about the Eritrean resistance, it could not construct a bold strategy for prying the Dergue loose from Moscow. Instead, U.S. policy seemed to rest on the hope that despite a $4 billion dollar Soviet arms investment and the influx of several thousand Eastern bloc advisers, who, among other duties, ran Ethiopia's security services, the Dergue could be bribed away with grain, much of which was going to areas that Mengistu had a strategic interest in starving. It was a naive hope, not a realistic calculation.

In a world of imperfect choices, where the United States often finds itself supporting regimes and resistance movements of limited caliber, the Eritrean guerrillas would appear to be useful proxies in a "low intensity war" to make Mengistu cry "uncle." Liberals on Capitol Hill would have fewer complaints about a group whose exemplary treatment of the eight thousand POWs under its charge has been documented by the International Committee of the Red Cross and whose competence in the field of famine relief during the 1984–1986 period is a matter of public record. (The only deserved stain on the EPLF's reputation was the group's 1987 attacks on famine relief convoys in heavily contested areas of Eritrea. Without trying to justify these unjustifiable actions, it should be stated that almost every day since the late 1970s, MIGs and other Soviet-made planes take off from Ethiopian government airfields and bomb anything that moves in EPLF and Tigrean guerrilla zones, thereby effectively stopping famine convoys from traveling during daytime hours. After a decade of avoiding retaliation, which got the EPLF absolutely no Western recognition in return, the guerrilla organization changed its policy and was condemned around the world for doing exactly what the Dergue attempted on a daily basis. It reminds me of the situation two decades ago in Biafra—as described by Dan Jacobs in *The Brutality of Nations*—where the international community looked the other way at massive Nigerian government human rights violations but lambasted the Biafran rebels on the few occasions when their behavior was insupportable.)

Unlike Nicaragua, no advisers were needed to train an army. The Eritreans have taught themselves to use all the Soviet equipment they have captured; they might even be able to teach the U.S. military a thing or two. In the spring of 1984, for instance, an EPLF attack on the Asmara airbase resulted in the destruction of two Soviet IL-38

MAYS long-range naval reconnaissance planes, thus forcing the Soviets thereafter to do all their monitoring of the U.S. Indian Ocean fleet from bases in South Yemen. Nor would the EPLF require many different kinds of weapon. Western intelligence experts confirm that the guerrillas capture from the Dergue much of what they need with the exception of shoulder-fired antiaircraft guns, which the Dergue doesn't have available for capture because the EPLF has no aircraft. In few other places would the sale of a few hundred antiaircraft guns have such dramatic effects as in Eritrea. A sale might accomplish more than all the aid to the Nicaraguan, Cambodian, and Angolan rebels combined, and the effects would be primarily and demonstrably humanitarian in nature (another thing liberals would like) because an air cover would allow cross-border relief convoys already being financed by U.S. taxpayers to roll twenty-four hours a day rather than just at night. In addition, there would not be much debate about the likelihood of the EPLF winning because the guerrillas have no pretensions about toppling the Dergue the way the contras do about toppling the Sandanistas or Savimbi's rebels do about toppling the Marxist Dos Santos regime in Luanda. The EPLF wants to change Eritrea, not Ethiopia, and might even be satisfied with an autonomy agreement like the one under Haile Selassie, provided that this time it was respected. Moreover, there is so much building dissatisfaction inside the Ethiopian military about the war and the Dergue's exclusive reliance on the Eastern bloc that the EPLF need not even be victorious for Reagan Doctrine planners to get their money's worth. The EPLF only might have to fight a degree or two better than it presently is in order to create the conditions necessary for a coup or policy shift in Addis Ababa; conditions that millions of tons of Western-donated grain have not been able to create.

But perhaps the most attractive aspect of assisting the EPLF is that unlike the muddled realities of Nicaragua and Angola, the Horn of Africa offers more clearcut distinctions between good and evil, the recent EPLF attacks on food convoys notwithstanding. The 1986 *World Human Rights Guide* gave Ethiopia the lowest rating of any country in the world. Human rights investigations by the U.S. State Department and Amnesty International turned up similar results. Besides the usual evidence of torture, the murder of children, and unlawful detention common to all the most brutal Third World regimes, the Dergue has been guilty of deliberately denying food to large segments of its population and of collectivizing millions of ethnic Oromos against their will. This is a regime with few defenders in Washington. No serious person, liberal or conservative, would deny that almost anyone would be preferable to the current leaders in Addis Ababa. True, many would say that the regime of Haile Selassie wasn't all that much better, but lacking the guidance of Eastern bloc security advisers, it was not nearly so lethally competent as the Dergue is in carrying out a policy of repression. In any case, the rule of the emperor, which collapsed in 1974, is not the issue. The issue that needs to be explored is why the United States—while supporting insurgencies in Afghanistan, Angola, Cambodia, and Nicaragua—is not supporting an insurgency in Ethiopia, whose population of 42 million is larger than that of all those other countries combined. Why, as Yonas Deressa, president of the Ethiopian Refugees Education and Relief Foundation, has asked, is the United States allowing the Brezhnev Doctrine to be implemented in the Horn of Africa rather than the Reagan Doctrine?

The ready answer offered by officials at the U.S. State Department and National Security Council is that the Eritrean guerrillas "are Marxists just like the Dergue" and thus cannot qualify for U.S. military support. Interested members of Congress, such as Senator Orrin Hatch, the vice chairperson for foreign policy on the Senate Republican Steering Committee, also have branded the EPLF with the "Marxist" label. In an editorial column in the *Wall Street Journal* (April 4, 1986), Hatch recommended that because the EPLF is "Marxist-oriented," and wants "to secede from the country," the United States should fix its hopes instead on the "non-communist, non-secessionist" Ethiopian People's Democratic Alliance (EPDA).

The use of the verb "secede" is questionable in this context, given that the region in question has been largely outside the Ethiopian government's control for a quarter century already and for a decade before that was officially declared "autonomous." More to the point, notwithstanding the democratic virtues of the EPDA, its army is small, and its role in fighting the Dergue is marginal compared to that of the EPLF, or even to that of the TPLF. The EPDA is simply not a viable substitute for the Eritrean guerrillas in the task of destabilizing a regime that Moscow has built into its most powerful ally on the African continent. But Hatch and others won't even consider helping the EPLF because it is "Marxist."

Responding to these charges, Isaias Aferworki, the number two man in the EPLF hierarchy after Ramadan Mohamed Nur—but reputedly the real power in the organization—told me that "we totally reject any labeling from any quarter. We have our own realities and we begin from there to solve our social and political problems. We are a broad democratic front struggling for national liberation. A national liberation struggle cannot be a Marxist struggle since it must accommodate all viewpoints." It was the same answer that he and Ramadan Nur had given to the handful of other journalists, almost all European, who had interviewed them. Unlike leaders of the Palestine Liberation Organization, EPLF leaders have no record of backtracking or contradicting themselves. Nevertheless, the EPLF cannot deny that it has a Leninist command structure, with its leadership organized around a "politburo" and a "central committee." Aferworki admitted that in its early stages, the EPLF was influenced heavily by Soviet literature, which was a reaction against Western colonialism in Africa. Such terminology "was all we knew," he claimed. Concerning the United States, Aferworki said "the standing of America here has always been positive. The food aid to Eritrea is what we expected from a people of noble ideas, and whatever the motives of the U.S. government in giving the aid, the fact is we have really benefited from it." However, he is bitter about the U.S. refusal to recognize Eritrea as separate from the rest of Ethiopia.

Aferworki, said to be in his later thirties (he says he does not know his exact age), met me in a protected veranda furnished with broken furniture at the EPLF command outpost of She'eb, three hours by Land Cruiser southeast of Orotta. The interview was scheduled for 10 A.M. on October 15, 1986. At ten exactly, he arrived on foot with no escort, dressed in a khaki safari shirt and blue jeans. With short black hair, a clipped moustache, and a cold, authoritative style of speech, Aferworki affected a military disposition.

Was he leveling with me about the EPLF's non-Marxist orientation? There is no action that the EPLF has taken within the area under its control that would suggest otherwise. The most left-wing concepts ever pushed by the organization's economic department were a mild land reform program, designed to narrow the gap between peasants and a few rich merchants, and aid to rudimentary worker organizations. Moreover, EPLF officials do not evince the coercive manner of approach to the civilian population that is so apparent in all communist societies. While in Addis Ababa, one often hears phrases like, "*This is what we're going to do*"; in Eritrea, it is more common for someone in authority to ask, "*How do we convince people to do it?*" Marxism, or capitalism for that matter, is simply not the issue in Eritrea. In a place with no heavy industry, no circulating currency, and only a rudimentary class structure, such terms have far less relevance than they do in Washington. The ideology I've heard professed by Eritreans is so vague that it seems little more than a form of the social contract theory developed by Jean-Jacques Rousseau in the eighteenth century.

In addition, after the experience of being bombed for a decade by a Soviet-supplied air force, Eritrean dislike of the Soviet Union is comparable with that of the Afghans. Moscow is constantly being condemned by Eritreans at all levels of society, from field commanders to peasant women. Amputees sometimes are referred to as "Mr. Gorbachev's work." The depth of hostility toward the Eastern bloc was made clear to me on my second journey into Eritrea (October 1986), at an ERA service station in the heart of Sudan's Tokar desert, where vehicles transporting grain from Port Sudan to Orotta were repaired. Due to the combination of a flat tire, reports of flooding further on, and the fear of being attacked by MIGs if caught on the road in daylight, I was held up there for seventeen hours. There were no toilets, nothing to eat, and only a few containers of expired Turkish mineral water to drink. Therefore, it was a pleasant surprise when a young Eritrean entered my hut and asked me if I wanted to watch a video. He led me to a clearing between a water tanker and a refuse heap where about two hundred people, many of them children, were seated on makeshift benches before a VHS unit hooked up to a generator. It was an EPLF propaganda film. After the usual scenes of marching soldiers, the camera switched to a ceremony where Ethiopian leader Mengistu Haile Mariam was smiling and shaking hands with the then-Soviet foreign minister Andrei Gromyko. At the sight of Gromyko, there was a distinct hiss from the audience, which grew more audible as the camera focused closer on the Soviet official's chiseled and stony face. The looks of burning hatred registered by some of the older children would have made President Reagan's eyes water, had he been able to visit this desert hovel. In a continent infected with a double standard on nonalignment, it seemed that these people were drawing the proper distinctions.

One would have to search far and wide for another issue on which official Washington appears as unknowing of the facts on the ground as in the case of Eritrea. Ironically, this ignorance continues despite the recent media attention lavished on the Horn of Africa, at a time when undermining Soviet client states in the Third World is particularly in vogue. But it is easily explained. No U.S. government official has visited the EPLF base area because the United States still recognizes Ethiopian sovereignty there, and so few correspondents of major U.S. media have made the trip that the amount of secondhand information available to people in Washington is incredibly sparse. A handful of analysts with access to satellite photographs at the State Department, the Defense Intelligence Agency, and the CIA are knowledgeable of the EPLF's military capacity. But even they lack a feel for the organization's ideology and the way in which the guerrillas and their leaders view the world and the superpowers.

A senior Reagan administration official admitted that "the general view held about the guerrillas is not an educated view." People in Washington see "these guys as leftists and as essentially separatist, while groups like the Contras are attractive because they openly declare an intention to topple a communist government." The official said that few in Washington realize that in terms of U.S. interests a "separatist" struggle in Ethiopia may be just as effective.

Nonetheless, the Marxist seal affixed to the Eritrean guerrilla movement is so easily disputed that it may be just a Washington excuse for inaction. The State Department and the White House are not under any pressure from any quarter to reevaluate their basic assumptions, so they don't. Why formulate a new policy if the current one is not under attack? One would expect Soviet involvement in such a populous and strategically placed country as Ethiopia, coupled with a record of human rights violations by the government with few precedents in Africa, to shake the U.S. bureaucracy out of its inertia. But the media are uninterested and no influential lobbies are at work. Although the tactics the United States uses in some parts of the world are the subject of endless scrutiny, often sparking official debate, other equally strategic regions are strangely ignored. (The U.S. role in Angola, which is of no greater strategic value than is the Horn of Africa, has been written about extensively.)

Although the Ethiopian famine resulted in lengthy public discussions about relief policy, little interest was stirred up about the administration's overall strategy in the Horn. The upshot, incredible as it may seem, is an official U.S. posture based on a 1950s situation when there was a pro-U.S. regime in Addis Ababa with a growing separatist movement in Eritrea that was encouraged by the Soviet Union and was oriented heavily toward the Arab world. This situation threatens Israel's fragile, newly born right of passage in the Red Sea and the construction of U.S. military facilities in Massawa and Asmara. Not much else would explain the U.S. government's defense of the Dergue's claim of absolute sovereignty over all of Eritrea. U.S. diplomats retort that despite Moscow's gridlock on the Dergue, the United States still can count the mass of Ethiopian people as its friends, so why alienate a population by recognizing its enemy? Besides, giving military support to one of the two sides in the Eritrean war only could add to the suffering, and encouraging the territorial dismemberment of any country is a destructive policy.

These are fine words, except that in the opinion of many, if not most, Amharas, the enemy is not the Eritreans but the Dergue. Not that it really matters. There is no case of a Third World dictatorship, assisted to such a large degree by the Soviet and East German security services, being dislodged by the popular will. As the Soviets proved in the late 1970s, the road to influence in Addis Ababa runs through Eritrea. Furthermore, in a military sense, Ethiopia is already a divided land, and giving the guerrillas defensive weapons would probably decrease the suffering, rather than increase it. Granted, these arguments may not be without flaw, but they certainly are worth a public debate.

*   *   *

"The Amharas are slaughtering our people, and the bombs of their MIGs and the shells of their tanks are burning our fields. Such is the situation. Why is everyone quiet? These are the things I want to know. . . . America must stop the flow of Soviet weapons." It was not what I expected to hear from a sixty-five-year-old Moslem peasant woman. According to media accounts, she should have been talking about the drought and the sacks of grain from abroad that saved her family from starvation. But this woman's home village, Af-abet, forty miles south of Nakfa, at one point had been overrun by the Ethiopian army, and the place where she lived now, Adishek, much closer to Nakfa in the EPLF zone, was so near to the front line that built into a low ridge were little corrugated iron bunkers for the chickens. Her world was one of war and ethnic hatred. Although grain from the United States was feeding her village, the gift of food wasn't on her mind when she spoke to me—guns were. She was no fighter, just a helpless peasant.

Although not sponsored by the Reagan Doctrine, Eritrean guerrillas nevertheless have managed to tie down and bleed a three-hundred-thousand-troop, Soviet-supported, black African military that otherwise would be a threat to all of East Africa, especially Kenya and Somalia. These are vital U.S. allies offering base facilities to the U.S. Indian Ocean fleet. Yet few members of the U.S. public even have noticed.

The most recurring vision I have of Eritrea is, paradoxically, not one that I myself saw. It was described to me by a British colleague, John Murray Brown. He was sitting outside one night when he noticed an EPLF guerrilla, lying on his back, searching the starscape. Brown asked the soldier if he were looking for anything in particular. The soldier replied that he was looking for satellites, claiming that they were easy to pick out in the clear night sky. The satellites gave him comfort, the soldier explained; they meant that at least somebody somewhere was paying attention to the war.

TIGRE: EXILE AND REPATRIATION

The Mercedes truck staggered up one hill and down the next, bucking the field of craters that passed for a road through the brush. The glare of the headlights was diffused by thick clouds of dust kicked up by the wheels of all the trucks in front of us: even with the windows shut it was like crawling up the wrong end of a vacuum cleaner. Everyone sweated and coughed. I held a damp rag over my nose and mouth. The sound of grinding gears helped to drown out the loud, scratchy music that the Tigrean driver insisted on playing.

After several hours of driving, the convoy halted. With the help of a half moon and starlight, I was able to get my first good look at northern Gondar, which the TPLF was using as a corridor into Tigre from its rear base on the Sudanese border. It was a ghostly landscape; the ravages of war and drought had left only shadows behind. Every object in view looked shriveled and burned like the remnants of a house after a great fire. The plain was dotted with carob and acacia trees, but all the branches were completely bare; it might as well have been a field of skulls. The grass was dead, and the lack of topsoil made the ground a vast carpet of dust.

Out from behind the rocks and crevices emerged little groups of men and women dressed in khaki shorts with Kalashnikov assault rifles slung over their shoulders like picks and shovels. Some wore bandage-like cloths on their heads as turbans. Their low chattering in Tigrinya had the effect of hundreds of birds waking. We now were an armed convoy of about twenty grain-laden trucks completely financed by U.S. taxpayers and protected by a group of self-declared Marxist rebels.

In theory, the U.S. government did not deal with these guerrillas. Rather, it dealt only with REST, which was supposed to have complete control over the trucks and the grain. But this trail in Gondar was a long way from Washington, and legalistic divisions tended to get submerged beneath the overpowering imperatives of war in this remote corner of Ethiopia. Not that there was evidence of grain being diverted to the soldiers. But, as I was to learn (during my trip in February 1986), nothing was easily verifiable in TPLF areas. The conditions in Tigre were even more primitive than those in Eritrea. Water was not always available even for washing. After living for days on crushed biscuits and marmalade, I felt ill more often than not. In such a state, traveling only at night and sleeping much of the day, it was difficult for an outsider to judge just what was going on. The guerrillas and our Tigrean guides often were not cooperative. The successive scenes of biblical-like migrations, patrolling soldiers, and trucks moving in the night created an imagery so rich it may have concealed as much as it illuminated. In Tigre, there were no trenches defining areas of control, no tanks or artillery pieces indicating troop concentrations, and no set-piece battles whose results were a matter of record. The TPLF, with an estimated fifteen thousand soldiers and no heavy equipment, was waging a classic insurgency campaign similar to those being waged in Cambodia, El Salvador, Mozambique, and elsewhere. The Dergue was responding in kind: crops were burned, markets razed,

and drinking wells poisoned in the midst of a drought in order to
"deny the enemy valuable resources and cover." Villages frequently
changed hands, meaning that peasants were caught in the middle even
more than occurred in Eritrea. This was a small-scale version of
Vietnam and Afghanistan, except that there was a famine here as well.

Unlike Eritrea, this wasn't a war of conquest on the fringes of the
empire. This was the empire devouring its own heart. Ethiopia, as an
imperial concept, grew up out of Tigre. Axum, in the northwest of
the province, was the legendary birthplace of Ethiopia's first emperor,
Menelik I, son of the Hebrew king Solomon and the queen of Sheba.
Only a century ago, a Tigrean emperor, Yohannes IV, ruled all of
Ethiopia from Makelle before Addis Ababa was built by the Amharas.
Now it was the same old story: the Amharas—who prevailed in the
Dergue—were fighting the Tigreans, who resented the domination. In
a sense, little had changed since the Scottish explorer James Bruce
visited Gondar and Tigre in 1770, when, as Alan Moorehead wrote
in *The Blue Nile,* there were "endless marchings and countermarchings
of futile little armies," with an "atmosphere of *Grand Guignol . . .* of
horror piled upon horror until everything dissolves into a meaningless
welter of brutality and bloodshed." Western journalists in the 1980s
found northern Ethiopia as baffling and incomprehensible as Bruce
must have found it more than two hundred years earlier. The TPLF,
like the Dergue, was the product of a secretive, self-contained culture
that for centuries eschewed contacts with the outside world. One could
draw fewer conclusions from a tour of Tigre than from a tour of
Eritrea.

Yet basic patterns did emerge. Not everything was unclear. Much
that was clear went unreported, and much of what was reported was
not properly explained. As in the case of Eritrea, one could visit the
government-held areas of Tigre on a day trip from the Hilton in Addis
Ababa, with a box lunch to go along. Or, one could visit the TPLF
side from Khartoum; it took two weeks, the food and accommodations
were even worse than in Eritrea, and the trip was less rewarding.
Thus, while legions of journalists followed entertainers and politicians
to Makelle, on the government side, where RRC officials lectured about
the Dergue's ability to provide the entire province of Tigre with relief
supplies, the TPLF roamed the countryside all around Makelle, and
in response, the Dergue was literally burning crops and blasting peasants out of their *tukul*s (huts) in places such as Abbi Adi, sixty miles
from where all the journalists stood.

For most correspondents on the government side, the TPLF was
never more than a vaguely defined, evil-bent force whose only goal,
it seemed, was to disrupt the RRC's relief efforts. The March 1986

killings of two Ethiopian employees of World Vision by the TPLF provided ample justification for this view. But if one looked beyond the "policies of relief" to the politics of war, the guerrillas' hostility to the presence of Western relief workers in Alamata was not difficult to fathom.

From a relief standpoint, World Vision's actions were unassailable. The private charity was transporting food as close as possible to the TPLF front lines and feeding as many people as could be fed. However, looked at another way, World Vision's role was not so benign. The Dergue, with Soviet financial and technical help, in the early months of 1985 had completed a successful offensive that seriously disrupted relief work in TPLF-controlled areas. The MIG bombings of transit camps along the escape route to Sudan and the capture of the Hermi gorge, which linked the densely populated central highlands with western Tigre, trapped thousands of starving peasants in places where no help was available. The towns of Abbi Adi and Sheraro also were taken. Abbi Adi reportedly was bombed on market day, March 1, 1985, and according to eyewitnesses in Sheraro, the hospital was destroyed and the wells were poisoned. Next, Mengistu had to consolidate his battlefield victory, and the Tigre part of the northern initiative that USAID was then pushing on him, as a complement to the cross-border program from Sudan, would help him do just that. Having gotten the Soviets to bankroll the military side of the offensive in Tigre, the Ethiopian leader now got the United States and World Vision to pacify the populations of the newly won areas with grain handouts. As Paul Vallely wrote in *The Times* of London (June 4, 1985), it amounted to "a bizarre *de facto* alliance between the United States and the Soviet Union." Not that USAID or World Vision went to the alter innocently. They were aware that the northern initiative might further the Soviet aim of defeating the TPLF, which, although avowedly Marxist, was fiercely anti-Soviet on account of Moscow's ties to the Dergue. But that was the price of feeding hungry peasants. The TPLF was not so sentimental. The guerrillas approached the World Vision employees in Alamata as they would have Soviet advisers—through the crosshairs of a rifle.

The media paid scant attention to the Alamata killings. (Blaine Harden's article in the *Washington Post* was a notable exception.) But two other events of even greater significance involving the TPLF that occurred around the same time received almost no coverage at all in the United States because they could have been reported only from the TPLF side: the Makelle prison break and the repatriation of eighty thousand refugees in Sudan back to Tigre. Between midnight and 3 A.M. on February 8, 1986, the TPLF stormed the prison at Makelle, the same town where RRC officials had assured throngs of journalists, politicians, and entertainers that the government's hold over the entire province was secure. The guerrillas claimed to have freed one thousand eight hundred prisoners. Without disputing that figure, Western diplomats in Khartoum confirmed that at least seven hundred prisoners escaped, many of whom had been detained for political reasons by the Ethiopian regime for more than a decade. The break was preceded by two diversionary attacks, one on the Makelle airfield and the other on a main road leading out of town. These attacks drew off two brigades of government soldiers. This was a painstakingly planned operation of great cunning and dramatic execution behind enemy lines that demonstrated what Western military analysts already knew: although lacking the equipment and infrastructure development of their Eritrean guerrilla counterparts, the TPLF was still one of the best-trained, nongovernmental fighting forces in the world.

The freed prisoners provided a fount of information about jail conditions in Ethiopia. The Paris-based International Federation of Human Rights sent an Anglo-French legal team, led by Alex Lyon, a former minister in the British Home Office, to take evidence from the former detainees. According to an article by Colin Legum, a noted expert on African affairs, that appeared in the *International Herald Tribune* (May 20, 1986), "The lawyers found that the civilian population of Tigre were victims of arbitrary arrest and torture, and detained without charge in overcrowded, insanitary conditions. Evidence from people who had been in other prisons showed that conditions in Makelle prison were not exceptional." Several different methods of torture were employed, which included submersion in a barrel of hot, dirty water and beatings with a leather whip called the "ox penis." Legum wrote that one prisoner "said he was forced to confess to murder by having a rachet screwed into his hand." Lassa fever and typhoid reportedly were common.

The same week as the prison break, REST began a three-month program of repatriation of Tigrean refugees from camps in eastern Sudan. It was a benchmark event of epic proportions that signified the end of the famine emergency in northern Ethiopia: eighty thousand of the three hundred thousand Tigreans in the border area were trekking several hundred miles back to their homes in an operation planned by their own relief organizations with little outside help. In political terms, the return exodus was the last in a series of referendums in which a large peasant population, by voting with its feet, expressed absolute fear of the internationally recognized government in Addis Ababa and complete faith in a guerrilla group recognized by nobody. The first round was conducted in late 1984, when two hundred thousand

Tigrean refugees stampeded over the border into Sudan, joining another one hundred thousand Tigreans already there. Like the Eritreans, the Tigreans were escaping war and drought. They preferred to dodge bombs from MIG runs on refugee columns during the eight-week journey on foot from central Tigre rather than go to nearby government feeding centers for help. *Time* magazine (January 21, 1985) reported the story of Mohammed Idriss, sixty, and his family of eight.

> The house they left sits on a hill overlooking one of the Ethiopian government's largest refugee camps and emergency feeding centers. Almost from his doorstep, Idriss could see trucks and aircraft ferrying in some of the thousands of tons of foreign relief supplies that are now flowing into the country every day. Yet he preferred to shepherd his family for 23 days across mountainous wasteland to the relief camp of Tekl el Bab, the newest of three centers that have sprung up near the Sudanese town of Kassala, 20 miles from the Ethiopian border.
>
> Why? "We were afraid," says Idriss. "If we went to the feeding center, the government would ask us for papers; they would turn me away. But first they would take my sons and send them to work on state farms in the south or draft them into the army."

The feeding centers would give food only to those with identification cards indicating membership in a government peasant association. Because people from TPLF-controlled areas had no such documents, they were denied food and sometimes beaten. For many, if not most, of Tigre's 5 million inhabitants, the food that the international community was donating in late 1984 and early 1985 may as well not have been given because it was delivered to the wrong address—that of the Ethiopian government, which was not so much governing Tigre as fighting a war with it. The Reagan administration, in addition to some private charities operating from Khartoum, already was aware of this problem and had begun planning a cross-border feeding program, in cooperation with REST. But others, particularly the United Nations, persisted in believing the Dergue. As late as September 21, 1985, the office of Kurt Jansson, the U.N. emergency coordinator in Addis Ababa, without even consulting REST released a report maintaining that 80 percent of the famine victims in Tigre were receiving help from the RRC, the International Committee of the Red Cross, and Western donor agencies operating from government-held areas. In light of the refugees' own accounts of what really was happening at government feeding stations, coupled with the fact that the TPLF controlled most of the countryside in the province, the U.N. claim seemed preposterous. As Allen Pizzey of CBS News reported on March 22, 1985, "Three weeks of travel across rebel-held Tigre have shown clearly that the government has no administrative presence . . . and is not distributing food aid."

Having escaped to Sudan, the Tigreans entered a new kind of hell. More than 1 million of Sudan's 22 million people were refugees, and the Khartoum government—destitute from civil war, drought, and its own corruption and mismanagement—was unable to offer the Tigreans anything except the assurance that they wouldn't be sent back across the border to Ethiopia. The refugees thus were dependent upon the mercy of international organizations, mainly the United Nations High Commissioner for Refugees (UNHCR), which, having dragged its feet on U.S. government predictions in 1983 of a mass influx of refugees the following year, was ill-prepared for the human flood. The Tigreans were packed into a number of holding camps strung out along a dun-colored moonscape near the towns of Kassala and Gedaref. The largest was Wad Kowli, southeast of Gedaref on the Atbara River, a few miles from the Ethiopian border. According to the Sudan Commissioner's Office of Refugees, there were as many as ninety thousand Tigreans at Wad Kowli in early 1985. Gayle Smith, the author of two books on Tigre, who visited the camp in March of that year, said in a telexed report to Grassroots International that the camp presented a "microcosm of an entire society dying out." More than one hundred people were dying a day of measles, multiresistant shigella, and a host of other diseases. The daily death rate at the camp was 14 per 10,000—the highest anywhere in the world, reported UNHCR field officer Jean-Michele Goudstikker. UNHCR explained that due to "a declining and deteriorating supply" of water from the Atbara River, the camp had to be serviced by tanker trucks. The situation was so bad that on February 17, according to Barbara Hendrie, a representative of Grassroots International who was there, Wad Kowli had "one day of surface water left." The refugees couldn't even bathe. Hendrie also reported "tremendous shortages of clothing, blankets, cooking utensils and salt and pepper for food."

The Tigreans were degraded in other ways as well. The refugees' presence sparked resentment among local Sudanese, who on several occasions stoned whole groups of camp inhabitants. Tigrean women were frequent targets of rape attempts by Sudanese soldiers. The night of February 10, 1986, after men in the camp had tried to help the women resist the soldiers, the army sealed off Wad Kowli and arrested 166 people. All of the men detained received five lashes each, said a UNHCR source. (In a May 16, 1985, dispatch, Paul Vallely quoted a Sudanese official at another camp as saying that "every Ethiopian woman who crosses the border deserves to be raped as the price of admission.") Therefore, one could hardly blame the fifty-seven thousand Tigreans, who in May 1985, despite continued drought and war conditions in Tigre, elected to return home against the advice of REST and other agencies.

By February 1986, however, drought conditions in western Tigre and parts of central Tigre had improved enough for REST to launch a repatriation program. A large crop in the west the previous spring and the likelihood of early *belg* (light spring) rains on the eastern escarpment of the central highlands meant that refugees returning to those areas would be able to sustain themselves until the first harvest of maize and sorghum, expected in June. The returning refugees were divided into groups of forty, according to village, and each peasant was given water, 100 grams of sugar, and five days worth of biscuits upon leaving Sudan. In addition, the International Rescue Committee in Wad Kowli distributed chloroquin for use against malaria contracted along the way. The TPLF, in cooperation with REST, had set up relief stations every three days walk, where fresh rations were provided along with medicine for the sick. At the last relief station, tools and seeds were to be distributed for planting. Those who lived in the central highlands had a month of walking ahead of them.

From the moment the Tigreans left the thatched *tukul*s at Wad Kowli there was no shade. It was a never-ending climb into the highlands. The passage through the vast ocean of dust in northern Gondar was as monotonous and unfriendly as a sea voyage. Some had donkeys. But most slung their sacks and plastic jerry cans on sticks over their shoulders. One old man had a leg injury and could barely walk, yet somehow he was walking. They were all half-naked in their ragged *shamma*s. But this was no march of sorrow. These people were going home and, according to relief officials, were healthier than they had been in years. But because they were not visibly starving, it was not a news story.

I followed the returning refugees across Gondar almost as far as the border with Tigre, riding in a grain convoy that closely paralleled their route. I saw firsthand what food aid specialist Jack Shepherd of the Carnegie Endowment said was unique in the Third World: a guerrilla army that was feeding its people rather than feeding off them.

At dawn, two thousand refugees straggled into the TPLF relief station at Gichew, where I had arrived the night before after a five-hour truck journey from Wad Kowli. I had slept out on the open plain and was awakened in my sleeping bag by the sound of feet pounding nearby. Except for the shrill racket of cicadas, there were no other noises: the refugees were too tired to talk. Gichew was one of the transit camps set up by the TPLF in late 1984 to aid starving peasants escaping to

Sudan. Now it was being used for the second time to assist the same people coming back. The site was selected because the thick brush made it hard to spot from the air and the high ground made it difficult to attack. Otherwise, Gichew was indistinguishable from the rest of the Gondar wasteland. My recollections of it are in black and white; drought had drained the color out of the landscape. All the trees looked stunted. Only the termite hills appeared tall (some were as high as six feet). The relief station was manned by sixty TPLF fighters and ten staff members of REST. The commander, Alem Ayel, was twenty-six years old.

The guerrillas doled out water to the refugees from oil drums. The line was silent and orderly. People sought out shade in *tukul*s and in the folds of the hills. In an underground slate bunker, chloroquin, Tylenol, rehydration salts, antibiotics, children's multivitamins, and an iron supplement were available. Grain was distributed by the TPLF in the afternoon, and in the evening a cup of flour was given out to each group leader; the flour was supposed to be enough to make dinner for forty. A guerrilla soldier with a notebook went around making sure every group was accounted for. Beads and silver charms dangled from black shoelaces around the women's necks as they prepared the *enjerra*. The smoke from the cooking fires at dusk drew a charcoal veil over the darkening tableau. "It is obvious we are afraid our relatives have died of hunger or have been taken by the government soldiers. So we are in a hurry to get back to see how they are," said Lete Gebreal, thirty-three, of Damo village, which was nearly a month's walk from Gichew.

It was an eight-hour journey by nighttime convoy from Gichew to Kaza, where the refugees would arrive after another three-day walk. Kaza had been firmly in TPLF hands since early 1984, and 100 guerrillas and REST personnel now occupied the cluster of *tukul*s on a flat-topped mountain (amba) overlooking a stream bordered by white oleanders. The meager trickle of water and the blooming, poisonous shrubs, along with a pack of colobus monkeys shrieking in the acacia branches, brought a sparkle of life to an otherwise dying landscape. The trees concealed 1,200 50-kilogram bags of U.S.-donated grain from the eyes of Ethiopian pilots.

In addition to being a relief station, Kaza functioned as a hospital and as an orphanage for 112 children whose parents had died of starvation en route to Sudan in 1984. The word "hospital" was misleading because a few basic medicines and bedding for up to 130 people were all that was provided. (In this respect, as in many others, conditions in Tigre were far more primitive than in Eritrea.) Haile Geremesken, the local TPLF commander, said that of the first nine thousand returning refugees who reached Kaza, eight hundred had spent at least one night in the hospital and three had died along the way. He showed me a notebook full of names as proof. This was relatively close to a normal death rate. If the commander's figures were even partially correct, it meant an extraordinary achievement for REST and the TPLF.

The returning refugees arrived at Kaza one night after plodding through a dust that filled their nostrils and attacked their eyes and throat but was only a few feet away from clear water and oleanders. Although the drought was over, the villages that these refugees were going back to were by no means secure. From the standpoint of the Ethiopian government, these villages were "strategic hamlets" in the middle of a war zone. The government aim had been to depopulate them by starvation and aerial bombardment, thereby driving the people to the main roads and government reception centers, where many were separated from their families and sent to resettlement camps in the southwest of the country. This policy still was continuing.

The fact that these Tigreans were voluntarily marching back to perhaps the same destiny owed much to the awful conditions in Sudan and to their all-consuming desire to learn the fate of their relatives left behind in Tigre. But the march also required an astonishing degree of faith in the TPLF. Some of these marchers—maybe one thousand of them—actually had been in resettlement camps and were among the lucky few to have escaped to Sudan. They now were completing a circle of migration: from village to government reception center to resettlement camp to safety in Sudan, then north along the Sudanese border to Wad Kowli or one of the other sites near Gedaref or Kassala, and finally back to the same village where the nightmare had started, and where it conceivably could start all over again.

As these refugees filed past with everything they owned tied up in bundles slung over their shoulders, it seemed to me that this repatriation revealed a lot more about the political preferences of a people than did all the rigged and semirigged elections that were forever taking place in Africa and elsewhere in the Third World. It seemed to me that TPLF, upon which these returning refugees in fact were staking their lives, warranted a closer look by U.S. policymakers concerned with turning the tables on a Soviet-backed tyranny whose actions had caused the famine in the first place.

*   *   *

The TPLF was borne out of ethnic conflict and a system of economic exploitation that even the most rapacious Western capitalist barely could imagine. For more than one hundred years, Tigre's 5 million people, 70 percent of whom are Christian and speak Tigrinya, have been on a treadmill of war and famine that makes the 42,500-square-mile province (the size of Ohio, Liberia, or East Germany) an environmental disaster zone. In fact, by the second half of the nineteenth century, subsistence-level agriculture was being ravaged by fighting among various feudal armies. The orgy of violence left Menelik, the Amhara negus of Shoa, the most dominant of the warlords. In 1889, he became Emperor Menelik II, succeeding the Tigrean Yohannes IV, who died in a battle with the Sudanese. Tigre bore the brunt of the Amhara emperor's war with the Italians. In 1896, Menelik led an army of one hundred thousand soldiers northward through Tigre as far as Adowa, where he defeated an Italian force that was poised to expand Italy's colonial claim beyond Eritrea. In the words of the Minority Rights Group report on Tigre, authored by James Firebrace, Menelik's "army fed itself from local food supplies leaving grain and seed stocks empty, and slaughtering the oxen used for ploughing. Seven years of famine followed [in Tigre]."

Imperial exploitation intensified under the rule of Menelik's successor, Haile Selassie, which led to a peasant revolt in 1943 against both the emperor and Tigre's own feudal aristocracy. The rebellion was put down with the help of a British bombing raid on Makelle, and reprisals were swift in coming. The peasants were disarmed, dispossessed of their land, and burdened by a brutal onslaught of taxation that filled the coffers of the emperor, the local nobility in Tigre, and the Coptic church. There was never any investment from any of these quarters back into the province, which is why there is no industry and almost no working class. There is so little money in circulation that halite (rock salt) is often used as currency. More than 90 percent of the people are peasant farmers, who have overworked the soil merely to eke out a living from it. The result has been five famines in the past thirty years alone. In 1959, ninety thousand Tigreans starved to death. In the 1972–1973 period, two hundred thousand in Tigre and nearby Wollo died.

It was from the exceedingly thin strata of educated people that an underground resistance was formed in the early 1970s, which was active in the overthrow of the emperor. After the coup, the local aristocracy, led by a descendant of Emperor Yohannes IV, Ras Mangasha Seyum, established the Tigre Liberation Front (TLF) to oppose the new rulers in Addis Ababa. But as the revolution progressed, the TLF itself became radicalized, adopted a Marxist program, and changed its name to the Tigre People's Liberation Front. War was declared on the Dergue in February 1975, after it had become clear that Mengistu and his cohorts, although ideologically in step with the TPLF, were bent on the same imperial approach to Tigre as was used by the deposed emperor. As usual in the Third World, Marxism counted for little when pitted against centuries of ethnic hatred.

In typical Ethiopian fashion, the late 1970s in Tigre saw another pageant of internecine bloodletting, as macabre as it was incomprehensible, with the TPLF fighting not only the Dergue, but two other Tigrean groups as well: the royalist Ethiopian Democratic Union of Ras Mangasha, and the Marxist Ethiopian People's Revolutionary party, which was estranged from the TPLF because of hair-splitting disagreements about liberation doctrine. But taking place as they did in the atmosphere of paranoia accompanying the Dergue's Jacobin reign of terror, these theoretical debates between different sets of hunted extremists led to armed clashes. Thanks partly to help from the Eritrean guerrillas, the TPLF defeated the other groups in 1978, thereby allowing for an expanded war with the Dergue, which, in the early 1980s, equaled anything transpiring in Southeast Asia or Central America for sheer horror.

Firebrace, in the Minority Rights Group report, describes the government's 1980–1981 offensive against the TPLF.

> Continuous aerial bombardment with cluster bombs, incendiary bombs and napalm left dry fields ablaze. Further plots were burned by government forces wishing to . . . put a squeeze on civilian food supplies. At the same time, thousands of infantry soldiers on the move with heavy Russian-built T-54 and T-55 tanks left huge tracts of cropland flattened in their wake.
>
> Tens of thousands of peasants were forced to flee their homes, and many had to seek shelter in damp caves where the incidence of disease was increased by overcrowding. Essential parts of the cultivation cycle were abandoned.

That offensive was a failure. The next, in western Tigre in early 1983, occurred just after the harvest season in the only part of the province with a grain surplus. As Firebrace related, "Grain was seized, grain stores and fodder supplies burnt, oil presses and mills removed, and whole villages destroyed." Once more, it was all for naught, as the TPLF regained the area after two months. While relief and rehabilitation aid requested by the government from the U.N. poured into other war-torn provinces during this period, nothing was allocated for Tigre, because 85 percent of the countryside was in guerrilla hands. The legacy of mass destruction combined with neglect triggered the 1984 famine, which most of the media would ascribe to "drought." For journalists arriving in Addis Ababa direct from Europe and the

United States, not only the distant past in Tigre but the recent past too might as well never have existed. The "war"—it rarely got more specific than that one word—was listed as just another reason for the calamity in the north.

Allen Pizzey was one of the few U.S. journalists who traveled in TPLF territory in order to explain the relationship between war and famine. Pizzey reported that "the Ethiopian government calls the rebels terrorist, but here they're more like Robin Hood figures, protectors of the traders. Almost every teenager in Tigre wants to be a fighter. Recruits come in as fast as refugees stream out." Although Pizzey's account reached millions of viewers on the *CBS Evening News with Dan Rather,* it is questionable how much effect the March 22, 1985, report had. It was a one-shot item lost in a barrage of countless other reports about Sudan and Ethiopia that barely mentioned the war and if they did, dismissed both the Eritreans and the Tigreans as "Marxist rebels."

From a public relations point of view, the TPLF had much more working against it than did the EPLF. With the Eritreans, the problem was mainly one of getting the whole truth out. But the truth about the TPLF, even if one could get it out, was not wholly palatable. Unlike the Eritreans, the Tigrean guerrillas never disowned the Marxist label. In fact, the TPLF underwent a further radicalization in July 1985, when the Marxist-Leninist League of Tigre was established in the "liberated" area. The league's founding document, which attacked "revisionism of all hues," evoked the perverse extremism of the Albanian communists. This created another barrier to U.S. support for Tigre at a time when the outside world was just beginning to recognize REST as an exemplary force against famine. But nobody need have been surprised. The TPLF was created out of the same crucible of revolutionary violence as was the Dergue. Language and group loyalty, not ideology, have separated the two. The fact that the TPLF does not share the Dergue's penchant for indiscriminate brutality may be merely a matter of circumstances; the TPLF does not have to police an unwieldy empire of disparate ethnic groups. The TPLF has only its own peasants to worry about, and its battlefield success partially depends upon their well-being, but the killing of the two Ethiopian relief workers in Alamata does indicate what the Tigrean guerrillas are capable of when they are not dealing with their own kind. Although the Eritrean revolt was born during the rule of the emperor, the one in Tigre was very much a child of the revolution.

But the circumstances under which the TPLF operates are not going to change. Tigre and some depopulated areas of Gondar are all the guerrillas want, or ever need, to control. Thus, the issue—for donors

interested in famine relief and for strategists interested in knocking a
Soviet piece off the board—is how the TPLF fights and how it treats
its own people in its own backyard. Marxist pretensions notwithstanding, the TPLF land reform program, the guerrillas' emphasis on wom-
en's rights, the creation of a rural health service, the building of schools
to augment a literacy campaign, and other infrastructure improvements
undertaken by the TPLF in the countryside are exactly the kinds of
things that USAID encourages every government in Africa to do.
"Marxism" in Tigre is—for example—little different than the sum of
U.S. government proposals for the development of western Sudan.
Although the Sudanese authorities never accepted U.S. advice, the
"Marxist" rebels in Tigre have. Since 1975, a veritable societal transformation has taken place. Democratically elected councils at the village
level have been set up. Firebrace, in the Minority Rights Group report,
noted that "local power has shifted to those traditionally excluded from
power—the poor peasants, women and particular groups who experienced discrimination such as Muslims in the highland areas and crafts-
men." According to Jon Bennett, a frequent traveler in the province,
writing for the British journal *The New Statesman* (June 17, 1983),
"What is unique here . . . is the extent to which the TPLF has captured
the imagination of the Tigrean peasantry and managed to translate
political consensus into participation." Such policies helped account
for why escaped peasants previously victimized by the Dergue in Tigre
trusted the TPLF enough to risk going back. However, recent attacks
by the TPLF on food convoys and feeding camps have undercut the
deservedly good reputation the organization has forged among knowledgeable people. But it is worthwhile to keep in mind that these attacks
notwithstanding, the human rights record of the TPLF on the whole
has been a great deal better than that of the Dergue.

*   *   *

What the famine emergency revealed, for the few who cared to look,
was that in terms of development policy at least, the guerrillas in both
Tigre and Eritrea stood alongside the United States, which, by virtue
of its massive economic assistance programs, usually has acted in the
interests of the African peasantry. The Soviet Union, on the other
hand, tended to support urban elites who exploited the peasants. Whatever the case in Nicaragua and El Salvador, in Sudan and Ethiopia
at least, the U.S. government was on the right side of a long-brewing
historical conflict. Unfortunately, the Reagan administration's conservative supporters never really emphasized this aspect of the famine
story. Nor did they take advantage of opportunities to undermine the
Ethiopian government by promoting guerrilla groups whose fighting

records have been superior to those of other insurgents whom the administration supported. Conservatives never really focused on the guerrillas because the media didn't. Although conservatives generally are more critical of the establishment media than are liberals, in the case of the famine conservatives were just as manipulated by the media. The major newspapers, and especially television, determined the agenda for political debate in the United States. Eritrea and Tigre— ravaged by Africa's bloodiest war and home to half the Ethiopian famine victims—never made it as hot items on the media's list.

FOUR

the African killing fields

I have never been a "village politician," was never enthralled by romantic notions of "the land," but it bothered me when we communists abruptly turned our backs on the peasants and subjected them to economic and police pressures.
—Milovan Djilas, *Rise and Fall*

It is sad that hundreds of thousands of people can be killed by governments with hardly an international murmur.
—R. J. Rummel, professor of political science at the University of Hawaii at Manoa, writing in the *Wall Street Journal*

Mao Zedong said that a guerrilla army "swims in the sea of the people." Another communist theorist (according to Peter Niggli's report for Berliner Missionswerk), this one a young cadre of the Workers' Party of Ethiopia, explained the corollary to that argument to a group of Tigrean peasants at Makelle after he had lost his temper with them: "If you dry out the sea the fish die."

He continued, "We will dry out Tigre and force the bandits to give up. You are the backbone of the bandits, so we have to break you first; then we can also destroy the marrow." Added another party cadre to another group of captured peasants, "We will not stop with the people, but we will destroy the whole land unto the last tree."

Ethiopia's communist rulers were aware that the Tigrean guerrillas could not be defeated by military means alone. So the government's office for nationalities, run by Ethiopian Amharas assisted by Soviet advisers, came up with a plan at the beginning of the 1980s to exterminate the TPLF's rural power base. But the plan didn't really get rolling until the famine-inspired Western relief effort did. Here is what happened to one of the fish in the sea.

Woldeselassie Gebremariam, a Tigrean priest in his late thirties, was one of fifty Ethiopian refugees interviewed in March 1985 at a camp in eastern Sudan by Peter Niggli, a Swiss investigator for the German church group Berliner Missionswerk.

My village is in the TPLF area. A cattle plague broke out last fall [1984] in the whole region. . . . The animals screamed, didn't feed anymore, they shit blood, fell away to the bones and finally died. The government announced it was going to vaccinate all the cattle free of charge at Adwa [in the north-central part of the province]. . . . The TPLF gave us permission [to cross into government territory] for the vaccination. We rounded up 750 head of cattle in our village and started off.

Woldeselassie, expecting to return home in a few days, left his wife and three children back in his village. This was about the time that a *Newsday* report (December 9, 1984) entitled, "New Start for Chosen Few" by Josh Friedman, indicated that a number of resettlement abuses, including the forced separation of families, had ended.

We arrived in Adwa on December 6 [1984] and were surrounded by soldiers in the middle of the town. [Woldeselassie explained how the soldiers picked out the youngest and strongest looking of the peasants and took them to prison.] We shouted, "Who was going to take care of our cattle?" . . . They answered it would be no loss if we lost our cattle, the government was going to resettle us and would replace our cattle in the new settlement."

There were more than 1,000 people in the prison at Adwa. A cadre by the name of Debesai was responsible for our registration. He declared that Tigre was only stones and rocks and the soil had lost all fertility, therefore the government had to bring us to more fertile areas. . . . We shouted all at once and started a big row which enraged our cadre Debesai very much. Debesai went to the administrator. . . . That man got angry too, came to prison and called us out, insulted us and finally ordered us to crawl back into the prison yard on our knees. The soldiers watched over the execution of his order and beat us as we crawled. . . .

We were kept in the prison for ten days. There was an absolute shortage of water. I don't know whether the old, the sick and the women got any at all. Every time the water was brought, a fight . . . started and only those who had the support of young, strong men received some water. . . . Some people tried to break out . . . my friend Makonnen, for example, but he was recaptured . . . and beaten the whole night. . . . The next morning he had to roll in the dirt before our eyes, water was poured over him until he was covered with mud. Then they ordered him to crawl back and forth on his elbows and knees. . . . He had to shout with his breaking voice that this would happen to anyone who tried to run away. He was not allowed to clean himself the whole day and his wounds were not treated.

For food, the prisoners were given two pieces of bread a day. The soldiers reportedly ate from grain bags, whose markings indicated they had been donated by the European Economic Commission and the governments of Canada and West Germany. On the eleventh day, Soviet pilots transported Woldeselassie and the others from Adwa to Makelle by helicopter. They couldn't go by land because the countryside in between was controlled by the TPLF.

> We were kept in an open field. There was no shade during the day and no shelter from the cold at night. The field, which contained 7,000 to 8,000 people from all over Tigre, was surrounded by three rows of soldiers. . . . Water was brought to the camp in two pipes. One pipe was reserved for the soldiers. The other pipe was for us but also served the soldiers if they wanted to wash their clothing. When they washed, we didn't get water. In between there were long queues. . . . When it was your turn, you ran to the pipe and tried to scoop up as much water as you could with both hands and also to drink a few drops—there were no containers for water. Meanwhile the next person was already pushing. . . .
>
> There was a camp prison for those who protested. . . . I was there. . . . Altogether, we were about 70 prisoners and we had to clear away the excrements every day.

Others at the camp explained how on account of catastrophic sanitary conditions, people fell ill with diarrhea and vomiting. Many died before even leaving Makelle. But when foreigners, including journalists, visited near the camp, the Tigreans temporarily were moved elsewhere.

> During the eight days I was there the cadre Debesai hung about [Woldeselassie continued]. He was brought in an official car in the morning and picked up in the evening. When he could no longer stand the stink that covered the field he had the car [pick him up in the afternoon]. Debesai was young and he wore a nice army jacket of the style the Russians wear. . . . He loved to say that today we were complaining about resettlement, but tomorrow, after we had been resettled, we would beg them to send our families. . . .
>
> Then the trip continued to Addis by plane. Trucks came to bring us to the airfield. The old and the sick were thrown onto the trucks like sacks by the soldiers: one held only the legs, one by the arms. . . . Then the healthy people were pushed on. But this was still bearable.

Soviet-made Antonovs, provided by the Soviet Union and Libya, were used in the operation. The planes, whose unpressurized cargo bays were designed for 50 paratroopers, carried 300–350 people on each flight to Addis Ababa. As Woldeselassie and many others described it, the sick people were laid on the floor in the middle of the plane, then the healthier ones were packed in. "We stood like sticks tied together. Those stretched out on the floor in the middle suffered most. People stepped on them, fell on them, squashed them. One person died before my eyes." Bonnie K. Holcomb, who worked alongside Niggli interviewing survivors, told *Spin* magazine that people "were crushed to death on the impact of takeoff and landing. They were suffocating, throwing up on each other, literally being asphyxiated. . . . Children had to be held over people's heads so they wouldn't be smashed. Women miscarried and bled." At Bole airport in Addis Ababa, troops carried off the dead bodies, and a fire brigade hosed out the pool of vomit and piss from the floor of the plane.

Although water was not scarce, the peasants were given only one cup of water each before being packed tightly onto buses for the long journey to Welega, a province in western Ethiopia astride the border with Sudan. "We were simply dropped off in the middle of the jungle, all around nothing but grass and bamboo of a man's height. I felt like garbage that had been dropped in the middle of nowhere," said another captured peasant, who like Woldeselassie, was used to living in the highlands of Tigre.

The jungly no-man's-land was near Asosa, a town about twenty-five miles from the Sudanese border. Woldeselassie said that no food was provided for two days after his group had arrived. He and other Tigreans tried to escape. But after three days in the bush they were caught by Berta tribesmen and brought back to Asosa. "The administrator asked us why we tried to run away. 'No one had forced us to come,' he said. . . . We nodded in agreement, hoping to reduce our punishment: yes, we had all come here voluntarily. Then we complained that there was no food, how should we survive? He answered that the government was begging other governments to feed us."

Woldeselassie was fortunate, however. A few days later, he made a second escape attempt and this time succeeded in reaching Sudan, where Niggli interviewed him at Damazin on March 6, 1985.

*   *   *

At this time, forty-two thousand people already had been relocated to the Asosa region, mainly east of the Dabus River, in order to make escapes to Sudan more difficult. Not a single installation awaited the peasants, and food and water were scarce. For those not lucky enough to escape soon after arrival, several months of hard labor followed: savannah grass had to be cut, trees were felled, and bamboo forests were cleared. Houses of corrugated iron were built for the militia and party cadres, and large grass huts were put up for assemblies. Only afterward were the peasants allowed to build smaller grass huts for themselves. In the intervening period, the peasants either slept out in the open or in the larger assembly huts, where two hundred to three hundred people were squeezed together, side to side, each night. Because the grass was so dry, fires were frequent. It is possible that some of the fires were set by Tigreans as a form of protest. In any case, the consequences were horrific. Hundreds of people reportedly were burned. Those who died were buried in mass graves. Among the victims were women and children, who on account of being ill from starvation, couldn't run fast enough from the flames. Others who were not hurt had their clothes destroyed. Because new clothing was not available, the cadres handed out empty sacks to the peasants so that they could make new garments.

The work day began at six, but most had to rise by three in the morning in order to stand in line for a cooking pan to roast the little bit of peeled grain that was distributed. Except for a short break in the middle of the afternoon for a second, similar meal, work continued until dusk, when graves were dug for those who had died during the day. New settlers usually received unground wheat. Only sometimes was wheat flour distributed. According to Niggli, the wheat rations varied considerably, from eleven pounds per person per month to fifty-five pounds. (A person needs at least sixty-five pounds per month to meet his or her minimum protein requirement through wheat alone.) Special food for the cadres and militia troops was brought in from the town.

The peasants were divided into work brigades of twenty-five, called a *guad*. Twenty *guad*s equaled a *tabia* (center in Amharic) of five hundred people. An *amba* (village) usually consisted of about seven thousand people, or fourteen *tabia*s. Each *amba* was commanded by seventy militia troops, who in turn were under the power of fourteen armed cadres from the Workers' Party of Ethiopia. A study prepared by Cultural Survival, an independent human rights organization staffed mainly by Harvard professors, explained how the militia troops lived in fear of the Marxist cadres.

In some cases, militia were beaten in front of the camp residents. . . . One escapee reported that three militia in his site had been accused of letting colonists escape. They were summarily hanged and then shot in the head. The militia took the examples to heart. As one escapee reported, "The main job of the militia is to kick us." . . . Beatings occurred, reportedly, when people urinated without permission or . . . if they slowed the rate of work in the fields.

Two escaped peasants told Niggli that the troops "liked to order their victim to lift his arms, look into the sun and spin around quickly. Blows with bamboo sticks ensured the proper acceleration, until the victim lost his balance and fell to the ground." Another punishment was to make a person walk around the *amba* holding his (or her) excrement in his (or her) bare hands.

Of course, there were shortages of everything, especially farm implements and medicines. However, a hospital for 100,000 settlers was being constructed in Asosa with Soviet aid, and Soviet doctors already were at work during this period. One Tigrean peasant whom Niggli interviewed said those who were caught trying to escape had to dig latrines for the Soviets.

*   *   *

When Niggli, Bonnie Holcomb, and the research director of Cultural Survival, Dr. Jason W. Clay, arrived in Sudan in February 1985 to interview the Tigreans and others who had escaped over the border, the resettlement issue was an interesting sideshow to the main famine story. Western journalists and diplomats in Ethiopia had caught glimpses of people being herded onto trucks and airplanes. One U.S. diplomat went so far as to say that "the selection process recalled Auschwitz." From the little that could be discerned, resettlement appeared to be yet another indication, if any was needed, of the Marxist regime's insensitivity to its own people. But there the issue ground to a halt for lack of evidence. Resettlement areas simply were off limits to almost all foreigners, except those on prearranged tours to model camps. The government denied that the program was not voluntary or that it was motivated by any factor besides the humanitarian desire to relocate drought-stricken peasants to more fertile areas in the west and southwest of the country. Western relief officials stationed in Addis Ababa, whose presence depended on the good will of the local authorities, tended to back up the regime's assertions. The obfuscations no doubt influenced Friedman's *Newsday* article, as well as a report aired April 1, 1985, on ABC's *World News Tonight* by correspondent Lou Cioffi, who depicted resettlement as a necessary evil.

Despite all the accusations, the government is going ahead with resettlement. The land in the north is dry and dead, nothing grows there. In the south it is rich and fertile. There is plenty of water. In this camp with proper irrigation, they can grow two crops a year. . . . This settlement [near Jimma, in Kefa province] has become for them a showcase, a demonstration that despite difficulties the resettlement program can be made to work. . . . As for the settlers, there are personal problems. Many are homesick, others are concerned about families they left behind. . . . This massive movement of almost one and a half million people will not be easy. But even those western officials who are critical of the program admit there may be no other way.

Jimma, as it turned out, was one of the camps about which Cultural Survival had obtained first-hand information concerning massive human rights abuse.

For the two months that they were in Sudan, Niggli, Holcomb, and Clay were relatively unobtrusive. They went about their business quietly and didn't socialize with the crown of journalists and relief workers in Khartoum. A year later, when the results of their research were being hotly discussed, few could even remember them. (I was fortunate to be tipped off to their operation by a diplomat, who casually mentioned that "there was this guy here from Harvard a few months back, Jason Clay, conducting research on resettlement, who seemed a lot more serious and professional than the others passing through this place. You ought to get in touch with him.")

Cultural Survival, based in Cambridge, Massachusetts, came to Sudan with especially impressive credentials. Founded in 1972 by a group of social scientists at Harvard University, its reports on endangered ethnic groups in Africa, Asia, and Latin America have criticized right-wing and left-wing governments alike and have been utilized by the World Bank, USAID, and foreign governments to judge a country's human rights record and need for development assistance. Clay's team interviewed 277 Ethiopian refugees at six sites in eastern Sudan (Fau II, Tawawa, Wad Kowli, Damazin, Kirmuk, and Yabuus) using local translators who were not connected with the TPLF. (Bonnie Holcomb, who speaks Oromo, helped with some of the translations.) All interviews were taped and then translated a second time by other translators back in the United States. More than half those interviewed were selected at random and, in almost all cases, involved more than 5 percent of the total population of each camp. This was a statistically huge sample. (Harris Polls, for instance, rely on .0004 of 1 percent of the U.S. population.) As Clay told me in a letter, "Methodologically, you cannot touch [criticize] the data that we collected" about conditions in Ethiopia "as it relates to the refugees in Sudan."

Nevertheless, by the time Clay and his team completed their work in Sudan at the end of March 1985, between three hundred thousand

and four hundred thousand peasants from the north of Ethiopia already had been resettled, according to the authorities in Addis Ababa. From a strictly scientific point of view, as Clay admitted to me, his findings could not claim to provide a wholly accurate picture of what was happening to those still in Ethiopia, who did not escape. This is because the Ethiopian refugees in Sudan, for a variety of reasons, may not have been representative of those who were resettled. Clay said, however, "the information that we collected was so similar on so many fronts, that it has to be taken seriously" regarding the present situation inside Ethiopia. Although this obviously was a researcher's opinion of his own work, Clay's words found an echo in the remarks of author William Shawcross, in *The Quality of Mercy,* about the situation inside Cambodia in the mid-1970s.

> Although it was hard to find a rationale for the Khmer Rouge conduct that the refugees described, their testimony was the same as that given to other people along the border. And their stories rang true; I just could not believe that these people had invented their tales or that they were simply being manipulated by the CIA or by Thai military intelligence. Refugees fleeing dictatorships—Stalin's USSR, Hitler's Europe, Pinochet's Chile, Husak's Czechoslovakia—have all been reliable witnesses of the states they left behind.

Clay told me that he tried to get permission for Cultural Survival to conduct research inside Ethiopia itself, but his queries never were answered. Nevertheless, certain scientific reservations notwithstanding, the work carried out in eastern Sudan by Clay, Niggli, and Holcomb was not only more thorough and unrestricted than was any other investigation of Ethiopian resettlement practices, but the work also stands as one of the most richly detailed, academically guided studies of the actual process of forced collectivization and its attendant human rights abuses in the reality of the Third World. To my knowledge, no study of the Great Leap Forward in China or the actions of the Khmer Rouge in Cambodia was as well packaged as was Cultural Survival's *Politics and the Ethiopian Famine 1984–1985,* a two-hundred-fifty-page monograph, served up with an array of attractive maps, whose results—if you could wade through the overwhelming details (few could)—were absolutely devastating.

"All those interviewed insisted that they had been captured by government troops and forced to resettle. . . . Ten per cent of all those interviewed reported that they witnessed people being killed who tried to escape." More than 40 percent said they were beaten. More than 85 percent said they had been separated from at least one member of their immediate families; 70 percent were separated from all members of their immediate families. Amete Gebremedhin, a Tigrean in her early forties, stated that after she and a group of other captured women protested to the militia about being separated from their husbands and children, "the soldiers laughed and said: 'What do you care about your children, you will find new ones in Asosa.'"

According to the report, resettlement often occurred in the process of fighting between the government and the TPLF. The government would surround a village, burn the crops, take the animals, and round people up. But in other instances, various lures were used; as in the case of Woldeselassie, the government would advise peasants to bring their oxen to a certain place for vaccination and then abduct those peasants. The most common lure was the promise of food at government feeding centers. Here Western grain deliveries played a direct part in the resettlement process. It also explains why hundreds of thousands of northern peasants, mostly Tigreans, ran away from the food that U.S. relief workers were donating in November 1984, rather than toward it, and trekked for weeks on foot to Sudan instead.

More than 30 percent of those taken for resettlement, according to Clay's report, "were held in regular prisons with common criminals or in military barracks until transport was arranged. . . . People reported that as many as 20 per cent of those captured at the same time from their village died in the holding camps even before beginning the trip." Relatives trying to bring food to those in holding areas were denied entry and were beaten by soldiers.

Some of the peasants were held in proper feeding camps, accessible to Western journalists. But "only the meek, quiet people were allowed to see the journalists. Group leaders and known resisters were moved out of camp areas where journalists were permitted to roam." In one case, an Ethiopian government official announced that "white guests are coming. . . . Whether you speak positively or negatively we will translate positively to the journalists." Tsegay Wolde Giorgis, a Tigrean in his fifties, said that in November 1984 "the inmates in the camp at Makelle were told to select ten speakers who should talk to western journalists. The speakers were supposed to talk about drought and famine that had affected their villages . . . and that they had no other desire but to be resettled." Another Tigrean, Haili Kelela, claimed that in front of a group of "white people" who had arrived in "a white car with a red cross painted on it," he and seven others told party cadres that they didn't want to be resettled. The cadres assured them that "we will give you food . . . and lead you back to your village." But after the "white people" had left, he and the others were thrown in prison and beaten until "I had to vomit blood."

Everyone interviewed said people had died en route to the resettlement sites; 60 percent said they actually saw people die. Clay's analysis of the death figures was the most comprehensive and the most controversial part of his research.

The death rates reported by the refugees ranged from 33 deaths per 10,000 people per day to 270 deaths per 10,000. These rates are extremely high given that the camp populations were comprised almost entirely of adults. Such figures were consistently reported from a number of different refugees from different areas. Furthermore, they were relayed by people who did not know each other. Some of the resettled people were undoubtedly malnourished as a result of declining agricultural production in their homelands, but many had not experienced famine until they were captured for resettlement. . . . Perhaps it is more important to note that the settlers received minuscule amounts of food for as long as a month before they arrived in the resettlement camps and then were expected to work 11 hours each day for six and a half days each week. . . . Many of the settlers were forced to sleep in open fields. . . . Finally, there were probably a number of diseases to which colonists had little or no resistance. . . .

These figures raise . . . the question of how many of the 400,000 people who were resettled by June of 1985 are still alive. If even the most conservative estimates of the death rate (33 per 10,000 per day) are halved and then halved again (i.e., reduced by 75 per cent), then 50,000 to 100,000 of those resettled in this massive program may already have been dead by July 1985.

The figure of "50,000 to 100,000" dead set the aid communities in Khartoum and Addis Ababa ablaze. It was a higher death rate than that at the emergency feeding camps on the Sudanese border at the height of the famine, and most of the Ethiopians who perished in Sudan were children and old people—of which there were very few in the resettlement program. Father Jack Finucane, the head of Concern, an Irish aid group in Addis Ababa, saw the death rates in an article I wrote for the *Wall Street Journal* about Cultural Survival's report and told a group of sixty foreign aid workers assembled on October 19, 1985, at the RRC headquarters, "I've read it and I don't believe it." Finucane said that in visits he and other members of Concern made to the resettlement area, there were no indications of any such horrors. But as it turned out, one month earlier, at a private meeting at the Hilton Hotel where only Western ambassadors and some aid officials were present, Finucane told a different tale; about a half million people were being displaced in "horrible conditions." Of seventy-seven resettlement areas, only two or three had succeeded, he had said. In

a July 29, 1985, letter to his home office, Finucane wrote it was safe
to assume that 25 percent—or one hundred twenty-five thousand—of
the settlers had died.

Finucane's reversal, whereby he independently confirmed from the
Ethiopian side the main points of Cultural Survival's Sudan-based
research, only to deny it all at a public forum in the presence of
Ethiopian officials, was laid out in a November 3, 1985, article by
David Blundy in the *Sunday Times* (of London). When Blundy, then
one of the paper's leading foreign correspondents, asked the chair of
the Band Aid coordinating committee in Addis Ababa, Brother Au-
gustus O'Keefe, about the discrepancy, O'Keefe replied, "That was a
private meeting [the meeting between Finucane and the ambassadors].
I won't talk about it. The press have done a lot of damage here. I
have never heard about any problems with resettlement."

It was a familiar pattern: back up the research of Cultural Survival
and Berliner Missionswerk in private, but condemn it in public. The
Red Cross League, for example, did a study on resettlement in the
summer of 1985 that corroborated much of what Clay's resettlement
study had found, including the death rate. But the report was kept
secret. (Oddly enough, the Canadian Embassy in Addis Ababa was a
true believer in resettlement, even in private. One Canadian diplomat
actually told me that the West had to get involved in a big way in
resettlement, in order to have "influence here." When I mentioned to
another Canadian official, whom I met in Sudan, that Canada was
assisting resettlement through funding to private agencies involved in
the program, he got very angry and proceeded to launch a tirade
against U.S. human rights abuses in the Third World. At the time I
knew of no other country about which the views of the Canadian and
U.S. governments were as divergent as on Ethiopia. Officials in the
U.S. State Department and National Security Council had been extremely critical of Canada's policy toward resettlement. In Addis Ababa,
the two embassies literally represented opposing camps. Some of the
Canadians I met appeared absolutely driven about proving that—at
least as far as Ethiopia was concerned—they had a foreign policy truly
different from that of the United States. In Canada itself this policy
was criticized. This was one of the stranger aspects of the famine
emergency.)

The spinelessness of the aid community in Addis Ababa was demonstrated a few months later, in December 1985, when the inevitable
happened—one of their own went public about the appalling consequences of resettlement. Medecins sans Frontieres published a report
entitled, "Mass Deportation in Ethiopia," alleging that with a death
rate of 20 percent, as many as three hundred thousand people were

likely to die in the resettlement program, of which up to one hundred thousand already had. The report noted that "one of the most massive violations of human rights" was "being carried out with funds and gifts from international aid." The French group quickly was expelled from Ethiopia, while the rest of the aid community chastised the group for getting involved in "politics" when it should have been keeping its nose to the grindstone of relief work. Apparently, nobody in Addis Ababa was drawing the distinction between "politics" and gross violations of human rights. The kiss of death to the French group's presence in Ethiopia was administered by the United Nations, which publicly defended resettlement by saying that the French organization's charges could not be taken seriously because it was the only group in the field making such accusations.

The U.N. statement, reported January 30, 1986, on the BBC's hourly broadcast, was yet another example of the aid community closing its eyes and ears to unpleasant facts that would have further complicated its working relationship with the Marxist regime, although these facts were easy to come by. Relief workers saw six hundred people at Korem, in Wollo province, being herded onto trucks by militia troops using sticks and whips. Within twenty-four hours, ten thousand other peasants fled the Korem camp fearing their turn would be next. Relief workers also knew that women and children were being denied food at Korem as punishment by the government because the husbands had escaped from resettlement camps. It was no secret that thousands of other women and children were being cut off from intensive feeding programs in Wollo in order to pressure people to volunteer for resettlement.

In early 1986, MSF took its case to the court of U.S. public opinion, which barely paid attention, even though the United States was providing almost as much aid to Ethiopia as was the rest of the world combined. A Washington press conference, among other activities, got the French doctors onto the front page of the *New York Times* for a day and into the editorial pages of several important dailies. But the story had difficulty making the evening news on the major networks because there was no footage of the settlers being abused. Also, this was the period of the Challenger disaster. Therefore, the impact of MSF's revelation on the general public was marginal. And as one refugee official in Washington explained to me, "Suzanne Garment of the *Wall Street Journal* was the only big columnist to write about it, so everyone around here dismissed it as just a right-wing issue." As limited as MSF's effect was, it was still greater than that of Cultural Survival. This was in a way unfortunate because MSF, a relief group whose investigation was not as well grounded academically proved a much softer target for supporters of resettlement than did the Harvard-based Cultural Survival. Because the resettlement debate began in 1986 to swirl around MSF, it was assumed by many that the accounts of human rights violations were exaggerated. Most observers forgot that the French doctors' report was merely part of a growing body of evidence corroborating what Clay's group initially revealed. The daily news media, by this time obsessed with the southern part of the African continent in place of the Horn, did little to put the findings into perspective or to investigate the matter further. The editorial page of the *Wall Street Journal* was a constant exception to this rule, but like all opinion pages, it didn't have quite the credibility of a hard news section, and the page's conservative slant meant that liberals often distrusted it. A breakthrough of sorts occurred in early March 1986, after a visit to the Damazin refugee camp by Blaine Harden of the *Washington Post* and Charles Powers of the *Los Angeles Times.*

The refugees on whom Cultural Survival's study was based were at Damazin for months in 1985, but few members of the media had bothered to interview these refugees. Even after Clay and Holcomb's report was published, journalists tended to write about the skeptical reaction in the relief community, rather than to hunt down the actual victims in order to hear their firsthand accounts. Harden had planned to do this, but as he explained to me, "I had a whole continent to cover and after several straight months in Ethiopia and Sudan, just as I heard about the Damazin story, I had to do a stint in West Africa." By the time Harden was able to return to Sudan, the refugees had been scattered to other locations, but another group of about one thousand had arrived from Ethiopia, and this group had been through an experience that was far more horrible than the experience of the people whom Clay, Niggli, and Holcomb had interviewed. As Harden wrote in his story, which ran March 11, 1986, in the *International Herald Tribune:*

> The dismal odyssey of the young Ethiopian mother began last spring with a false promise of free food in the Ethiopian government resettlement program. . . .
> En route, she said she was forced by Ethiopian soldiers to abandon her two children. She said she watched her husband die of disease in an overcrowded transit camp. After fleeing Ethiopia, she said, she was robbed, beaten, raped and held as a slave by Sudanese rebel soldiers.

The rebels belonged to the Ethiopian-backed Sudanese People's Liberation Army (SPLA), which was at war with the Khartoum government and in control of the jungles on Sudan's southeastern frontier. The escapees from resettlement fell prey to the rebel soldiers in the bush just as the Vietnamese boat people fell prey to pirates on the high seas. According to interviews conducted by Khartoum-based relief officials, several hundred Tigrean women and children escaped from resettlement camps only to be taken into captivity by the SPLA. The women and girl children were raped repeatedly, while the boys were forced to become fighters.

Harden pointed out in his article that "the stories told here . . . come not from outsiders, but from peasant farmers [who] in 13 separate interviews . . . told a remarkably consistent story." He and Powers spent two days at Damazin doing nothing but interviewing a completely new set of refugees, and both reporters came up with exactly the same information as had Clay. In the lobby of the Khartoum Hilton, Harden told me that despite his reservations about aspects of the Cultural Survival report, he found nothing in Damazin to contradict the basic tenets of Clay's research. Referring to the large-scale human rights abuses in Ethiopia, Harden shook his head and said, "It's really happening over there."

Harden's report triggered a moving editorial in the *Washington Post* a few days later, but not much else. The television networks as usual were preoccupied elsewhere. Yet what I find particularly disturbing was that at no point in 1985 or 1986 did the *New York Times* send a reporter to Damazin. Neither Clifford May, Nairobi-based Sheila Rule, nor anyone from the *Times* Cairo bureau had ever gone there. Even the best newspapers cannot be expected to cover every single story, but the refugees at Damazin were at the center of the whole resettlement controversy, and they were available to journalists for months at a time. The *Times* dutifully editorialized about resettlement and reported the controversy in the relief community surrounding it, but the most prestigious daily in the United States never really probed the issue in the same aggressive manner in which it had probed human rights violations and other misdeeds of far lesser magnitude in other areas of the world, particularly the Middle East and South Africa.

In spring 1986, a few weeks after the *Washington Post* published Harden's Damazin dispatch, former RRC head Dawit Wolde Giorgis, who had defected to the West several months earlier, admitted publicly that "force had to be used [in the resettlement program], and a vast number of people were herded like cattle, loaded on trucks and airplanes, and sent to the south. The whole operation was run by the Workers' Party and its cadres in the various provinces." This was the same Dawit who consistently had defended resettlement at the height of the famine emergency, and many of the media reports that had cast a somewhat favorable light on the program had made use of statements from him, and his chief assistant in the RRC, Berhane Deressa, who also defected.

Around the same time that Dawit was recanting what he previously had told scores of journalists, the Ethiopian government announced that as of December 1985, five hundred fifty-two thousand peasants had been resettled. Yet the previous summer, the government had claimed that as of May 1985, five hundred forty-seven thousand had been resettled. Clay thus put the question: "What happened to the 100,000 to 250,000 people that were surely moved in the last few months of 1985, but who are no longer in the resettlement camps?" Not only did nobody have an answer, but few others were even aware of the question.

*   *   *

It is intriguing that resettlement received so little attention in the United States. After all, as I've demonstrated, the body of evidence was substantial. It is possible that more blacks were killed in the program in less than two years than had been killed directly by South African security forces in forty years. The manner in which Ethiopians died evoked the well-known slaughter of millions of Cambodians by the Khmer Rouge in the mid-1970s. Yet not only was the U.S. public more concerned about the abuses in South Africa, but both the media and the public also evinced more interest in the fate of a few hundred South Korean students, who had been detained by the police, than about tens of thousands of peasants in Ethiopia who had been starved, beaten, and worked to death in a veritable jungle gulag.

In the opinion of Chester Crocker, the U.S. assistant secretary of state for African affairs, the lack of public awareness was the fault of the media. In a conversation with me in Washington in early 1987, Crocker explained that in the mid-1980s

there was a rapid growth of American public interest in Africa due to two radically different events—one, the unrest in South Africa, became a white hot, made-in-Hollywood media issue; the other, Ethiopia, affected millions yet had less of a profile because of the problem: who do you blame? The media is very dependent on access, and access to resettlement areas in Ethiopia was more restricted than to most places in South Africa.

Crocker, of course, was a very embattled figure during the Reagan years because of his controversial policy of "constructive engagement" toward the white minority regime in South Africa. The media was relentless in its pursuit of that story, and Crocker's general attitude toward the Fourth Estate could not have been particularly warm.

Although it's true that the magnitude of the abuses warranted more dramatic coverage than the story got, more than "access" was involved. As I see it, the fundamental flaw in the resettlement story was that it was a foreign news item with no domestic spinoff. Because the United States, despite its generous aid, was not influential in Ethiopia—and had not been for a decade—it was a tragedy for which the Reagan administration bore absolutely no responsibility. Although private donations to certain charities were indirectly assisting resettlement, as were public donations from other governments, USAID always was careful to channel U.S. aid to relief operations unconnected with the program. Thus, there was nothing to dig up against the administration, and the herd instinct in the media never was activated. Even after the MSF visit, journalists almost never raised the matter at State Department briefings. Ethiopia had been "lost" years before, and U.S. interests were not being jeopardized by the inhuman actions of Ethiopia's regime. The country now was part of that zone of darkness where literally anything could happen away from the television cameras. Had the deaths occurred at the hands of a colorful madman, like Idi Amin or Muammar Gaddafi, or even someone less well known but just as crazy, like the former "emperor of the Central African Empire," Jean-Bedel Bokassa, the story could have been rescued from oblivion. But Mengistu was far too efficient a killer to be distracted by buffoonery, so his crimes had little mass market appeal.

The media, however, bore only part of the responsibility for the limited public response. Elliott Abrams, a former assistant secretary of state for human rights and humanitarian affairs in the Reagan administration, told me that

> there has to be some kind of pressure from a human rights group for a human rights issue to be considered legitimate. U.S. government statements alone can't do it. And for a long time, human rights groups were saying nothing about resettlement because a lot of democratic governments were assisting the Ethiopian Marxist regime. Human rights groups of the left were certainly reluctant to criticize. The U.S. government's criticism therefore looked political rather than humanitarian. And remember, at the time we were in the middle of a struggle over South Africa. You have to ask: if the Reagan administration hit the government of Ethiopia hard, who would support us and who would criticize us? Would the main effect be to help the people of Ethiopia, or merely to add fuel to the fire over our Africa policy? I think part of the problem is the reluctance of human rights organizations to criticize left-wing governments.

Abrams remarks contained a subtle, deliberate, and fascinating, contradiction: first, he suggested that the Reagan administration did attack the Ethiopian government for its resettlement practices, but then he implied that the administration didn't. I strongly suspect that Abrams, one of the more ideologically motivated of Reagan's political appointees, felt that as much as the administration did to publicize human rights abuses in Ethiopia, it could have done even more. I think he, as well as others, felt that had the administration wanted to pull out all the stops, it had it in its power to make resettlement a big media issue.

On the face of it, the Reagan administration did all that normally could have been expected. Crocker and Vice President George Bush spoke out against resettlement on a handful of occasions. USAID administrator M. Peter McPherson rarely missed an opportunity to bash the Ethiopian authorities over the head about it. McPherson made resettlement his pet issue, telling me that "from the start, we were totally disgusted with the Ethiopian regime." Richard Shifter, who replaced Abrams as the human rights undersecretary (when Abrams became assistant secretary for inter-American affairs), made the investigation of resettlement abuses a priority. Finally, there was Alan L. Keyes, the assistant secretary of state for international organization affairs, who as a black was perhaps in a better position to publicly articulate what many others were saying only privately. On March 6, 1986, Keyes told the Senate Subcommittee on African Affairs that

> those who condemn the white government of South Africa for its injustice against Blacks but who do not even wish to verify the injustices that may be perpetrated by Ethiopia's Government against its people obviously imply that a higher standard of human rights is to be applied to whites than to peoples of other races or colors. We reject this implication. If it is racist not to care when Black people are denied their rights, then it is racist not to care when Black governments deny them.

Nevertheless, if ever there were an issue tailormade for a president who was forever searching his file cards for examples of why fighting communism around the world was not just a strategic imperative, but a moral one as well, it was resettlement. Here was a difficult-to-dispute example of an undeniably Marxist Third World government mistreating its people on a grander scale than had any right-wing regime anywhere, particularly those in South Africa, the Philippines, and Chile. Here was an example of what happens to people when their country is "lost" to the Soviet bloc. Resettlement constituted powerful *moral* ammunition for the Reagan Doctrine. But when did President Reagan ever speak out about it? Maybe he did, once or twice. If so, it was a reference too obscure for even Ethiopia experts to remember. Re-settlement was the issue Ronald Reagan had been waiting for all his presidency.

If not Reagan, why not Bush, at least? As one State Department official observed cynically, "Bush should have taken on resettlement as *his* issue. If ever there was a guy who needed—and was always looking for—his own issue it was Bush." Resettlement, which Bush criticized in the context of his trips to Africa but never really jumped on in Washington, was perhaps the only cause available to him at the time that was original and would have helped to shore up his credentials as a presidential candidate among conservatives, without alienating moderate elements in the Republican party.

Some felt that the reason resettlement never made it past the door of the State Department was because Chester Crocker stood in the way. According to this theory, Crocker's overriding obsession was his South Africa policy. He had gotten his job on account of his views on South Africa, and his performance as assistant secretary was being judged solely by how he implemented them. The last thing he needed was another complication to further erode his already strife-torn policy toward that country. Therefore, he seemed to some observers to be gun-shy about having the White House launch a frontal human rights attack against a black African regime at a time when President Reagan was being chastised for his indulgence of the white minority government in Pretoria. One State Department official explained the situation to me this way: "If you don't have an issue that you can fully justify and explain in ten or fifteen seconds before a TV camera, then you don't have an issue. It would have taken longer than that to show why there was nothing hypocritical in attacking Ethiopia harder than South Africa." Alan Keyes went a step further: "If the Ethiopian government does away with tens of thousands of people nobody is interested, while if the South African government does away with thousands of people over a period of several years you can't keep the media away."

But, again, it wasn't only the media, nor even just the human rights organizations that weren't interested, but Western governments as well. Keyes said that at a meeting of the U.N. Human Rights Commission in February-March 1986, he

actually got the feeling that the Europeans wanted it all swept under the rug. They didn't even want to investigate. . . . The Western Europeans (and Canadians) didn't like us harping on resettlement, because they saw it as harming the famine hostages in Ethiopia. It came through pretty clearly that their attitude was, "What's all the fuss about? This is the way the Ethiopian government has treated its people for centuries."

In fact, as a National Security Council staffer revealed, after the United States got independent intelligence confirmation of the main findings of Clay's report, Secretary of State George Shultz was ready to enter a U.N. resolution condemning the Mengistu regime, but backed down after receiving absolutely no support from the United States' Western allies, who did not want their aid programs in Addis Ababa jeopardized.

*   *   *

The oft-heard argument of all of those who discounted the conclusions of the U.S. government, Cultural Survival, MSF, Berliner Missionswerk, and others was that resettlement was a necessary step toward the prevention of future famines, even if, for the time being, it was being carried out badly. This was the line of thinking transmitted to the public by the media, as in the case of the ABC *World News Tonight* report by Lou Cioffi, who along with many other journalists heard this argument from relief workers and diplomats in Addis Ababa. I don't know how many times it was pointed out to me that resettlement was originally a USAID–World Bank idea proposed to the Ethiopian government in the late 1960s during the reign of Haile Selassie. The question I usually asked in return was, So what? Isn't it beside the point if it was a great concept in the abstract? Weren't the goals motivating USAID and the World Bank very different from those motivating the Ethiopian authorities who now were in charge of the program? For this was the most startling and convincing, albeit ignored, finding of the Cultural Survival report—more significant in a way than even the extrapolation of death rates. Interviews with dozens of peasants revealed that the drought and famine were of marginal relevance to the resettlement program. The report stated:

> The majority of those interviewed who had fled the resettlement camps had not been hit hard by the famine. On average, those taken from Tigre who were interviewed claimed that they had produced 80 per cent of their subsistence cereal needs in 1984. They had possessed on the average more than 22 head of livestock at the time of their resettlement. Those taken from Wollo, while having experienced severe food shortages and absence of rainfall, cited government policies of confiscating surpluses critical to survival in a transitional zone as the underlying causes of their plight.

Niggli wrote that of the Tigreans he interviewed who had escaped from resettlement camps, "only 14 per cent . . . had had no harvest in the last year and can be regarded as drought victims or famine victims." Of the rest, many had had an average harvest prior to being resettled, and some even had had a good harvest. Niggli mentioned there were even "absurd cases" such "as Tewolde Gebregziabher who had owned an irrigated fruit plantation and who was a rich peasant by Ethiopian standards" prior to being forcibly removed to the south. The studies indicated that most of the abducted peasants lived not in the worst, drought-affected regions, but in the vicinity of roads strategically vital to the government's war effort.

The criteria the government used in the resettlement selection process had more to do with a peasant's potential for assisting guerrillas than with his or her need for fertile land. For example, although most of the Amharas in Wollo were Christians, most of the Amharas taken for resettlement were Moslem Oromos, whose fathers and grandfathers had Oromo names, and who traditionally had supported warlords and other insurgents against the ruling Amharas of Shoa. Rather than a catastrophe—as it had been for Haile Selassie—the famine was a godsend for this regime. The famine created a pool of millions of peasants, who whatever their political leanings, now had no choice but to rely on the government for help. The government now had a legitimate excuse to relocate those it thought to be hostile, as well as the wherewithal to do it, partly because of relief supplies pouring in from the West.

Rather than work to alleviate the famine, the regime appeared to deliberately exacerbate it for the peasants targeted for eventual resettlement. Said one farmer, "The Dergue is the best friend of the pigs and the monkeys. He allows them free access to the fields while we sit imprisoned in useless harangues about paying more tax out of the crop that at that time is mostly eaten by animals." Remarked another, "They should put the baboons in the meetings and let us go to farm the field. Then we could eat and get fat like the animals do." In addition to the problem of animals, more than a quarter of those interviewed by Cultural Survival said that the army had stolen their farm equipment (plows, seed bags, leather straps, and other tools).

Not only did the resettlement program destroy the livelihoods of peasants in the north, but the program destroyed those in the south, too. Many of the new sites in fact had been successfully farmed for years before the indigenous inhabitants had their land expropriated by the state to make way for the new arrivals. The rationale for this seemingly irrational act was military and political: most of the sites were located along access routes used by the Oromo Liberation Front in its war against the government. Thus, not only would the Tigrean rebels in the north be deprived of their base of peasant support, but so would the Oromo rebels in the south. Moving people around became another way to prosecute a war. Amhara imperialism simply had evolved into a more sophisticated form. A look at the placement of resettlement sites on a map reveals a pattern strikingly similar to the military expeditions of Menelik in the late nineteenth century.

Because restoring agricultural productivity was not the aim of resettlement, the government put up with miserable results without attempting to change the program. About three-quarters of all the tractors at the new sites reportedly were out of order in 1984, and the production level of the resettlement camps was even lower than at the state farms. Yet the government, backed by segments of the aid and diplomatic community in Addis Ababa, kept insisting that "there was no other way."

In Cambodia in the mid-1970s, a horde of primitive peasants, the Khmer Rouge, brutalized an urban elite. In Ethiopia in the mid-1980s, an urban elite brutalized a class of primitive peasants. Although for several years, until the release of the film *The Killing Fields,* the crimes of the Khmer Rouge were partially obscured by the closure of Cambodia to the outside world and the shadowy nature of the group's leader, Pol Pot, there was never really a tendency in the West to portray the forced relocation of urban Cambodians to the countryside as anything less than wholesale murder; nor was it really necessary to prove that that's what the relocation was. The Khmer Rouge, because they were primitive peasants, lacked the sophistication to con Western relief officials into subsidizing the reorganization of a society along Stalinist lines. But in Ethiopia, not only were Western officials dealing with an urban elite, but with the most sophisticated, Westernized stratum within that elite, composed of people who were able to convince others of what they themselves did not wholly believe. Forced collectivization thus was marketed successfully as famine relief.

*   *   *

Resettlement, however, was just one aspect of collectivization. The other, much larger, component was villagization. In 1984 and 1985, the government managed to resettle about 500,000 of the 1.5 million people targeted; the program was resumed again in 1987 after the last unsteady flickers of the media spotlight had been snuffed out. But in roughly the same time frame, 1984–1986, ten times that many people— approximately 5 million—had been forcibly uprooted through villagization, with another 27 million scheduled for the same fate by the mid-1990s.

Villagization—a more grandiose, amorphous, and incomprehensible program than resettlement—made even less of an impact in the outside world. Villagization happened deep in the bush, far away from the diplomats, television camera crews, and other Western monitors, and it was too great a cataclysm to be grasped through the medium of print alone. (I think a main reason why Stalin's war against ethnic Ukrainians made less of an impact in the West than did Hitler's war against the Jews—even though the former may have claimed more lives—was because there were far fewer pictures of it; as with villagization, the destruction of the Ukrainian peasantry happened in secret, inside the sealed perimeters of a Marxist police state.)

Moreover, the most descriptive and penetrating article about villagization was an October 3, 1986, cover story in the French news magazine *L'Express,* which isn't read in the United States. Although effectively written articles and editorials on the subject did appear (notably in *Newsweek,* the *Washington Post,* and the *Wall Street Journal*), almost all were published in mid-1986, long after the Ethiopia story had been submerged by developments in South Africa. If resettlement came to light too late in the day to make a strong impact, villagization came to light even later.

However, unlike resettlement, villagization had no real defenders in the Western relief community in Addis Ababa. Even the Swedes, who in the past had been the most sympathetic to Marxist-style agricultural experiments, publicly criticized villagization and reduced their aid budget in Ethiopia on account of it. The reasons for this more realistic attitude were several. First, villagization did not become an issue until the very end of 1985. By then, the defection of Dawit, the publication of the Cultural Survival and MSF reports, and the demonstrated refusal of the Ethiopian regime to moderate its policies in the face of famine all had a cumulative effect on those, who the year before, had been willing to give the regime the benefit of the doubt. Second, the very size of the program—designed to affect three-quarters of the country's entire population—denied it credibility. Third, the RRC, in the throes of high-level defections, was less successful in selling it. (Once in exile, Dawit condemned villagization as "another ill-conceived policy.") Fourth, and most importantly, villagization was more blatantly ideological than resettlement was. Mengistu had spoken out openly against "kulaks" and, in a separate study done in Somalia, on escapees from villagization, Cultural Survival reported that, indeed, all those interviewed had been relatively prosperous farmers prior to being "villagized."

> None of those interviewed in the camp were drought victims. . . .
> Half used gravity-fed irrigation. They laughed at the suggestion that they
> might be famine victims. Those interviewed produced more than 670
> kg. of cereals, grains and beans, per person, for extended families which
> were twice as large as their nuclear families. While this level of production
> is more than three times basic subsistence needs, those interviewed

insisted that these crops were not their primary food staple. Instead, they relied on a variety of yam, which . . . was interplanted with other crops.

Most of the respondents grew chat, potatoes and red onions as cash crops, and half produced coffee and groundnuts. . . .

More than 92 per cent of those interviewed owned livestock. . . .

When asked why production had declined . . . 25 per cent said that drought had reduced production but that it had not caused significant declines. Some 30 per cent reported that uncompensated, forced labor, required by government or local officials, did not allow them enough time to cultivate their fields. Most said their herds had decreased because they were forced to sell animals to pay taxes . . . and because local officials stole their animals.

In the face of these realities, nobody believed that the program was meant to combat drought, famine, and underdevelopment, as the Ethiopian government authorities claimed. Ray Wilkinson reported in *Newsweek* (May 5, 1986) that diplomats and relief officials told him that "villagization is really a smoke-screen for collectivization of the sort that Soviet leaders forced upon Russian peasants in the 1930s. The Ethiopian government's real aim . . . is to herd peasants into centralized communities where the Army can keep them under control—and where communist cadres can indoctrinate them in Marxism-Leninism."

The basic outline of the fate of millions of peasants, mostly Moslem Oromos, under villagization was not in dispute. The army would move into a group of villages, requisition the crops and livestock, and force the inhabitants to tear down their huts piece by piece. Then the peasants were made to walk, with the remnants of their homes on their backs to a new, central location that had been selected by the party cadres. The new site almost always would lack a mosque, a school, and an adequate, nearby water source. But it would come equipped with a guard tower, a red flag, and a banner of the Workers' Party of Ethiopia. In the Hararghe region of eastern Ethiopia, thousands of such villages sprung up in the mid-1980s, each with several hundred rebuilt huts put up in straight rows. Gilles Hertzog, a French relief official writing in *L'Express* (October 3, 1986), described the new sites as "black rectangles where the huts are aligned like on parade." Hertzog asked, "What kind of crazy vision [has been] imposed on one of the oldest inhabited regions of Africa?" The tearing down and rebuilding usually occurred at harvest time at the peasants' own expense, when they should have been in the field bringing in their crops. Just the time wasted on relocation served to lower agricultural productivity.

"As we understand human rights in the West, this program is a gross violation of those rights," a Westerner in Ethiopia told Wilkinson; "This country's communist rulers are breaking up a centuries-old culture, and the only people they asked are themselves. On these grounds alone the program is indefensible." Yet, although nobody defended it, no Western government really condemned it either. Even the Reagan administration's criticism was muted, compared to the way it attacked resettlement. Rarely in modern times have so many people had their human rights abused in so organized a fashion with hardly a whimper of real protest or sustained media coverage than in the case of villagization.

The utter brutality of the experience was far worse than the *Newsweek* and *L'Express* articles had suggested. In the first months of 1986, fifty thousand Moslem Oromos escaping villagization stampeded over the border into northwestern Somalia, where they were held temporarily in a squalid refugee camp, located a few miles from the Ethiopian frontier, called Tug Wajale B. In the spring, Jason Clay of Cultural Survival and Lance Clark of the independent, nonprofit Refugee Policy Group in Washington, D.C., went to Tug Wajale to interview the new arrivals about their experience in Ethiopia. All the Oromos interviewed told a similar story of a whole way of life being systematically destroyed, not only by the razing of ancestral villages, but through a deliberate policy—implemented by the army—of wrecking mosques, raping women, and removing children to far-off schools. Lance Clark reported the following testimony from a "woman of about 35 years of age."

My husband is one of those who leads the prayers in the mosque. One day when another man was leading prayer, some military came. They threatened to kill anyone who prayed, anyone whose head touched the ground (in prayer). The prayer leader began to pray, and they shot him. The troops said that anyone who touched his body would be killed also. They then took his body outside of town and threw it out for the hyenas to eat.

Said another "woman of about 45 years of age":

The government says . . . that there is to be no religion, that your child does not belong to you, is not under your control. We had a good crop this year, but then the government came and even took away our oxen. But we have not left because of hunger, but because of freedom.

A "man of about 40 years of age" told Clark:

The problems began when all of our things were nationalized; all of our resources, and our women. There is to be no individual and no religion. The government cadre began talking about this three months ago, but when they actually started to do it, we had to leave. The government has been attacking our religion—they are making mosques into stores, and into toilets.

One woman told Clay "that in her village the standard rape ratio was five militia per woman and that the militia were 'turned loose' twice a week." As to the food supply, the Oromo refugees "insisted that they had been told [by the cadre] not to give milk to their children; since all cows belong to the state [and] it is the state's responsibility to feed the children."

Officials at the State Department in Washington said that the main reason why a greater protest wasn't made against villagization was because unlike in the case of Cultural Survival's resettlement study, the United States was unable to verify independently the stories told to Clay by the refugees in Somalia. I was told that the U.S. Embassy in Addis Ababa mounted a special effort to investigate villagization in the Hararghe region but was unable to confirm, or to deny, the accounts about mosques being destroyed and women being raped. I then asked myself, How are observers based in the Ethiopian capital supposed to find out about the specific acts of militia troops in small places out in the bush when the entire relief community in Addis Ababa knew nothing about the flight of the fifty thousand Oromos to Somalia while it actually was occurring? (As thousands of Oromos were pouring over the border, international observers in Addis Ababa were telling their counterparts in the Somali capital of Mogadishu that it shouldn't be happening because they had no information about it!) Moreover, because the basic facts about how the program was being administered were already well known and chilling enough, was it really necessary to have independent verification for every gory detail before the State Department could scream bloody murder? Even in the most controlled and manipulated circumstances, journalists who were taken to showcase sites in Hararghe with Ethiopian government guides could not escape the feeling that something awful was taking place. One doesn't have to read in between the lines of Sheila Rule's June 22, 1986, story in the *New York Times* (buried on page 11) to get this message.

There is little free access to the new villages and Government escorts, or "minders," are everpresent. The authorities choose the areas that visitors are allowed to see. . . .

> An elderly woman, asked for her views [on villagization], replied at
> length, her words sounding as though they were steeped in anger. When
> she finished, the [government] interpreter's translation was: "I don't know.
> I am an ignorant woman."

I decided to go to Somalia (in October 1986) to hear the refugees'
stories firsthand. It took me a week to get a visa from the Somali
Embassy in Nairobi and then to get on to one of the twice-weekly
flights to Mogadishu. Once in Mogadishu, the UNHCR office assisted
me with the rest of my journey, which included another plane flight
to the steamy port of Berbera in the north; from here a UNHCR
Land Cruiser drove across the entire width of northern Somalia, first
to Hargeisa, where I spent the night, and then, finally, to Tug Wajale,
where I slept in a sleeping bag inside a drafty tent on the freezing,
windy plateau. The return journey to Nairobi took just as long. Several
members of the Nairobi-based foreign press corps also made the journey
at one time or another in 1986. But because Tug Wajale, on account
of its location, could not be done as a "quickie," practically no one
from outside Africa came in to do the story. (The only exception I
am aware of was Philip Revzin of the *Wall Street Journal,* whose
report was published May 26, 1986). Thus, only a handful of articles
appeared about the testimony of the Oromo refugees, and almost all
of those were buried on inside pages.

I interviewed fourteen refugees at Tug Wajale B and another nearby
camp in three days at the end of October 1986. Almost all of the
interviews were done in isolation; the refugee was moved by Land
Cruiser to an area out of earshot from his or her compatriots, where
I spent, on the average, about ninety minutes talking to the person.
The translator I used was not a member of the Oromo Liberation
Front or any other political organization I know of, and he had been
highly recommended to me by several foreign relief officials. I tried
hard to avoid asking leading questions, and I sought constantly to
ferret out inconsistencies in the stories I heard, so much so that one
of the women I interviewed accused me of being hostile. Despite all
of these precautions, I was impressed with the consistency of the
accounts. All, interviewed separately, told more or less the same story;
the gruesome tale of Fatma Abdullah Ahmed, described at the beginning
of this book, was repeated many times during my stay at Tug Wajale.
Nothing I heard was substantially different from what Jason Clay or
Lance Clark had reported, even though some of the people I interviewed
had arrived at different times and were in a different batch of refugees
from the ones Clay and Clark interviewed. I was warned that refugees

were prone to invent tales of political persecution, so that they will be considered by the U.N. as bona fide "refugees," instead of just as drought victims, who were liable to be sent back to their country of origin after agricultural conditions improve. But my interviews proved otherwise. These escapees, who had lived in isolated villages, spoke only Oromo, and probably encountered white foreigners for the first time in their lives at Tug Wajale, simply were not sophisticated enough to recognize bureaucratic distinctions that not every relief official could recognize. It simply strained logic to believe that what these refugees were saying was not essentially true. Yet not only did few want to believe them, as in the case of resettlement, few even wanted to listen.

*   *   *

Villagization went on unabated and thereby paved the road to the next famine by uprooting the way of life of the country's most successful group of farmers. In 1987, foreign donors were helping to make up cereal deficits in twenty-two of thirty-nine regions of Hararghe, which prior to villagization traditionally had registered surpluses. Thus, large amounts of Western aid were subsidizing communism, albeit indirectly, while charities such as Live Aid were serving to buttress a ruling elite that had destroyed the lives of more of its own people than had any other government in this decade, with the sole exception of Iran's, and that consistently had refused to negotiate a truce in a war that killed hundreds of thousands. Clay's frequent assertion that Western aid in the long run could kill more people than it saved in the short run was neither farfetched nor unfair.

Meanwhile, partly on account of the uproar raised by the U.S. government and MSF, resettlement ground to a halt in January 1986. But it got rolling again in March 1987. The first mention of this appeared near the bottom of a story on Ethiopia, written by correspondent James Brooke, in the *New York Times* (March 13, 1987). The article labeled resettlement "controversial." The *New York Times* correspondent also noted that the Ethiopian government planned to resettle only thirty thousand people a month, which was half the rate of the 1984–1985 period, thereby indicating perhaps that resettlement would be less "hurriedly executed" and therefore somewhat more humane. If it eventually turns out that resettlement—if not villagization— was truly reformed, then the Reagan administration and a few human rights and relief groups deserve the credit. The media's overall response to Ethiopian collectivization was remarkably passive.

FIVE

strategic fallout

Capitalism prefers to proceed by various forms of economic and cultural penetration, because they are easier, cheaper, and less reprehensible. But they are also less permanent. The Soviets, by contrast, "are keeping to the much safer and time-proven system of territorial annexation and direct appropriation."
—Paul Johnson, in *The New Republic*,
quoting from Jean-Francois Revel's book, *How Democracies Perish*

The only thing necessary for the triumph of evil is for good men to do nothing.
—Edmund Burke

It was a typical U.S. performance: bighearted, extravagant, and, ultimately, somewhat naive. Close to forty tons of durra were being anchored onto cables that dangled from three Boeing 107 helicopters, hovering several hundred feet in the air over the Sudanese town of Nyala, 600 miles west of Khartoum in the very center of the African continent. It was late August 1985, and although the drought had broken, the desert of western Sudan had been transformed into a vast arterial watershed by the heaviest rains in more than a decade. Tens of thousands of starving peasants were trapped by floods in the weeks prior to the harvest, and because many airstrips were washed out, the only way to get food in was by costly, fuel-consuming helicopter drops. On this particular day, August 29, the durra was being flown into the savanna region of Buram, one hundred miles south of Nyala, which had gone without grain deliveries for almost three months. On hand to take part was USAID administrator M. Peter McPherson.

The suspended durra moved through the air at a crawl. After an hour and a half of flying, small clusters of wattle huts began appearing amid the flood-soaked, green desert canvas below. Using a VHF radio, a Save the Children Fund field officer guided the pilots toward the drop zone, which we could see was filling up with dark, seminaked figures running in the same direction as our helicopter. McPherson and I already were on the ground when the second and third helicopters released their loads. Had the scene been staged in Hollywood it couldn't have been more stirring: mobs of barebreasted women, armed with spears, tore into the mountain of grain, fighting over the individual sacks while shrieking "*esh* Reagan" (Reagan's bread). There practically was a riot. Within a minute or two, every sack was gone. McPherson, an old Peace Corps hand, was ecstatic. I still can picture him sweating in his white shirt and exclaiming how happy President Reagan was going to be when he heard about this. McPherson said something to the effect that these people were going to remember what the United States did for them for years to come. Later, in Washington, another USAID official actually described the Buram peasants as new political allies of the United States.

Sending a squad of helicopters to deliver a relatively small amount of grain to a few thousand hungry Falata tribespeople, stuck in the middle of nowhere 115 miles from Sudan's border with the Central African Republic, was indeed a daring and generous act. All over western Sudan as well as in Ethiopia that summer, the United States was winning hearts and minds with similar feats. According to Brussels-based columnist Giles Merritt, writing in an October 1985 *International Herald Tribune,* 1985 was "the year when the United States went into Africa, one of the few remaining areas of the world it had managed to stay out of. In the past Washington has been glad to leave much of Africa under the influence of the former European colonial powers. But three million tons of U.S. food aid . . . changed that." Merritt feared that such a generous outpouring of emergency aid was bound to get the United States involved in "the quagmires of African politics. The sacks of emergency grain and the seed that the Sudanese have named 'Reagan' may prove as sure a hook as President Kennedy's handful of military advisors in Vietnam."

If only the columnist's fear had been borne out! For if the United States had become a factor in "the quagmires of African politics," then the helicopter drops might not have turned out to be one-time-only, quixotic acts that had no effect on the destiny of the region. Even though U.S. aid in Ethiopia and Sudan, on account of the famine, shot up fourfold in one year and cost almost $1 billion, in political terms the aid achieved nothing. At the same time that the United States was putting food into the hands of starving peasants in the wilderness, Libya was putting cash into the hands of Sudanese politicians in Khartoum. As it turned out, 1985 was the year when both Libyan and Soviet influence in the region, already substantial, increased dramatically, while U.S. influence actually decreased, despite the fact that the Libyans and the Soviets provided almost no relief aid.

There was nothing ironic or contradictory about this. Famine aid helps peasants, who in postcolonial Africa have no political power. In fact, it is largely because peasants have no power that famines occur in the first place. The urban elites who run African nations know that peasants do not start coups. Coups are started by disgruntled city dwellers. One way African politicians keep city dwellers satisfied is by providing them with cheap bread obtained from peasant farmers who are forced to sell their grain at artificially low prices. (In Ethiopia, as we have seen, this economic exploitation has overlapped with the imperial strategy of the ruling ethnic group.)

African rulers by and large—unlike the bureaucrats at USAID—are not interested in the kind of rural development (the building of roads, drainage systems, and grain storage facilities) that helps peasant farmers feed themselves and the rest of the country even during times of flooding and drought. For three decades, African rulers have been more interested in brutally maintaining power. The Soviets and their allies simply have created opportunities for themselves by becoming directly involved in either supporting or putting down the rebellions that arise in response to this brutality.

Despite what African rulers say, the lack of an imperial tradition in the United States has hindered, rather than helped, its ability to be a force for positive change in Africa. For instance, in recent years, France intervened in Chad more boldly than did the United States in Angola, yet France suffered far less opprobrium, even though the Marxist government in Luanda that the United States has been trying to topple is more ill-suited than Muammar Gaddafi's regime in Libya to better the lives of the people under its control. The drama played out between the United States and Libya in the mid-1980s in Sudan highlighted the tactical disadvantages of employing only humanitarian means to deal with problems that are in essence humanitarian, even if they have been narrowly defined as "strategic."

*   *   *

Sudan, like Ethiopia, although for different reasons, never has been a nation in the modern sense. While Addis Ababa functions not only as the capital of a country but of an empire, Khartoum, at the other extreme, functions as neither. Khartoum, a dust-ridden city of 2.5 million at the confluence of the Blue and White Niles that teems with hungry beggars and Mercedes Benzes is more a trading post than a political center, a base from which Arab merchants traditionally have exploited the seminomadic tribal configurations, some Arab and some not, in the vast stretches of desert under their tenuous control. Although Sudan is as large as the United States east of the Mississippi River, the sole bond joining a place such as Buram, in the westernmost province of Darfur, to Khartoum is an arbitrary line on a map drawn by a European colonialist at the end of the last century. The physical and psychological links between the famine-stricken west of Sudan and the capital of Khartoum are infinitesimally more slender than, say, the links between New York City and the Midwest corn belt. As a Western diplomat said, "The people of Akron, Ohio, care more about the people of Darfur than do the people in Khartoum." Or, as a certain politically active, Khartoum University professor said to me on the eve of the April 1985 coup that toppled President Jaafar Nimeiri, "We don't care if millions starve, so long as we get rid of Nimeiri."

Libya, in every sense, acted according to an understanding that Sudan was a country in name only, whose politicians could be bought for a price, which was best paid in military assistance to fight southern rebels rather than in food for drought victims. The United States, which saw Sudan in more charitable terms, was no match for such a strategy. As a result, by 1987, Darfur peasants were in an even more pathetic position vis-à-vis their own government than they were at the start of the famine in late 1984. From then on, the most humane thing the United States could do for Sudan was to work with the Egyptians to replace the democratically elected regime of incompetent, insensitive landowners with a more efficient group of politically moderate soldiers, who, because they would be more dependent on U.S. support, might be forced to help peasants in a manner that Western donors always have recommended.

Call this interpretation cynical, meanspirited, or right wing if you like, but first take a look at what actually has happened in Sudan: for at least twelve of the sixteen years that Jaafar Nimeiri held power, he was, by the continent's own dismal standards, one of its better rulers. His May 1969 military coup was popular at the time because it ushered in a period of relative stability after five changes of government and two general elections in five years. Democracy may have been wonderful in the abstract, but for a sprawling, largely illiterate country fractured by tribal divisions it meant stagnation, chaos, and death. Although Nimeiri came in as an Arab radical, in 1971, after surviving a Soviet-inspired attempt to topple him, he turned toward the West, and the following year, by granting local autonomy to the black south, he managed to end a seventeen-year civil war that had cost more lives than had all the Arab-Israeli wars put together. Throughout most of his rule, Nimeiri's dictatorial style was generally benign. Despite having ninety-eight Libyan-backed mercenaries executed in 1975 for trying to depose him, three years later he granted an amnesty to all his political enemies and allowed them to return home from exile abroad. From the vantage point of 1980, *Los Angeles Times* Africa correspondent David Lamb was able to write in his book *The Africans* that "while other presidents have solidified their power, Nimeiri has loosened his. . . . He . . . has given his people a precious gift, a sense of unity and purpose that grew from the ashes of a shattered nation." During the middle period of Nimeiri's rule, Sudan was closer than it ever had been to achieving the illusive goal of becoming a real nation.

By the early 1980s, however, ten years of absolute power had taken its toll on Nimeiri's personality. He was becoming increasingly cruel, corrupt, and paranoic. Had African or Arab politics evolved to the point where rulers could safely hand over power after a limited period in office, Nimeiri might have gone down in history as one of the continent's few political success stories. But it was not to be. Looking back, September 1983 is as good a date as any to mark Nimeiri's transition from a U.S. asset to a U.S. liability. That was when Islamic Sharia law, henceforth known in Sudan as "the September laws," took effect. Banks no longer could charge interest. Anyone convicted of stealing the equivalent of $50 could have his right hand amputated at the wrist. Even non-Moslem foreigners could be whipped in public for being found in possession of alcohol. (Not only liquor, but rubbing alcohol became difficult to obtain.) Nimeiri sought to apply the Sharia statutes in the non-Moslem south as well as in the north. This and his inexplicable decision to abrogate the 1972 autonomy agreement with the non-Moslem south helped ignite a renewal of the civil war in 1984. When I interviewed Nimeiri in December of that year, a few months before his overthrow, he was a hated and desperate figure. I remember him leaning back in his chair behind his desk eyeing the entrance to his office with the look of a punch-drunk prize fighter. Bedecked with medals and slurring his words, he seemed like the worst, comic book stereotype of a Third World dictator. When I asked him about Islamic law, he delivered what amounted to a temperance lecture about the hazards of alcohol consumption.

Nimeiri, at this point, was being kept in power by the thirty-thousand-man Al Amen al Goumi (the State Security Force), a financially pampered group of plainclothes thugs, whose budget was as large as the sixty-five-thousand-troop regular army. With 6,000 cars and 400 safe houses, the security force was described in Sudanese as "a holy state within a state." But in comparison with other Arab and African security forces, the Sudanese force was a group of choirboys. Disappearances, torture, and executions were rare. The newspaper articles and human rights reports about Islamic law far outnumbered the actual number of amputations, which was about fifty in the eighteen-month period between the implementation of the September laws and Nimeiri's overthrow. Although Sudan in the last days of Nimeiri's rule still was one of the freest societies in the Arab world, nearly every Sudanese I met in Khartoum in December 1984 heaped abuse on him. The fact that they were able to do so without risking prison proves my point. I cannot imagine anyone so openly criticizing a ruler in Libya, Syria, Iraq, or Saudi Arabia in the company of a foreign journalist. Yet to read what was being written about Nimeiri in the foreign press, one would have thought he was infinitely worse. One of Nimeiri's last acts before being toppled was to turn a blind eye to the transfer of seven thousand five hundred starving Ethiopian Jews to Israel via Sudan. After the coup, when Nimeiri's vice president and security chief, Omar el Tayeb, was dragged off to jail for his role in the operation, he had less blood on his hands than almost any other security chief in the entire Moslem world.

Nimeiri's overthrow was more like an abdication. On March 27, 1985, the day after taking the financially practical but politically dangerous step of removing the subsidies on basic commodities, Nimeiri—dressed in a white suit and Panama hat—flew off to Washington. As his presidential jet wheeled over Khartoum and adjacent Omdurman, "bread riots" already were in progress. Peaceful, well-organized demonstrations by underpaid urban professionals followed a few days later. The United States could do nothing to save him. Khartoum, in the throes of revolt, paid no attention to his audience with President Reagan. The $60 million in aid that finally was released to Nimeiri following the meeting did the embattled Sudanese leader absolutely no good because he never had admitted to his own people that the aid had been withheld in the first place. As for the awarding of an additional 225,000 metric tons of wheat and sorghum to Sudan while Nimeiri was in Washington, this also had no effect because a famine hundreds of miles away in the far west of the country was making no impact on strike organizers in the capital. During the three weeks I spent in Khartoum before, during, and after the coup, I rarely heard any discussion about the famine among Sudanese. At Khartoum University, the center of political activity, the students and professors hotly debated everything, except the famine. While millions were dying from hunger in Darfur, Khartoum's educated elite spent hours discussing the type of democracy a country that still was almost totally illiterate should have. It was a noble preoccupation, but a selfish and unrealistic one, too. While journalists like myself, in the 100-degree heat of the moment, were emphasizing the noble side of the whole drama, diplomats and aid experts already were worrying about it being too noble.

Painted in the broad brush strokes of newspaper copy, the unfolding events in Khartoum should have heartened U.S. policymakers. The

1985 coup was about as bloodless and orderly a transition of power as Africa ever has seen. No radical elements, either Islamic or secular leftist, played a significant role. Nimeiri never returned and instead went into exile in Egypt. Power was transferred for twelve months to a military council headed by General Abdul Rahman Swareddahab, who deliberately maintained a low profile and proved sincere in his pledge to hold parliamentary elections the following year. After twelve days of orderly voting in April 1986, in the freest elections ever conducted in the Arab world, the Umma (Nation) party leader, Sadiq al Mahdi, was chosen prime minister. Sudan couldn't have done better, at least so it seemed. A former prime minister in the 1960s who was pardoned by Nimeiri after leading the 1975 Libyan-backed coup attempt, Sadiq—as he is known in Sudan—had more political savvy than did any other Sudanese politician and by 1986 had clearly established a reputation as a political moderate and Islamic modernist. During his years in exile in London, Oxford-educated Sadiq had spoken out on such matters as the nature of Islam (about which he contributed an essay for a *Festschrift* in honor of the late Jordanian prime minister, Abd al-Hamid Sharaf), and he was on record as favoring the liberalization of the harsh Sharia code promulgated by Nimeiri. Sadiq also had personal magnetism based on inherited historical legitimacy. He was the great-grandson of the fabled Mahdi, whose Ansar warriors ejected the British from Sudan in 1885, killing General Charles George Gordon in the process. From a distance of a few thousand miles, Sadiq certainly must have appeared as the very culmination of a Western Arabist's, or Africanist's, dream come true. The manner of Sadiq's ascension, and the résumé he brought along with him, provided an answer to all the mudslinging about the Arabs' and Africans' penchant for violence and tyranny and their inability to create modern political systems.

During this momentous period in its history, Sudan in fact became one of the few countries in the Third World to be praised by Amnesty International for a dramatic improvement in the human rights situation because of the release of political detainees and the banning of amputations and other extreme aspects of Sharia law after Nimeiri's departure. But while the new, liberal procedures may have directly benefited a few thousand people, if that many, millions of others suffered. What from a comfortable distance was a textbook case of political modernization was in point of fact causing chaos in the relief effort, penetration by hostile neighbors, and the total abdication of responsibility regarding economic and agricultural reform.

Nimeiri's ouster did not satisfy the strike leaders. A few hours after the coup was announced, a political science professor from the black

Christian south, Kunijwok Gwado Ayoker, told me, "We have knocked two teeth out of the monster's mouth; now we have to knock out the other thirty." The strikers eventually forced the ruling military council to disband the State Security Force. This made a lot of people feel good, including myself, who along with three British journalists had been detained for several hours and held at gunpoint by Nimeiri's strong-arm men prior to the coup for the crime of watching an anti-Nimeiri demonstration. At the time, it didn't occur to me that I actually was lucky. Had I been in any one of several other countries in the region, the circumstances of my detention almost certainly would have been far worse. But nobody, except a few diplomats, was doing any serious thinking during those first, heady days of democracy.

Nobody realized then that among the first people to take advantage of the freer political climate in Khartoum would be the Libyans. The State Security Force, which had a strong presence at Khartoum airport in addition to having the task of monitoring foreigners inside the country, was the only organized line of defense against Gaddafi's advance men. After the security force was disbanded, the Libyans poured in by the hundreds and set up "revolutionary committees" that operated slush funds for aspiring Sudanese politicians. In their "surly, unctuous" manner, as a Western ambassador described it, the Libyans had a good streetwise understanding of local politics; they knew that behind the breezy statements about democracy and nonalignment lay many a broke politician and political party sorely in need of ready cash for an election to be held within twelve months. One man whom the Libyans were rumored to have quickly placed in their pocket was the new defense minister, Brigadier Osman Abdullah Mohammed, who spent more than a week in Tripoli after the coup and returned home with a "protocol" providing for Libyan help with "logistics, transport, equipment, training programs" and "aspects of navy and air defense." Brigadier Mohammed told Sudanese journalists that Libya also would be helping to arrange peace talks between the Khartoum government and the rebel SPLA.

Following the coup, everyone assumed that the SPLA would call a truce because the overthrow of Nimeiri was what its leader, John Garang, had been demanding. But Garang, a U.S.-educated Dinka tribesman, obviously was not going to be satisfied with one group of northern Arabs replacing another in the presidential palace in Khartoum. Garang, whose African southerners for years had been supported by Gaddafi against the pro-U.S. Nimeiri, called the new regime "the hyena with new clothes" and went on fighting. The civil war, rather than dying down, dramatically intensified. The military council responded by marching a four-thousand-troop unit of the Sudanese regular army northward from Juba, the capital of Equatoria Province, in order to capture the SPLA stronghold of Bor. The operation was a "total, utter failure," according to one Western diplomat. Garang, whose total forces numbered less than twenty thousand, attacked the government column, and those soldiers who weren't killed refused to march any further. Sudan Airways stopped flying for a time to Juba, and the only way in and out of the city was by chartered plane. Next came an SPLA attack on Renk, barely two hundred fifty miles south of Khartoum on the White Nile, the closest the SPLA had ever come to the capital. Garang then appeared capable of cutting off Khartoum's power supply by blowing up transmission lines connecting the city with the Roseires Dam to the southeast. The government could do nothing; it had virtually no air force and was so short of fuel that it had to requisition diesel fuel from famine relief organizations to run military patrols.

Financed by Gaddafi and headquartered at Itang, just inside the Ethiopian border, the SPLA was a creature of two Soviet allies. It was to them that Sudan's new leaders were forced to make obeisance—not to the United States, which only was helping to feed starving peasants, a matter farther down on the list of Sudanese government priorities. Neither Libya nor Ethiopia was about to let up the pressure just because Sudan, in the words of some Western commentators, was on the road to becoming a "fledgling democracy." Quite the contrary: for Gaddafi and Mengistu, a weak new government in Khartoum, which by its own definition was only "transitional," represented an easy target rather than a credible negotiating partner. It was about this time that the Sudanese defense minister went to Tripoli to sign the "protocol." Meanwhile, the United States, which was occupied with helicopter drops and other acts of mercy in the far west of the country, was merely a bystander to this whole process.

The Libyans also were active in the west; they took bold, strategic advantage of the famine while U.S. citizens, journalists in particular, were looking the other way. On the Sabbath Friday, August 23, 1985, six days before the Buram helicopter drop, a Libyan relief convoy of forty-three trucks and trailers, escorted by Libyan soldiers, rolled into the Darfur capital of El Fasher with an undisclosed number of weapons hidden beneath sacks of grain and dried milk powder. Around the same time, tribal chiefs from other parts of Darfur and adjacent Kordofan were being invited to Tripoli as guests of Colonel Gaddafi. There was nothing inspired about Gaddafi's designs on western Sudan, a forward base for his ill-fated adventure in Chad and a place from which to outflank Egypt. It is a tract of desert whose seminomadic Arab and African inhabitants are more likely to know the names of their tribal heads than that of the current ruler in Khartoum. "No umbilical cord links us with the central government," explained the commissioner of northern Darfur, Abdul Hafiz, who was communicating with Khartoum by radio from El Geneina, a beau geste town about fifteen miles from the Chad border. If not for relief flights operated by international agencies, it would have taken Hafiz nearly a month to travel by land to Khartoum.

Gaddafi couldn't have picked a more logical target. Darfur was the last unconquered part of Sudan and had resisted all foreign invaders, including the French based in present-day Chad, until May 1916, when an ·Anglo-Egyptian force of more than two thousand troops backed by airplanes finally defeated the Fur tribespeople of Sultan Ali Dinar. Darfur thus became the westernmost province of British-controlled Sudan, rather than the easternmost province of Chad. Afterward, the British gave the local tribal chief complete control of internal affairs. "It was a government within a government," recalled the present sultan, Abdul Rahman, who occupies a dilapidated villa in El Geneina overlooking a cubist landscape of whitewashed walls and desert. Even today, the people of Darfur harbor little loyalty toward Khartoum. Economically, the flow of people and goods is more in the direction of Libya than of Sudan's Nile River heartland. The goods on sale under the wattle stalls in El Geneina's market come by way of Libyan and West African ports, rather than via Port Sudan. Many a woman in El Geneina has a husband working in Libya, where oil wealth makes the salaries much higher. Of course, the United States, because of famine aid, also was making friends in the region. But the U.S. presence was transitory, and in any case, the power in Darfur, as everywhere else in Africa, lay in the bigger towns, such as El Geneina, El Fasher, and Nyala, where nobody was starving except Chadian refugees, about whom none of the locals really cared.

The void in the western desert that the Libyans planned to fill had been deepened by the drought and famine of the past several years, which had forced the migration of Kababish tribespeople out of the area toward the Nile in the east and the savanna lands in the south in search of food and water. Many of these fabled desert warriors, who had a historic tradition of fighting rival Libyan tribes, would not return to their homes. So if Gaddafi decided to invade, he would have found this quadrant of Sudan emptier than ever.

The Libyan convoy that stormed into El Fasher in August 1985 stayed for about a year. It was forced out not by any U.S. pressure, which would have proved useless, but by intimidating French air sorties carried out from bases in Chad. However, by the time the Libyans had left El Fasher, they had installed themselves elsewhere in western Sudan as part of a front against French-backed Chadian government troops. The most unsettling aspect of the whole affair was the speed with which the convoy was able to get to El Fasher: it took only twelve days to cover the fourteen-hundred-mile distance from the Mediterranean port of Benghazi. In the same period, USAID was taking two weeks to bring food to El Fasher from Khartoum, only six hundred miles away. The Libyans had the advantage of driving through areas unaffected by flooding. However, no roads were available for much of the journey from Benghazi.

Libya apparently was having an easier time of it in Darfur than was the United States, whose helicopter drops were among the few bright moments in a season filled with frustration. Flood conditions were so bad in places that a truck convoy with emergency grain supplies took the better part of a month just to travel from El Fasher to El Geneina, a distance of less than two hundred miles! Other convoys were being attacked by Beduin bandits, and relief organizations funded by USAID even were having trouble finding local drivers willing to attempt the journey out west. Expanding the scope of the helicopter operation was impractical because of the tremendous fuel costs involved. As the Libyans proved, only an army could move supplies on land great distances in such a place, and the Sudanese army, strained to the limit battling the SPLA, was practically useless—even more so after the coup.

The root cause of these logistical difficulties was USAID's naive reliance on Sudan Railways. Jonathan C. Randal, the senior foreign correspondent of the *Washington Post,* in a memorable dispatch from Khartoum described what happened.

That notoriously inefficient, government-owned corporation, long impervious to outside pressure, was to have transported 1,300 tons of sorghum daily along the final 590-mile route from the White Nile city of Kosti west to Nyala in Darfur. After successful initial deliveries in December and January, Sudan Railways abruptly ceased honoring its contract despite the doubling of normal freight rates for the grain shipments. . . .

U.S. Agency for International Development officials continued to hope that Sudan Railways would resume functioning normally and delayed turning to road transport as a major alternative.

In recent weeks starving villagers have been reduced to breaking open anthills in search of grain, tearing leaves off trees and eating mochet, the green berry of a poisonous bush that must be soaked for three days and then boiled before it is edible. . . .

"We didn't think it was possible for Sudan Railways to fail entirely," an AID official said. "We thought they could manage at 30 percent efficiency."

U.S. officials said they remained at a loss to pinpoint reasons for the railway's refusal to deliver grain, despite repeated, well-publicized entreaties by Gen. Abdul Rahman Swareddahab, leader of the transitional military council. . . . But indifferent and incompetent management, possible union opposition to the weak, military government . . . widespread corruption and a higher priority for traffic destined for urban centers than for remote villages are often cited.

"In the old days we would have sent in the Marines to run the railroads," a U.S. official said, "but we cannot do that anymore."

In a word, countless peasants lost their lives because USAID officials were insufficiently cynical about the local reality. The railway union members who held up emergency food deliveries in order to put pressure on the government were among those in the streets of Khartoum demanding a return to democracy. But what value can democracy possibly have in a culture where civic responsibility does not extend beyond the bounds of tribe and kinship? The lethal impotence of the regime that replaced Nimeiri was clear for all to see on May 26, 1985, when General Swareddahab traveled to Nyala to witness the arrival of grain supplies on Sudan Railways. When the train pulled into the station, the freight that it unloaded was not grain, as was expected, but sugar for use in making the pastries and candies eaten by city dwellers at the end of the Moslem feast of Ramadan. Had the much-hated Nimeiri still been in power, the United States at least would have been in a position to bully the government and the railway into partially living up to their commitments. In Kordofan, several weeks before Nimeiri's overthrow, Vice President George Bush was able to make a triumphant visit to the provincial capital of El Obeid because massive amounts of U.S. grain had arrived just in time to avert a catastrophic famine. The difference between Kordofan in the winter of 1984–1985 and Darfur the following spring and summer was that in the latter instance, U.S. officials in Sudan were under greater constraints because of a new, widely acclaimed regime that insisted on more nonalignment in foreign affairs. Tens of thousands of peasants died proving this point.

In the fall, a bumper crop saved many lives, but not nearly as many as it should have because much of the grain was hoarded by local merchants in order to boost prices, thus denying food to the very people who desperately needed it. In Khartoum, meanwhile, the political situation was becoming increasingly chaotic, with communists, Baathists, Islamic fundamentalists, and Libyan-backed elements holding demonstrations and positioning themselves for the coming elections in April 1986. The *Washington Post*'s David Ottaway reported that the worsening security atmosphere forced the U.S. Embassy to take "extraordinary" precautions to protect its staff. The transitional military government informed the United States that it was unable to keep track of all the Libyans and their Sudanese allies filtering in and out of the country. In one instance, a U.S. official told Ottaway, "a plane arrived from Libya with 100 people on it, only 80 of whom had passports. The others slipped through the relaxed security at the airport." At this point, dozens of senior Sudanese officials were going back and forth to Tripoli, where they were being entertained in luxury hotels and guesthouses. Thousands of other Sudanese, including former members of Nimeiri's State Security Force, were being given salaried jobs in Libya. Libyan oil was pouring into the country to prop up the economy, which was collapsing because the transitional regime—paralyzed by strikes and demonstrations in the weeks prior to the elections—took no effective countermeasures. U.S. personnel were reduced to throwing their hands up in the air and barricading themselves inside the embassy compound while taking different routes to work each day. Said one diplomat in an exasperated tone, "The only thing worse than an African government that says it is going to hold elections and doesn't is one that says it is going to hold elections and actually does!"

The Libyans were less fatalistic. They acted. In March, as election fever mounted, the Libyans pulled off a brillilant campaign stunt. The SPLA had seized the important outpost of Rumbeck in the Bahr el Ghazal region of southern Sudan and then threatened to launch an offensive against the government. Having assisted the SPLA for many years, the Libyans now turned against their former allies and attacked the rebel-held town with two Tupolev-22 bombers. In the words of a senior U.S. State Department official, it was the old "good cop–bad cop" routine. No amount of helicopter drops could have impressed the politicians in Khartoum as much as did this air raid. In the midst of the April elections, the Libyans shot a U.S. Embassy communications clerk, which along with anti-U.S. demonstrations in Khartoum engendered by President Reagan's bombing of Libya, forced the evacuation of 250 U.S. citizens, many of whom were USAID personnel who had helped with the helicopter drops and other aspects of the relief effort and who still were vital to it. The gift of "Reagan's bread" was of little relevance to those urbanites shouting anti-U.S. slogans in the capital because these Sudanese never needed the bread in the first place.

For the United States, Sadiq al Mahdi's election as prime minister was the only positive development in the midst of all this humbling chaos. But anyone who had ever spoken with Sadiq and his followers at length could have foreseen that this was a misplaced hope. My introduction to the political values of Sadiq al Mahdi came on a September night in Khartoum, in the late summer of 1985, at the Syrian Club, where I and Jonathan Steele, a senior foreign correspondent for *The Guardian,* had been invited for dinner in order to meet several Umma party notables, in preparation for our interview with Sadiq. Over hoummous, tehina, delicious goat's cheese, and other delights of Middle Eastern cuisine we talked for several hours around a simple foldout table in a garden under the stars. I do recall spending almost all of the time discussing three subjects: the Umma party's strategy in the elections the coming spring, the civil war in the south, and Islamic law. Regarding the civil war, I remember thinking that our hosts were making no attempt to emphathize with the feelings of non-Moslem Africans in the south of the country or to even accept the fact that only half of Sudan was Arab. The subject of the famine, I believe, never was raised by our hosts. When Steele or I brought it to their attention, a few words were uttered, and that was that.

Steele, for some reason, could not be present at the interview with Sadiq. So I met with Sadiq alone, in the dim salon of his villa on the other side of the Nile in Omdurman. We spoke for about an hour. His sharp gaze, white turban, graceful, gesticulating hands, and excellent English made quite a regal impression. Sadiq certainly seemed to have an aura about him, and he sometimes spoke with poetic elegance: "democracy in Sudan is a lone bird surrounded by vultures interested in its flesh." On the question of Islamic law, he was intelligent and subtle. He said that although drinking alcohol was immoral according to Sharia precepts, it need not be illegal for those who do not agree that it is immoral.

On the famine and the future of the peasants Sadiq showed little interest, however. His answer to my queries about these issues came in a single sentence: "it is no longer a serious problem because international aid has been forthcoming." He considered famine a problem the wealthy West was obligated to solve, thereby leaving him free to deal with other matters, such as Sharia law and the war with the SPLA. As to the African southerners, he appeared to have no better understanding of what really bothered them than did his Umma party colleagues with whom I had met several nights before. I had the distinct feeling, which many other foreign observers also shared, that in all the years of his intellectually active London exile, Sadiq had not formed a specific blueprint of what he wanted to do once he returned to power. In short, he was very much the quintessential Arab politician— a man who used flowery speech to maneuver around difficult and complex issues without confronting them head-on.

Like every Arab ruler, Sadiq never seemed to doubt the primacy
of his own ethnic and religious group over others in the nation. This
was no particular flaw for a politician in Libya, Syria, Jordan, or other
Middle Eastern countries. But fate had cast Sudan as a polity that
was ethnically and religiously split to a degree greater than any of
these other places. Sudan lay across the fault line separating the Arab
and African worlds, but its Arab politicians, of which Sadiq was typical,
refused to countenance this fact. Sadiq also had one more unfortunate
trait that was typical of his part of the world: he was an urbanized
landowner with a demonstrated lack of interest in the problems of the
peasants. All the tragic weaknesses of Sudanese society were summed
up in this most respected of Sudanese politicians.

Once Sadiq assumed power, absolutely nothing changed. It was as
if General Swareddahab—an honest, well-meaning, but completely in-
effectual man—never had departed. Sadiq simply made no impact.
Order broke down further. Strikes remained common. Ministerial di-
rectives counted for little, and bureaucrats lower down were not listening
to those above. Advice from the International Monetary Fund was
ignored. Subsidies and commodity price-fixing, which virtually stole
income from peasant farmers, continued. Import-export controls increased, and the currency remained overvalued. In their speeches, Sadiq
and the other members of the cabinet hinted at all the right measures,
but deeds never followed. Said a Western aid expert, "We don't see
anything resembling a rational economic plan that could serve as a
reference point for donors." The prime minister's policy seemed to
consist of making trips abroad in order to hold out the begging bowl.
He tried Moscow and Tripoli first, looking for aid and help against
his nemesis, Garang and the SPLA. In Moscow Sadiq got little, except
a promise for deliveries of gas containers and soybeans, which some
people in Khartoum said, only half-jokingly, were radioactive. The
Soviets, who had a larger embassy staff in the Sudanese capital than
the British had—but did no relief work—were playing it smart. Why
should they supply arms and substantial assistance to a sinking ship,
whose descent was being deliberately quickened by its Libyan and
Ethiopian allies?

The Ethiopian air force had been dropping weapons and other
supplies behind SPLA lines inside Sudan, which was helping to tip
the balance in the civil war more and more in favor of Garang. In
mid-September 1986, Colonel Gaddafi made his second visit to Khartoum since the overthrow of Nimeiri. Several hundred Libyan security
personnel, each armed with both a pistol and an assault rifle, preceded
him unannounced and without bothering to get airport landing clear-
ance. Throughout the visit, Libyan planes constantly were landing and

taking off. Although Gaddafi's retinue was disarmed of their assault rifles, no one knows if other arms entered the country.

But Sadiq's slippery and insubstantial political style seemed to be perfectly suited to handling the Libyan threat. Sadiq dealt with Gaddafi the same way he did with all the Western diplomats, financial experts, and relief officials who came into his midst: he whispered sweet things in Gaddafi's ears and did nothing. A less experienced and less sophisticated politician might not have been able to generously accept Libyan aid while keeping Gaddafi at bay the way Sadiq did. In this regard, if in no other, the great-grandson of the Mahdi served his country well.

After Sadiq's visit to Washington in October 1986, about fifty of the U.S. personnel who had been evacuated the previous April were allowed by the U.S. State Department to return to Sudan with their adult dependents, which meant children had to be left behind. It was an impossible situation and reflected the ambivalence of the Washington bureaucracy to the atmosphere in Khartoum. Although the Libyan presence seemed to be diminishing slightly, Sadiq had not lived up to his promise to eject several known Libyan terrorists who were in the Sudanese capital. Because Sadiq also had not lived up to his pledge to present Western donors with an economic reform and development package, Washington took another half-measure: it released $71 million of money previously appropriated to Sudan in order to pay for food imports, but refused to appropriate any more funds.

As 1986 drew to a close, it was God who came to Sadiq's rescue in the form of the second bumper harvest in two years. Starving Sudan suddenly was drowning in grain, although as usual a lot of it was in the hands of rapacious merchants instead of hungry peasants. Nevertheless, in the opinion of most Western observers, the extra food stocks gave Sadiq another year in which to do nothing before the hangman appeared at the door.

In April 1987, on the second anniversary of the coup that toppled Nimeiri, the peasants of Sudan, the largest country in Africa, had little hope. Western-style parliamentary democracy had produced only another government of corrupt landowners. This government was worse than Nimeiri's, because at least Nimeiri, who did nothing for his people in his final years in office, did not hinder the United States and other Western nations from doing something. Under Swareddahab's and Sadiq's leadership, Western relief workers were encountering one bureaucratic and security hurdle after another in their attempts to get internal travel permits, to import supplies into the country, and to do other tasks vital to helping people whom the Sudanese government ignored.

On the other hand, the storm cloud raised by Gaddafi could very well vanish with the eternally shifting desert winds. In the first weeks of spring 1987, French-assisted Chadian government forces virtually ejected Gaddafi from the north of their country, and inside Libya itself, the mercurial colonel was facing what appeared to be an inexorable, albeit gradual, buildup of internal opposition. However, even if we should all wake up one morning to hear that Gaddafi has been overthrown, his bold moves to take advantage of a vacuum of power in Sudan in the mid-1980s should cure those in the West of the delusion that humanitarian means are sufficient to achieve humanitarian ends in Africa.

USAID officials have pointed out to me that the equation I make is an unfair one. Humanitarian assistance, they say, by its very definition is designed to have a humanitarian impact, not a political one. The real-life facts on the ground prove, however, that such logic is a cop-out because, first, it lets Third World leaders morally off the hook. If leaders like those in Khartoum and Addis Ababa placed as much priority on the well-being of their peasants as the United States does, there would be no question about granting a political payoff commensurate with the amount of U.S. famine aid.

Second, I believe the U.S. experience in Sudan, Ethiopia, and elsewhere forces the nation to question the very meaning of the term "humanitarian." Is it humanitarian to allow people like the Libyans or the Soviets to establish a foothold in a given country when experience demonstrates that the individual inhabitants, especially peasants, in their zone of influence tend to have far fewer freedoms than do those in the U.S. zone of influence (alarming exceptions such as Chile in the 1970s notwithstanding)? Experience likewise demonstrates—protestations of humanitarianism to the contrary—that relief aid to a politically powerless sector of a Third World population cannot compete in terms of influence with military and other kinds of assistance to the politically powerful. The argument that the West has an advantage in the Third World because it presents a more viable model for economic development is nonsense because the Eastern bloc provides a more viable model for political control, which is what ruling elites are interested in.

At the same time, calling certain kinds of humanitarian assistance "strategic" gives rise to another confusion. "Strategic" connotes a sinister intent because the word alludes to military, even nuclear, conflict. "Strategic" also implies a certain willingness to accept in the abstract that places like Ethiopia or Sudan, to say nothing of places like Iran, will be required for the defense of the Western world, an abstraction that many in the United States do not accept. It needs to be emphasized that what is "strategic" is also "humanitarian" and is often the most effective form of long-range humanitarian assistance. Conservatives trying to sell the Reagan Doctrine are a good example of this confusion in labeling. They sometimes have mistakenly marketed their product as a "strategic" response to Soviet expansionism. Although each individual case has to be considered on its merits, as a general rule, the Reagan Doctrine also can be called a "moral" response, which would be more attractive to the U.S. public at large. Otherwise, by declining to take direct action against aggression by the Soviets, the Libyans, and others, the United States in effect is consigning helpless people around the world to an awful fate.

*   *   *

No group of people was more ignorant of these hard facts of life than was the foreign policy team of President Jimmy Carter in 1977 and 1978. No one mentioned during the famine emergency that the wholesale loss of human life—not to mention the disregard of human rights—had important antecedents in the Carter human rights policy, in which pious, abstract moral precepts became a barrier to the kind of action necessary to save a population from being swallowed whole by the shadow of totalitarianism. Much of what has transpired in the past decade in the Horn of Africa can be traced to that folly of good intentions, and conservative pundits miss their chance to promulgate a rightist foreign policy when they attack the Carter administration's record in Iran and Afghanistan rather than in the Horn of Africa.

The Horn of Africa is a powerful allegory of U.S. foreign policy weakness precisely because what occurred there in the late 1970s was so entirely typical of how the United States, the Soviet Union, and Third World elites behave and interact. The United States was reactive and internally divided; policymakers argued about what forceful measures to take without actually taking any and expected the USSR to act as the United States would in the same position. The Soviets did not oblige. As is their wont, they employed proxy soldiers—in this instance, Cubans and South Yemenis—as tools in a crude, brazen, and not-altogether-well-thought-out policy. Despite what U.S. conservatives like to believe, there was no detailed Soviet game plan. The Soviets improvised as they went along. But because U.S. policy was based on and constricted by moral precepts that Soviet and African rulers only preached, the Soviets were able to operate in a vacuum of U.S. inaction that made it seem as if their moves were part of a bold, brilliantly conceived strategy. The behavior of the emergent-Ethiopian strongman, Mengistu Haile Mariam, also was not unique. He was neither a religious fundamentalist nor at the time a Marxist ideologue. He was simply the number one thug on the lookout for an alliance that would best serve to consolidate his control. He found it.

The Horn also was a pure, essentially in vitro case study of liberal foreign policy notions at work in the real world. It was the first turf battle between the United States and the Soviet Union after Jimmy Carter was inaugurated as president, and as a consequence, Carter's team was fresh and relatively undistracted by other crises. By the time that the shah's regime in Iran began to unravel in mid-1978, and certainly by the time of the Soviet invasion of Afghanistan in 1979, Jimmy Carter, hardened by his experience in the White House, was less of a liberal than he was when Ethiopia and Somalia grabbed his attention in early 1977. In Iran, whatever else his faults, Carter eventually tried force to free U.S. hostages, something for which the conservative editorial writers of the *Wall Street Journal* praised him. In Afghanistan, he took the unpopular, highly symbolic decision of boycotting the 1980 Moscow Olympics, despite little support from much of the Western world. Ideologically, the president's behavior in these later crises was harder to categorize. But in the Horn, the liberals and Africanists had their chance. In comparing what they predicted in the late 1970s with what had transpired by the late 1980s, they have nothing to hide behind.

In his memoir *Hard Choices,* Carter's secretary of state, Cyrus Vance, recalled that "we in the State Department saw the Horn as a textbook case of Soviet exploitation of a local conflict. In the long run, however, we believed the Ethiopians would oust the Soviets from their country as had happened in Egypt and Sudan." Carter's U.N. ambassador, Andrew Young, agreed with Vance, arguing that the Soviet presence in Ethiopia was not only temporary, but self-defeating because the Soviets would get bogged down in internal African problems. Young, who because of his passionate public interest became extremely influential regarding U.S. relations with African states, advised Carter not to get involved as the Soviets had. After all, Young was quoted as saying, U.S. policy toward Africa was now "more wholesome and healthy than it has been in a long time." Basically, Young and Vance wanted Africans to decide matters for themselves. If the Soviets were foolish enough to continue their military adventure, area experts in the U.S. State Department predicted that the Horn might become the USSR's Vietnam. According to a Baltimore *Sun* editorial (November 15, 1977), the United States "may yet come out with enhanced influence for non-involvement" in the region. One of the only dissenting voices was that of Carter's national security adviser, Zbigniew Brzezinski, who advised force as the only effective measure to counter the Soviet gambit. Brzezinski brought up various military-related options and recommended linkage between events in the Horn and progress on nuclear arms talks. Regarding the Soviets, Brzezinski wanted to be tough, while Young and Vance wanted to be reasonable. Reasonableness won out at every turn. Brzezinski's tragedy, as the Ethiopia-Somalia crisis was the first to reveal, was that of being a hawk in an administration dominated by doves.

Of course, "in the long run," as Vance put it, the Soviets will be forced to leave Ethiopia. As everybody knows, nothing is forever. But to judge Vance and Young by their own standard of concern for Africa and its peoples, even if the Soviets were ejected tomorrow, it would be too late and therefore irrelevant. One million Ethiopians already have died as a result of famine and of forced collectivization, which would not have occurred had the Soviet Union not implanted itself in Ethiopia to the degree that the Carter State Department was willing to allow.

Vance's belief that the Soviets would be ousted from Ethiopia the way they were from Egypt and Sudan was at no point a serious possibility simply because the Soviets weren't involved in Egypt and Sudan to the extent that they were in Ethiopia. In Egypt, from the late 1950s through the early 1970s, the Soviets gave substantial military and economic aid to a sympathetic regime, but they never sought to create a communist satellite as they did in Ethiopia. Moscow's involvement with Sudan in the first years of Nimeiri's rule was less dramatic than in the case of Egypt. But not only was Vance guilty of a false comparison, but of a particularly U.S., and even more particularly liberal, tendency of ascribing the lessons learned from one's own experience to that of another nation. The futility of seeking permanent domination over an African country was what the United States learned from the USSR's misadventures in Egypt and Sudan, not what the Soviets learned. What they learned was quite the opposite. As the French political philosopher Jean-Francois Revel explained in *How Democracies Perish,* "The expulsion of Soviet advisers from Egypt by Gamal Abdel Nasser's successors was a lesson to Moscow that no country can be held permanently unless it is given a Communist regime wholly shaped in the standard satellite mold. . . . In the Soviet view, the case simply proved that half measures can never guarantee anything."

The fact that Moscow was attempting to create a presence in Ethiopia so soon after the failures in Egypt and Sudan should have been a warning signal to Vance, and to Young, too, that this time the Soviets could be expected to be even more heavyhanded in their involvement. Rather than seek to create another Egypt, they would seek to create another Mongolia or Vietnam (in the sense of a Soviet satellite)—

which they did. But neither Young nor Vance ever appeared to be thinking along those lines.

A still-existent nineteenth century empire, Soviet Russia, was grafting itself onto another still-existent nineteenth century empire, Amhara-dominated Ethiopia, and old world notions of power were all that came into play. Yet the West was led by idealistic theoreticians who eschewed not only the use of force and punitive measures, but even the threat of using them. Young and Vance wanted an African solution for an African problem, which given the unpleasant realities of Africa meant a Soviet solution because the only Africans who mattered in Ethiopia were the kind who were more impressed by the Soviet concept of power and control than by the U.S. one.

*   *   *

The groundwork for appeasement already had been laid by the time Jimmy Carter took office on January 20, 1977. Unfortunately for the mass of Ethiopian peasants, the political cataclysms that were shaking their country had caught the United States in a mood of distraction and self-defeat unequaled since the country formally became a super-power at the close of World War II. The first phase of the Ethiopian revolution corresponded with the last phase of Watergate. Haile Selassie was forced out of the emperor's palace only a month after Richard Nixon was forced out of the White House. The final months of the emperor's life and the consolidation of the Dergue's power in Addis Ababa and other cities occurred concomitantly with the fall of South Vietnam in early 1975. The following year, Tom J. Farer wrote in *War Clouds on the Horn of Africa* that "in the wake of Vietnam, the air is filled with tests of will looking for somewhere to settle. The Horn is not an especially hospitable setting for human habitation. But as a venue for confrontation by proxy, it now shows real promise." There was a fear among the public that the United States might get entangled in another fruitless confrontation in the Third World. Hesitancy, coupled with a distinct lack of confidence, became the order of the day. Rather than fine tune its manner of involvement in distant corners of the globe, the United States chose not to get involved at all. For Americans, this was certainly convenient. For Ethiopians and others, it was not.

As Paul B. Henze, a Carter-era National Security Council staffer, wrote in *The National Interest* (Winter 1985-86), "The biggest gain for the Russians was the withdrawal syndrome that set in among Americans. Technological advances had made U.S. communications facilities at Asmara redundant by 1971, and a decision was taken to phase down operations. Ethiopia was not officially informed. One school of thought in the State Department held that Ethiopia would no longer be of importance to the U.S. once the Eritrean sites were closed." So when Mengistu and the Dergue came to power, the United States, under President Gerald Ford, began to distance itself from internal Ethiopian politics. William G. Hyland, a deputy assistant to President Ford for national security affairs, reported that

> this American reluctance to be too closely associated with the new PMAC [Provisional Military Advisory Council—the Dergue] was founded in some part on the belief that it would not last; it was tearing itself apart, executing and purging its own followers, and periodically threatening to execute the royal family. In fact, much American political capital was expended in convincing the PMAC to save Haile Selassie and his family. But at the same time the United States showed little sympathy for the new regime's fear of a Somali invasion, despite the continuing and growing Soviet military role in Somalia.

The United States already was beginning to forget the laws of nature. A regime that was executing and purging its own followers and threatening to execute the royal family was not a regime that was about to fall; rather, it most surely was going to survive against all comers, even if it had to execute half the population to do so. Didn't the Bolsheviks do the same during their first years in power in the USSR? Wasn't it apparent that given the kill-or-be-killed atmosphere in Addis Ababa, and the professed ideology of the combatants, that the individuals who were going to emerge on top at the end of all the bloodletting were going to make perfect bedfellows for the Soviets? The United States was dealing with professional murderers, and the only leverage it had over them—their well-grounded fear of an invasion from historically hostile Somalia—was not utilized.

The outgoing secretary of state, Henry Kissinger, tried to keep an iron in the fire by continuing military assistance to Ethiopia, even after the overthrow of Haile Selassie. Liberals, quite legitimately, questioned this approach. The Dergue had renewed the military conflict in Eritrea and from the very beginning had been treating its people with extreme barbarity. But Kissinger, at least, seemed to realize that if the United States completely forfeited its presence in Ethiopia, rather than hold its nose for the time being at the awful violations of human rights, the eventual result would be not only a strategic gain for the Soviets, but a more drawn out suffering for the people of the region.

Exit Ford and Kissinger. Enter Carter and Vance, with Young at the United Nations adopting a high public profile on African affairs. They wanted a policy that would demonstrate greater U.S. concern for black Africa, while being less heavyhanded at the same time. In the

Horn, this immediately translated into asymmetry because the Soviets were starting to be more enterprising and aggressive than ever.

When the Carter team took over the State Department, the Soviets, who had made Somalia into a regional military power far out of proportion to its size, already were beginning to sense opportunities next door in Ethiopia. Somalia was an example of how the Soviets, contrary to popular belief, understood Africa better than the United States did. The United States gave millions in development aid after independence in 1960 and then in 1962 offered Somalia $10 million in security assistance. The Somalis said no thanks and took a $32 million offer from the Soviet Union instead. Moscow used its entree to develop ties within the Somali officers' corp. In 1969 came General Siad Barre's coup, which the Kremlin very well may have had a hand in, and Soviet-Somali relations blossomed. Soon U.S. Peace Corps volunteers were being stoned in the streets of the Somali capital of Mogadishu thanks to a Soviet disinformation campaign. Between 1970 and 1975, the Somali army was increased from twelve thousand to twenty-three thousand soldiers. The Soviets supplied hundreds of tanks and fifty-five combat aircraft.

The presence of ethnic Somalis in Ethiopia's Ogaden desert made Somalia an irredentist state, and the Soviets obviously were taking advantage of Siad Barre's dreams of conquest and a Great Somalia. The six thousand Soviets in Somalia strutted about as if they owned the place. Naturally they were hated. It didn't matter. Their bull-in-a-china-shop approach never betrayed them. Although the Soviets eventually would leave Somalia, it was only because they had decided to jump ship to Somalia's number one enemy, Ethiopia, thus giving Siad Barre no choice but to accept the Americans as sloppy seconds.

As the revolution began to devour its children in Ethiopia, both the Soviets and the irredentist Somalis sensed great opportunities for themselves. Armed to the teeth by the Soviet Union, General Siad was finally in a position to attack his historic enemy, now weakened by revolutionary violence and turmoil. The Soviets, however, were becoming more and more intrigued by a different kind of opportunity: the line of bodies in Addis Ababa was forming a road for them to enter on. Ethiopia was always the prize of the region, which the United States had and which the Soviet Union now wanted. Somalia was but a country of 3 million people, mostly illiterate nomads, who lived and worked as if hypnotized by the merciless sun and humidity of the Indian Ocean. Ethiopia had ten times as many people, and many of those people were hard-working and culturally developed highlanders, whom the Soviets knew would make excellent fodder for the kind of mechanized African satellite state that they hoped to build. Regardless of a country's size and place on the map, in the final analysis it can be judged only by the talent of the people who live in it. (Israel is a perfect example.) The Soviets knew what every experienced Africa hand had long been aware of: that the highland Ethiopians—whether Amhara, Tigrean, Eritrean, or Oromo—were the hard-working, efficient people of black Africa. Somalia, a steamy, barely populated hellhole, never could be anything but a strategic bit of real estate suitable for a naval base or a landing strip. But Ethiopia . . . now there was a place that could be made into *something!*

The Kremlin initially thought it could create an entente between the two sworn enemies, with the Soviet Union guaranteeing the sovereignty of Ethiopia and Somalia under an umbrella of military aid; sort of like the arrangement the United States had with Greece and Turkey, both of whom were forever quarreling yet never actually went to war because each was dependent for supplies on the United States, which had bases in both countries. As with Greece and Turkey, the Kremlin wanted to make Ethiopia and Somalia part of a larger alliance that would include Marxist South Yemen and hopefully, someday, North Yemen and Djibouti as well, thus effectively choking off the West at its Red Sea oil windpipe.

In December 1976, the final month of Henry Kissinger's reign as the vicar of U.S. foreign policy, the Soviets offered $385 million in military aid to the Ethiopian Dergue while trying to reassure the Somalis at the same time. By this time, the Dergue already had switched ideological gears by declaring a commitment to "scientific socialism." But checkmate was still at least several moves away. The Dergue still was receiving M-60 tanks and F-5 warplanes from the United States, courtesy of Kissinger's foresight. Consequently, Mengistu was hesitant about going through the disruptive task of switching armorers for an entire army. Moreover, the Dergue still was receiving weapons and U.S. spare parts from an important U.S. ally in the region, Israel, whose position in revolutionary Ethiopia was somewhat better than its position later would be in revolutionary Iran. (The Mossad had trained Haile Selassie's secret service, and partly for historical and cultural reasons, Israel had developed close ties with the emperor. As with Iran, the relationship existed at so many levels of the Ethiopian bureaucracy that it never was severed totally after Haile Selassie was deposed, especially inside the military. But there the similarities ended. The mass of Ethiopians—Christians and Africanized Moslems—did not hate Israel with the same intensity as did the fundamentalist Shias in Iran; thus, the links with Israel that survived the Ethiopian revolution did not have to be denied by the new regime to quite the same degree as they have been by the authorities in Iran.)

In the early spring of 1977, as the Carter team was in the process of washing its hands of Ethiopia due to massive human rights violations, the Soviets had dispatched East German security police to Addis Ababa to help Mengistu consolidate his revolution, while sending Cuban leader Fidel Castro on a peacekeeping mission to both Ethiopia and Somalia. Admittedly, Carter faced a tough choice. Given the ongoing bloodbath in Ethiopia, it is doubtful whether any administration, liberal or conservative, would have wanted to, or would have been able to, continue delivering U.S. arms at an undisturbed pace to the Dergue. But considering the stakes for the United States and the people of the region, the military aid relationship did not have to be completely severed, as it was in April and May 1977. The situation still was not irreversible, however. As the Horn moved toward a momentous sequence of events in mid-1977, the United States would have other opportunities to remain engaged.

Carter's decision to cut off all arms deliveries apparently removed all further restraints from Mengistu and the Eastern bloc. In early April, Mengistu flew to Moscow for a week-long state visit where he signed the Declaration of the Foundation for Relationships and Cooperation, which laid the groundwork for one of the most massive Soviet arms transfers ever in the Third World. Within days, Cuban soldiers were sent to Ethiopia directly from Somalia, and tanks and armored personnel carriers began arriving from South Yemen. On May 1, the Red Terror began with the assistance of Mengistu's newly arrived East German security advisers. During the coming months, thousands of Ethiopian teenagers would be gunned down in the streets of Addis Ababa.

Following Castro's ill-fated attempt at peacemaking, Supreme Soviet Presidium Chairman Nikolai Podgorny paid an official visit to Mogadishu in another effort to get the Somalis to accept the new reality— of Soviet support for both them *and* the Ethiopians. But General Siad was having none of it. Somalia was in a better position than ever for invading Ethiopia, and the Somali leader was willing to risk his relationship with the Soviets rather than let the opportunity pass. Although for a little while longer the Soviets would find themselves the chief arms supplier for both countries, the Kremlin already had made the decision to forfeit Somalia if necessary in return for a bigger prize.

As the die was about to be cast, the Dergue still was maintaining contact with Israel, which had just elected a new prime minister, Menachem Begin. One of Begin's first acts was to communicate with Mengistu about the plight of Ethiopia's black Falasha Jews. This led to a series of messages whereby the Ethiopians made it known to the Israelis that they still desired a "Western option." In June, the long-awaited Somali invasion of Ethiopia's Ogaden desert began; regular Somali army units crossed the border to support WSLF guerrillas. Despite clandestine Israeli assistance and the new Soviet equipment, which had just begun to arrive, the Dergue, which also was occupied with fighting in Tigre and Eritrea, was not strong enough to stop the Somali advance. When Begin met Carter in Washington in July and urged him not to close the door completely on Ethiopia, Mengistu was in desperate straits and very well may have been amenable to certain U.S. demands on human rights and other issues if Carter was willing to resume, albeit on a low level, the military aid relationship. There was no question of blackmail. This was not Iran. Ethiopia never had taken any foreign hostages, and its revolution—leftist although it was— basically was devoid of any overt anti-U.S. sentiment, despite previous U.S. support for Haile Selassie. The United States thus had no axe to grind against Ethiopia when Begin offered Carter a second chance to salvage some degree of U.S. influence in black Africa's second-most-populous nation. But Carter rejected the Israeli leader's advice out of hand.

Carter very well may have felt that considering the growing Eastern bloc arms commitment to the Dergue, Mengistu was likely to take U.S. weapons without giving anything back in the way of policy concessions. But nor was Carter willing to put U.S. weapons in the hands of the Somalis as an alternate means of pressuring the Dergue. After all, through their own hell-bent irredentism, the Somalis now were providing Carter with yet another opportunity to muddle the outcome of Moscow's Ethiopia gambit. Apparently to placate Brzezinski, Carter did give General Siad indications that the United States was willing to supply arms. But by August, when Somali troops were on the verge of overrunning Jijiga, fifty miles inside Ethiopia, the United States announced that so long as Somali troops were illegally occupying Ethiopian territory, Washington could not supply them with arms. Vance, as usual, was applying Marquis of Queensbury Rules in the jungle. (One would think from the pious tone of the pronouncement that Ethiopia was a normal, friendly country.) The Soviets were less legalistic. They brought in Cuban and South Yemeni troops to slow the Somali advance while at the same time resuming arms supplies to Somalia and inviting General Siad to Moscow.

The Moscow meeting was a failure, however. The Somali leader, under pressure from his own conquering army and WSLF guerrillas, could not simply withdraw in order to accommodate Soviet strategy in Ethiopia. On November 13, 1977, the Somalis expelled their Soviet advisers and broke diplomatic relations with Cuba. Later in the month, the Soviets began airlifting thousands of Cuban troops to Ethiopia.

During the next four months, as Tom Farer reported in *War Clouds on the Horn of Africa,* Moscow would deliver more than $1 billion dollars worth of arms to Ethiopia, which was more than four times the value of all the arms the United States had delivered to the country since 1953.

The Somalis had no choice but to come running to the United States. "We advised them," related Vance in his book, "to accept OAU [Organization of African Unity] mediation of their dispute with Ethiopia, to seek a negotiated peace, and to offer their neighbors [Ethiopia and Kenya] assurances of respect for their territorial integrity." (This was basically what Moscow was telling General Siad to do.) The administration was taking the easy way out: preaching the Western version of morality from the sidelines while the Soviets, by trial and error, were muscling their way toward control over tens of millions of people.

At the beginning of 1978, the influx of Soviet arms and Cuban soldiers finally was taking effect. The Somalis were weakening. If the Ethiopians managed to completely eject Somali forces from the Ogaden, coupled with improved military fortunes in Eritrea, it would mean the consolidation of Mengistu's power and that of the Kremlin's in Ethiopia—an incredible display of Soviet military strength and determination in support of an ally. In this desperate moment, the administration, according to Vance, was only "prepared to support Somalia in a limited way, including the supplying of defensive arms, but only after the Somalis withdrew from the Ogaden." It was a classic example of the West being too civilized to defend its own values and interests. However badly the Soviets may have looked for deserting Somalia after building it up into a regional power, at least they were acting in support of their interests.

At this point, Brzezinski was urging several available options on President Carter, including deploying the U.S. Navy in the region, providing air cover for Somali troops, giving military aid to the Somalis and Eritreans, and linking Soviet behavior in the Horn to progress on the Strategic Arms Limitation Talks. None of these occurred. In his book, Vance outlined the strategy that took shape in early February.

- First, to work with our NATO allies to achieve agreed Western goals: a negotiated settlement; preventing an invasion of Somalia; preventing an increase in Soviet and Cuban influence in the area.
- Second, to ensure that other friends in the region—Egypt, Iran, Saudi Arabia, and Sudan—also understood and supported these goals and would urge them on Siad Barre.
- Third, to obtain Somali agreement to withdraw from the Ogaden.

- Fourth, to lay the diplomatic and political groundwork to help Somalia defend its territory, including supplying defensive arms after it withdrew from the Ogaden.
- Fifth, to keep pressure on the Soviets to stop the Ethiopians and Cubans at the Somali border and to support a negotiated resolution.

In other words, do nothing.

First, Soviet influence had grown so much in the region that the issue was how to reduce it, not to accept it at the present level as Vance indicated. Second, the "other friends" were nearly as powerless as was the United States in the face of a massive Soviet airlift of weapons and Cuban troops. Third, whether the Somalis agreed to withdraw from the Ogaden or not, the Ethiopians, Cubans, and Soviets were about to use force to kick the Somalis out. Fourth and fifth, the defensive arms that the United States eventually would provide General Siad were beside the point: the Soviets had no need for Ethiopia to invade Somalia because their position in Ethiopia would be secured merely by driving the Somalis out of Ethiopia and by turning the tide against the Eritrean guerrillas.

In mid-February 1978, the Ethiopians, fortified by Cuban armor, counterattacked. Somali forces were outflanked, and Jijiga was retaken by the Dergue on March 9. Farer wrote in his book that "President Carter practically simultaneously announced" the decision by the Somali government to remove all its troops from Ethiopia. One could say that it was a rare case of one superpower leader announcing a victory of the other. Vance still was not satisfied, however. Even after Somalia had withdrawn its troops, the United States, according to Vance, still was "not able to assist Somalia militarily at that time because Siad Barre reneged on his assurances that he would leave Ethiopia alone." Had the Kremlin been able to draft the script, it couldn't have done a better job.

The superpower flip-flop in the Horn of Africa now was complete. It was by no means a fair trade—either for the United States or for the people of the region. Instead of controlling a country of 3 million people whose nomadic lifestyle they virtually left alone, the Soviets now had control over a country of more than 30 million people, whose existences would be trampled on in the course of implementing communism. Although U.S. ideology had helped to restrain some of Haile Selassie's excesses, Soviet ideology would serve to intensify the worst excesses of the Dergue. In *Breakfast in Hell,* relief worker Myles F. Harris described the difference between the two Ethiopian regimes.

The old rulers kept the peasants poor, chained to the soil by debt so that no heads were ever raised in defiance. But at least the feudal lords knew something of the land, how much it would produce. . . .

But the new men, they were from the city and knew nothing of the soil. They had dead eyes and spoke in riddles. They took everything the peasant produced and for a price so low it brought death and withering of the crops, fear, and whispers. And the new man heard everything and forgot nothing, even what a man murmured in his sleep. Many a peasant went to jail wondering what it was he had said and against whom.

Carter's strategy emphasized human rights and diplomacy. The Kremlin interpreted this as just plain weakness. The USSR moved more than $1 billion in arms to take over a country while the United States did nothing except stand on ceremony. In coming years, hundreds of thousands would die as a result. Ethiopia obviously took up a significant amount of Carter's time at the beginning of his term in office. But it's difficult to find a reference about Ethiopia in his memoir *Keeping Faith.*

*   *   *

By the time Ronald Reagan took office, Ethiopia was well on its way to becoming Moscow's first African satellite. Although the maturation of the Eritrean and Tigrean guerrilla resistances offered Reagan the chance to destabilize the Dergue through the use of proxy armies, the conservative Republican president, while willing to arm less competent guerrilla groups in other parts of the globe, did next to nothing in Ethiopia. In 1981, Reagan authorized the Central Intelligence Agency to provide $500,000 yearly to the London-based EPDA in order to distribute antigovernment leaflets and audiovisual material inside Ethiopia. The EPDA was multiethnic and democratic, but it also had few guerrillas in the field. Countering Soviet guns and East German surveillance techniques with leaflets and soundtracks was the kind of gentlemanly course of action that Carter would have employed had he been reelected in 1980.

*   *   *

In 1984, the famine emergency gave the United States what it thought was an opportunity to weaken Moscow's hold over Ethiopia using peaceful means. While the Soviet Union provided less than 1 percent (10,000 tons out of 1.25 million) of the emergency food aid, the noncommunist world provided 99 percent. Mengistu was not impressed, however. During a November 1985 visit to Moscow, the Ethiopian leader, according to the TASS news agency, "expressed profound gratitude to the USSR for its . . . assistance in strengthening the economy and defensive capacity of socialist Ethiopia and in overcoming the consequences of the severest drought." No similar tribute was paid to the West.

In June 1986, Ethiopia released a draft of its new constitution. Aleme Eshete, an Ethiopian scholar, described it as "almost an abridged translation of the Soviet constitution of 1977. One does not see Ethiopia in it. The chapters of the Soviet constitution are all reproduced in order." The only major exception was the part dealing with the office and powers of the president, which was lifted almost straight out of the Romanian constitution, in order to give Mengistu the kind of absolute power enjoyed by President Nicolae Ceausescu.

The U.S. position in Ethiopia in the mid-1980s was worse than ever. Said a diplomat at the U.S. Embassy in Addis Ababa: "We could wake up tomorrow morning and find that we're being kicked out." Indeed, the record in Sudan and Ethiopia had made one thing clear: in the struggle against totalitarianism, bread alone was never enough.

CODA: THE TWO YEMENS

At the southern entrance to the Red Sea, across the shark-infested waters from Ethiopia and Somalia, lie North and South Yemen. The two Yemens offer a mirror image of the reality in the Horn of Africa and therefore provide another clue as to why the U.S. position in Ethiopia is worse than it ever has been, despite the generous outpouring of famine aid.

Although one often is confused with the other, the historical experience of the two Yemens has been markedly different. In 1839, the British occupied Aden, at the southwest tip of the Arabian peninsula, where they established a coal-bunkering port for ships sailing to and from India. A debilitating form of colonialism ensued. While Aden boomed, nothing was done to develop or, more importantly, to integrate the adjacent hinterland. Order was kept by bribing the local tribal chiefs. Not surprisingly, the radical guerrilla movement that ousted the British in 1967 was dominated by up-country tribespeople, who would use extreme methods to unify what had been no more than an assemblage of separate little protectorate states rimming Aden. The preconditions for the Marxist straitjacket in the country that came to be known as South Yemen thus were formed.

But neither the British nor anyone else could ever colonize the tribespeople in the high mountains and deserts in the far north—the legendary home of the Queen of Sheba. The Ottoman Turkish hold over this region was nothing more than a four-hundred-year-long series of bloody failures. Only in 1962 was the sultanate—as medieval as the court of Haile Selassie—abolished. Even so, North Yemen remains a stronghold of xenophobic traditionalism much like Ethiopia and Afghanistan, and like both of those countries, the first group of foreign invaders able to successfully penetrate North Yemen may turn out to be the Soviets.

The similarities between North Yemen and Ethiopia are, to say the least, unsettling. In antiquity, both places shared a storybook aura as civilizations existing in mountainous isolation at the very edge of the known world renowned for their gold, spices, frankincense, and precious stones. According to tradition, the line of Ethiopian kings that ended with Haile Selassie was started by the Yemenite Queen of Sheba and the Hebrew King Solomon. Axum, the first great Ethiopian kingdom, was established by colonists from Yemen, which was known to the Romans as Arabia Felix (Fortunate Arabia) on account of its wealth. In the intervening centuries, only the most intrepid explorers were able to scale the fortress of mountains that kept both Yemen and Ethiopia locked away in a cultural time warp. Exactly like Ethiopia, North Yemen was one of the few places in the Third World that totally withstood the bastardizing influence of the West until the second half of the twentieth century and even now is an anthropologist's dream come true. The Zaidi version of Shiite Islam practiced in Yemen was no less strange and unique than was the form of Coptic Christian orthodoxy practiced in Ethiopia. Visiting the area in the 1950s, the late British journalist David Holden wrote in *Farewell to Arabia,* "Secluded behind its mountain barriers, protected by its sheer lack of physical communications and the fitful hostility of its Imams, the Yemen maintained a reputation of unusual mystery, even for Arabia . . . a medieval survival, a kingdom of silence."

The same could be said for Ethiopia.

I was the only U.S. journalist in North Yemen following the bloody coup and tribal war in South Yemen in early 1986, and I was allowed in by mistake—the North Yemeni consul in Greece who gave me the visa was unaware that the Ministry of Information had banned news reporters from the country. It was very much as Holden described it: a land of iron-red canyons, basalt plateaus, and beehive-like villages tripping down mountain sides whose terraced green fields exuded an almost tropical remoteness. The men wore turbans, plaid skirts, and curved daggers thrust inside their belts and retired every afternoon to chew *qat,* a narcotic leaf whose affect is similar to marijuana. But there was nothing exotic about the politics. As in the Horn, the great nineteenth-century game of grand strategy was in progress.

The Soviets moved into South Yemen at the same time that they were moving into Somalia. A listening post, naval anchorage, and runway suitable for long-range reconnaissance flights were constructed at Aden; while on the South Yemeni island of Socotra off the Somali coast—at the very tip of the African Horn—submarine facilities were installed.

In 1979, on the heels of their successful Ethiopia gambit, the Soviets got interested in North Yemen, which with a population three times larger than South Yemen's was, like Ethiopia, the prize of the region. The Saudi Arabians offered the North Yemeni leader Colonel Ali Abdullah Saleh $300 million in aid to keep the Soviets out. Moscow responded with a $1 billion arms program spread over the next five years for the thirty-five-thousand-troop North Yemeni military, which consequently was Soviet trained and Russian speaking and equipped with MIG bombers, T-62 tanks, and SAM antiaircraft missiles.

Still, the Soviet position in North Yemen is insecure. True to their own past, the North Yemenis like to keep all foreigners at bay and have accepted aid from several Western nations, including the United States, as a brake against further Soviet influence. Marxism is definitely not to the North Yemenis' liking. Not even their own government has control over the local economy, which is based on smuggling and functions as a kind of unofficial, duty-free market: Rice Crispies and Frosted Flakes are available in corner groceries in the capital of Sana'a.

The discovery of oil in North Yemen in July 1984 by the Dallas-based Hunt Oil Company made the Soviets especially nervous, according to Western diplomats in Sana'a. At the time, the two Yemens were involved in unification talks (one of many attempts throughout the years to end the official division of 1934, when the British, in Aden, were forced to recognize the imam's sovereignty north of a line that is the present-day boundary between North and South Yemen). Moscow was worried that unification would allow the more populous, free-market country to the north, now buttressed by U.S.-exploited oil, to dominate and eventually submerge its smaller and poorer Marxist neighbor to the south.

Soon after oil was discovered in North Yemen, Moscow sent Abdul Fatah Ismail, the former president of South Yemen, home to Aden to rejoin the Politburo after a five-year exile in the Soviet Union. Even by South Yemen's insane standards, Ismail was a hard-liner, who in the late 1970s had signed a friendship treaty with the Soviets and made his strategically located country of 2 million an observer member of Comecon. The Kremlin's intention was for Ismail to sabotage the policy of rapprochement with North Yemen instituted by the current South Yemeni president, Ali Nasser Mohammed.

However, the Soviets underestimated the deep personal antagonisms, further aggravated by tribal differences, between Ismail and Nasser Mohammed. On January 13, 1986, guns were drawn at a Politburo meeting and Ismail was badly wounded. Although the details never will be known, Ismail may have walked into an ambush set by Nasser Mohammed similar to the ambush Mengistu set for his rivals nine years earlier. Fighting erupted throughout Aden, and the Soviets at first supported Nasser Mohammed, with Moscow Radio describing Ismail on three successive days as a "coupist" and "agent of reaction." But as the revolt against Nasser Mohammed gathered steam, the Soviets quickly switched sides. According to diplomats' accounts and published reports, Soviet ships delivered ammunition to Ismail's Laheej tribespeople. Soviet advisers helped direct tank and artillery fire, and Soviet planes bombed the airport in support of the rebels. When the dust cleared two weeks later, ten thousand people were dead and billions of dollars worth of property were damaged. As in Ethiopia the previous decade, it was another example of the Soviets brutally working their will while the outside world looked the other way.

Ismail himself was one of the casualties. Aden Radio gave several conflicting accounts of how he died. There is a strong suspicion that he may have met his end in Moscow, where some diplomats believe he was taken after being wounded in the January 13 shoot-out. Prior to the official announcement of his death, Soviet diplomats in Sana'a were saying that Ismail was "finished politically" because Moscow had "no interest" in backing a man "known throughout the Arab world as an extremist." Conceivably, Ismail was left to die, or even eliminated, once it was clear that the new, hard-line regime in South Yemen that he helped establish was firmly in place. It would not be the first time that Moscow had done in a socialist hero once he had outlived his usefulness.

At the very least, Ismail's death was convenient for the Soviets. In place of a shrewd, powerful leader such as Ismail, the Aden bloodbath had thrown up a group of gray men who were even more subservient to the Kremlin than the last bunch had been. The new South Yemeni president was Haydar abu Bakr Attas, a man of no political talent who commanded little popular support. His first act after assuming the post was to fly straight to Moscow for consultations. The Soviets had learned well from their experience in Somalia in the late 1970s: in taking over Ethiopia they had been forced to give up Somalia because Somali leader Siad Barre was still independent enough to force the Soviets to make a choice. But the new South Yemeni leader will be no Siad Barre. In their drive to dominate the Red Sea oil choke point, the Soviets will have fewer hard choices to make.

It was a messy operation and didn't go according to plan. Not even the Soviets were anticipating a tribal war that would cost ten thousand lives. But in the end, they still got what they wanted—a regime in South Yemen with absolutely no mind of its own, thus leaving the Soviets free to do whatever is necessary to further improve their position in North Yemen.

The 10,000-barrel-a-day refinery that opened in mid-1986 in North Yemen, along with a planned 250-mile pipeline to the Red Sea, could be vulnerable targets for Soviet-inspired sabotage. The oil fields are in the desert near the frontier with South Yemen where the border is not always secure or even delineated. It also should be remembered that the massive Soviet military aid program means that the USSR has influence in North Yemen where it counts. Even Western diplomats in Sana'a admit that Moscow's intelligence sources no doubt are better than theirs.

*   *   *

Mengistu's greatest fear was enacted in South Yemen in January 1986: the Soviets were prepared to shed blood, and lots of it, merely to replace one subservient ruler with an even more subservient one. Mengistu, a brawler by nature, at first fought back. In what may have been his only blatantly hostile act ever toward Moscow, for several days he supplied arms to Nasser Mohammed's supporters while the Soviets were arming the Ismail faction. But a visit of several high-ranking Soviet officials to Addis Ababa quickly brought Mengistu into line. Given the facts of life as brutally demonstrated in Aden, one of the last things the Ethiopian leader needs to do is to pay political tribute to the West for its famine assistance. His life depends upon what the USSR thinks of him, not what the United States thinks.

aid: rolling the rock of Sisyphus

None the less, he knew that the tale he had to tell could not be one of final victory. It could be only the record of what had had to be done, and what assuredly would have to be done again in the never ending fight against terror and its relentless onslaughts . . . by all who, while unable to be saints but refusing to bow down to pestilences, strive their utmost to be healers.

—**Albert Camus,** *The Plague*

Khawaja is a Sudanese Arabic word that means "a white foreigner." When a British aid worker in Khartoum told a middle-class Sudanese woman that millions of Sudanese were close to death due to a famine in the far west of the country, she exclaimed, "My God, are those *khawaja*s going to have a crisis on their hands!"

As the woman's reaction indicated, the famine was a crisis of conscience for the West only. The famine certainly wasn't a crisis for the Eastern bloc. Not a single rouble was collected for Live Aid, of which Dr. Anatoly Gromyko, head of the USSR's Africa Institute, said he never heard. (*Moskovskii Komsomolets,* a widely read Soviet youth publication, described Live Aid as a "tele-cosmic concert" on behalf of peace; the paper never mentioned the word *famine.*)

But from interviews I conducted in fall 1985 and spring 1986, it became clear to me that the famine did not prick the conscience of many Africans who were not starving. Ahmed el-Tigani, secretary of the Khartoum Doctors' Union, which was instrumental in overthrowing President Nimeiri, explained that Africans saw suffering all around them and therefore were immune to it. "For us, famine is not grossly abnormal. We have no curiosity. We don't feel a need to see the relief camps." "Nobody is thinking about famine or desertification," said Abdel Gadir Hafiz, chief editor of the local news section of the Khartoum daily *El Ayyam* (The Days). The shocking scenes of mass starvation witnessed by millions of U.S. citizens in their living rooms were not seen by Africans. When a Sudanese government minister saw a video film of the famine at the home of a Western relief worker, the minister was amazed—he said he had no idea it was that bad. This was in early 1986, a year after the start of the famine emergency in Sudan. Osama Fatouta, a twenty-four-year-old Sudanese who was educated in London, said the only people in Khartoum who cared about the dying peasants were foreigners. Fatouta told me he was motivated by shame to singlehandedly create the Sudanese Volunteer Services Association, a famine relief organization composed of young people like himself, wealthy enough to study abroad, who thus were inspired by Western notions of community service. "People I know think I'm crazy. They can't understand why I'm doing this. I've gotten little support," Fatouta said. Most Sudanese, or Ethiopians for that matter, couldn't be bothered. In *Breakfast in Hell,* relief worker Myles F. Harris likened the African middle class "to the aristocracy in prerevolutionary Russia. They could walk down a street crowded with beggars and see only people on it similar to themselves."

Fatouta, Harris, and others intimately involved in the relief effort knew an awful truth that many in the United States were afraid to face: that although God may cause drought, famine in Africa is caused by the power relationships among Africans. All the relief assistance in the world cannot change the values by which Sudanese and Ethiopians live. This is why although 1 million died, nothing changed. The Ethiopian death machine rolled on. Not one truly significant agricultural reform took place. In fact, the same production methods responsible for the 1984 famine have since been expanded through resettlement and villagization. Because the population of more than 42 million is increasing at a faster rate than is agricultural production, the conditions are ripe for an even greater famine catastrophe in the 1990s, according to a 1986 report by USAID. In Sudan, meanwhile, merchants continue to hoard grain, and peasants are forced to borrow money for seeds at exorbitant interest rates. As in Ethiopia, there have been no significant reforms of any kind.

Few relief workers I met in either country were ignorant of these realities. Like Sisyphus, the mythical king of Corinth, they labored in the hot African sun rolling a rock up the hill, knowing in advance that it was going to roll back upon them. "There are no solutions," said John Richardson, who worked for the United Nations in both Addis Ababa and Khartoum. Even successes were hard to gauge in the statistically unverifiable reality of Africa. Yet millions were saved, if only for the time being. As Martin Fletcher, of the NBC News Tel

Aviv bureau, remarked in Addis Ababa, "If you can extend a child's life for even six months, what's wrong with that?"

It almost doesn't matter that in the process of saving millions in Ethiopia, the West may have salvaged Africa's most chillingly brutal regime, thereby giving it the wherewithal to ruin the lives of even more millions during a long period of time. Graphic images of starving children simply couldn't be ignored. To ignore the starvation, even if it meant a long-term benefit for the population, would have entailed so harsh and painful a calculation that only the Eastern bloc—if the shoe were on the other foot—would have been capable of it.

Compassion, as the famine clearly demonstrated, was both the U.S. weakness and strength. Imagine the public response if the Reagan administration had—for the sake of toppling the regime—refused to give Ethiopia any emergency aid at all! Given the limitations imposed by our morality, we in the West did about all we could, and what we did was blunted severely by the conditions the Western aid worker faced the moment he or she got off the plane in Africa. Sudan, where Marxism cannot be blamed for the pitiful state of affairs, offers a particularly vivid picture of what relief workers were up against: there can be few experiences more jarring than to emerge from the cocoon of a Swiss Air plane, having just been pampered by elegant stewardesses, red Rhone wine, and Vladimir Ashkenazy on the headphones only to be thrust into the hellhole of Khartoum airport. My fifth arrival, in late 1986, was no easier than my first in 1984. Depression sets in even before the descent, when at 35,000 feet the thin air outside takes on a pasty hue and the plane shudders ever so slightly from the thermal winds and dust of the Sahara; a premonition of the defeating, pie crust emptiness below. In business class, passengers start gulping their drinks down before ordering one final glass. Given Islamic law, it's likely to be the last alcohol they'll see until leaving Sudan.

On the final approach, Khartoum resembles a pattern of rectangles etched in sandpaper, bordered by the White and Blue Niles, which are impressively wide from the air, but do not offer any surcease from the environment once the traveler has landed. The Sudanese capital, designed by the British in the shape of the Union Jack, turns its back on the two rivers. Stepping outside the air-conditioned Swiss Air cabin, the dry, suffocating heat of Khartoum grabs the traveler's lungs in a vise. Even at night, sunglasses are often necessary due to the dust.

On my last visit, prices of food and other basic commodities were up 50 percent from the year before. There were shortages of everything. Water and electricity cuts were more frequent. Making a local telephone call was harder than ever. The drainage system had become so bad that after a five-minute downpour many of the streets were impassable.

Khartoum literally looked mean. "All the drought did was expose just how bad the system always was here," said a Western diplomat.

Because the Western relief community's worst enemy was the Sudanese government, aid workers put up with the material hardships of the Acropole, where most of them stayed, in order to avail themselves of the services of the hotel's Greek managers, who dealt with Sudanese officialdom better than any Western embassy staff could. It may be an irony that while hundreds of millions of dollars of emergency assistance poured into Sudan, the only wedge between partial success and a complete breakdown of the relief effort was a trio of Greek brothers from the island of Kefalonia in the Ionian Sea, whose father had come to Khartoum in the wake of British rule. As journalist Edward Girardet aptly put it in the *Christian Science Monitor* (July 8, 1985), George, Athanasios, and Gerassimos Pagoulatos and their wives ran a fifty-room hotel, arranged visa extensions and internal travel permits, helped clear aid consignments through customs at Port Sudan, dispatched hand-carried documents throughout Europe, and otherwise ran errands for the relief effort all "with the courtesy and aplomb" of captains "of a luxury liner." Had the Pagoulatos family packed their bags and gone back to Greece in the mid-1980s as they originally had intended, then the Western relief effort simply might have collapsed. Few aid workers were capable of maneuvering through the corrupt and inefficient Sudanese bureaucratic treadmill by themselves. Many required the Pagoulatos brothers to hold their hands.

Emergency Palace was the sobriquet given to the Acropole by senior Associated Press correspondent Mort Rosenbloom. Some compared the hotel to Rick's American Cafe in the movie *Casablanca*. The dining room, usually jam-packed with journalists and relief workers, was decorated with Greek island watercolors and serviced by scowling, turbaned waiters who shuffled around among the tables. The only thing the Acropole lacked was liquor, a sacrifice necessitated by Islamic law. Nevertheless, the conversations that took place over the curried rice, Nile perch, and freshly squeezed lemon juice prepared by "Mummie," the matriarch of the Pagoulatos clan, had a delirious, intoxicated quality—an effect of the heat no doubt. Because many of the journalists and relief workers in Sudan also had worked in Ethiopia, the entire history of the famine was recorded in the Acropole dining room. When I last arrived at the Acropole in the autumn of 1986, there was only one topic of conversation—the south.

The famine relief story in the Horn of Africa in the mid-1980s had three parts to it. Acts One and Two were northern Ethiopia and western Sudan. Act Three, which in this case was the denouement of the drama, was the south of Sudan. As in Shakespearian and Greek tragedy, it was the part of the play when the protagonists—the journalists and relief workers—attained full awareness. The problem was that by the time they did so, the public was barely paying attention. The theater had emptied out before the final scene.

*   *   *

With 1 million square miles of territory, Sudan always was more like a vast subcontinent than an individual country, and of all its remote regions—western Darfur included—none seemed as remote as the jungles and savannas of the equatorial south. Even by African standards, the south was in the middle of nowhere, cut off from the rest of Sudan by the Sudd, the world's most formidable swamp, and bordering such dangerous, disease-ridden, and underdeveloped places as the Central African Republic, Zaire, war-racked northern Uganda, and Kenya's Turkana desert. A netherworld of violence and chaos, roamed by armed bandits and disaffected Ugandan soldiers, the south was a heartland of unreported atrocities as well as a breeding ground of leprosy, elephantiasis, and Green Monkey disease. Just the lost and vacant ring of the towns in the region (Yey, Tarakaka, Pibor Post) evoked distant planets and gave one the feeling that the south really was in deep space. It had no roads to speak of, and because of the civil war, planes flying into the region always were shot at and occasionally were shot down. On every trip to the south, Western relief workers literally took their lives in their hands. When I asked a U.S. diplomat how to get to a certain area of the south near the Ethiopian border, he gave me a mad look and said, "Parachute, I guess." Admitted an official of Sudan's Ministry of Information, "Nobody ever really knows what's happening down there."

Southern Sudan never had a chance. In the nineteenth century, Mohammed Ali and later Egyptian khedives gradually annexed the area to their Sudan holdings in a crazed attempt to control the headwaters of the Nile and expand their empire. The British, employing their usual divide-and-rule tactics—but also motivated by an instinctive realization that for the non-Moslem, African south to "work" it would have to be separated from the Arab north—did everything in their power to keep the south free of northern influence. Tribal consciousness was promoted. Arabs were excluded from the area, and Greeks and Armenians were brought in instead to run the shops. To encourage Christianity, the Verona fathers, an Italian Catholic order, were allowed in to proselytize. The cleavage soon became too deep to correct. As Michael C. Hudson indicated in *Arab Politics: The Search for Legitimacy,* of all the minorities in the Middle East, the black Africans of Sudan always have been the least assimilated, less so than even the

Jews in Arab countries, who, unlike the African southerners, spoke Arabic and were racially similar to the Arabs.

The Moslem Arabs in the north and the pagan and Christian Africans in the south were entirely in different orbits. Khartoum's Arab politicians wanted to own and exploit the south without having to do anything for it—they didn't even want to think about it. "To the Arabs, the southerners are just a bunch of spear-chucking heathens," said a Western official. When it dawned on the Arabs that the oil and hydroelectric resources of the region might never be utilized due to the civil war, voices were raised, beginning in late 1986, about it not being such a bad idea if the south were to formally split away. If Sudan had "less of a government than any other country on the continent," as the chief of United Nations Emergency Operations in Khartoum, Winston Prattley, told me, then southern Sudan had even less than that.

Neither the northern Arabs nor the southern Africans had any respect for the humanity of the other. So when years of fighting between the Khartoum government and the south's SPLA ignited a famine, neither side could comprehend why the *khawaja*s were kicking up such a fuss.

Journalists and aid workers knew less about the south than about anywhere else in famine-stricken Africa. The south was less safe, less accessible, and involved greater physical hardships than was the case in northern Ethiopia. Even those who managed to penetrate the area only were able to see an outpost or two. The going aid agency figure of those effected by famine was 2 million, but nobody really had any idea. Anthony Suau, a Pulitzer Prize–winning photographer on assignment for *National Geographic,* told me he had a feeling that the whole southern famine might be a hoax insofar as only tens of thousands might be threatened instead of millions. Still, while knowing and seeing less, by 1986 journalists and aid workers had learned a lot about famine in Africa, and consequently they had a more accurate insight into the realities of southern Sudan and other hunger-hit regions than they had about Ethiopia in 1984 and early 1985.

"War, Not Drought, Cited as Key Threat to Africa" was the headline in the March 28, 1986, *International Herald Tribune* for *Washington Post* correspondent Blaine Harden's dispatch. "It is no longer drought but rather war that has become the major factor in a continuing famine," wrote Harden in the lead paragraph. Another *Tribune* headline, on July 1, 1986, read: "War in Southern Sudan Heightens Food Crisis, Hampers Relief Effort." Underneath, *Washington Post* correspondent Jonathan C. Randal wrote: "The increasingly violent 'hidden war' in southern Sudan . . . has unleashed rival armies, marauding militias and bandit gangs and displaced hundreds of thousands of destitute and hungry civilians. Waged across an inaccessible area larger than France, Belgium, Switzerland and Austria combined, the fighting is destroying crops and livestock on an increasing scale."

Although it is true that drought was much less of an issue in the lush south of Sudan compared to northern Ethiopia, the primacy of human factors in the southern Sudan famine was not the only reason for the media's focus on the war there. In terms of size, strategy, and outside political relevance, it was a less interesting war than the one in Eritrea. Yet the media virtually ignored fighting in Eritrea, which was easier and safer to visit, while concentrating heavily on the bush battles between Sudan's regular army and John Garang's Ethiopian-backed SPLA.

*   *   *

Despite all the difficulties inherent in the terrain, the Western relief community in the summer of 1986 was prepared as never before for this famine. Northeastern Africa had just had a record harvest: 18,000 tons of food were available in northern Sudan and neighboring Kenya, with sixty trucks, painted in white with the U.N. emblem, all ready to roll into southern Sudan from the Kenyan border. Medical supplies also were in abundance. On account of increased stability in Uganda, following the coming to power of Yoweri Museveni in Kampala the previous January, a truck route from that country was open as well, and the World Food Program was ready to transport 90,000 tons of food into southern Sudan from there. Unlike Bangladesh, Cambodia, Ethiopia, and western Sudan, there would be no bottlenecks plaguing the emergency effort this time. Wrote columnist Jonathan Power in the *International Herald Tribune,* "This time, everything is in place—waiting."

It was practically all for naught, however, because it was not in the interest of either side in the civil war that people be fed. On June 1, 1986, twelve Kenyan truck drivers bringing food into the south from the Ugandan border town of Nimule were ambushed, presumably by SPLA rebels. The drivers were bound by ropes to their steering wheels, and then grenades were lobbed at the trucks. This put a virtual halt to the World Food Program's overland relief operation. Only 600 of the 90,000 tons had been delivered. Churches, private relief groups, and U.N. agencies appealed to both the SPLA and the Sudanese government for a truce in order to let food in. The calls went unheeded. On August 15, the SPLA banned all flights over southern Sudan, claiming that the government was using the Red Cross as a cover to resupply its army. (A Red Cross official called the claim "ridiculous.") To press the point, on the next day, the rebels shot down a Sudan

Airways plane after takeoff from Malakal, about 425 miles south of Khartoum, using Soviet-made SAM-7 antiaircraft missiles. All sixty civilian passengers on board were killed. The Khartoum authorities grounded all flights into the region. Now no food could get in by air either.

"We are not repentant," SPLA leader John Garang told Blaine Harden (*Washington Post,* September 19, 1986). "We warned that the airspace over War Zone I is closed." Garang, sporting a revolver and a knife along with an AK-47 assault rifle, said that too much publicity had been given to food shortages in government-held towns such as Wau, where one hundred seventy thousand starving refugees were reported to be besieged by SPLA troops after being driven out of their villages by cattle raiding gangs called *marahlin*.

While the SPLA was starving the towns, the Sudanese government was starving the countryside. Red Cross officials reported that hundreds of famine victims had testified to government brutality. Particular targets of the regular Sudanese army were villages occupied by Garang's Dinka tribe, which accounted for 40 percent of southern Sudan's population. Western diplomats said that whole Dinka villages were burned to the ground by government troops and their allies. Khartoum had fallen back on the old British colonial method of arming local tribes hostile to the Dinka, specifically the Messariya, Baggara, Murle, and Acholi. The Messariya and Baggara were Arab herders and nomads, known for their military prowess. Many of the Acholi were deserters from the army of former Uganda presidents Apollo Milton Obote and Tito Okello Lutwa, who a few months earlier had been defeated by the National Resistance Army of Uganda's new president, Yoweri Museveni. Because these Acholi deserters also were launching attacks across the border in Uganda, Museveni retaliated by banning relief shipments into southern Sudan, a move that further crippled the relief effort.

The situation had gotten desperate enough in southern Sudan for tens of thousands of Ugandan refugees of the Madi tribe to come back home. When I visited northern Uganda in mid-1986, the Madis already were building new huts and cutting the spear grass in preparation for planting maize near the banks of the Albert Nile. A Verona father, who had returned with the Madis, told me that utter chaos now reigned in southern Sudan; Acholi deserters were on the rampage in refugee camps "mutilating" their former Madi enemies, who had fought against the Acholis in Uganda's own, just-concluded civil war. Cruelty was being piled on cruelty in an obscure and complex tribal free-for-all that only the Western relief community was trying to stop. It was noteworthy that the refugees spoke only about the suffering of their

own tribe and when prodded about the fate of the others evinced little
or no sympathy.

Near the end of August, M. Peter McPherson lent his voice to the
call for a food truce. "As the condition of large numbers of innocent
people continues to deteriorate rapidly, I call upon the government
and the SPLA to allow desperately needed food to reach those in
need" (*Washington Post,* August 29, 1986). At this point, the only
supplies not in short supply in southern Sudan were salt, sweets, liquor,
and cigarettes, which until a few weeks before—rebel antiaircraft fire
notwithstanding—pilots had been willing to fly in on account of the
high prices these items fetched. Grain just brought in too small a
profit for a pilot to risk losing his life.

Fighting continued and neither side agreed to a truce. No amount
of diplomatic pressure seemed to work. Finally, U.N. officials and
others decided to shame the Sudanese authorities and the SPLA into
opening up the air space over the south. A $1 million, thirty-day shuttle
service, dubbed Operation Rainbow, was announced with much fan-
fare. The government-held towns of Juba, the capital of Equatoria
Province, Malakal, the capital of Upper Nile Province, and Wau, the
capital of Bahr el Ghazal were to be reached by flights from Khartoum.
Yirol, an SPLA-held outpost in Bahr el Ghazal, was to be supplied
by flights from Kenya. The foreign press corps in Nairobi was alerted
and encouraged to proceed to Khartoum to cover the departure of the
first flight.

The Khartoum authorities immediately objected to the relief plan
because it included rebel-held areas. So before even getting off the
ground, Operation Rainbow was scaled down to include government
areas only. Still, crews from the three major U.S. television networks,
among other media personnel, packed into the Khartoum Hilton for
the lift-off of the first relief consignment. Then the delays started. By
the time Sadiq el Mahdi's government gave its permission, the SPLA
raised objections. Then the government objected to the SPLA's objections. For several days in a row, the departure was called off at the
last moment. There also were reported problems with the company
insuring the plane. Few journalists were willing to take part in the
operation because who could be sure that some lone SPLA outpost,
in spite of an agreement not to shoot, wouldn't try to shoot the plane
down anyway? In the end, a flight managed to take off in early October,
with only enough grain to feed one decent-sized town for one day.

Through sheer doggedness, the Sudanese—the Arab government and
the African rebels both—had managed to blockade an entire Western
relief effort. A flight here and a truck there got into the south with
badly needed supplies. But that was all. Because so little out of so

much made it to its destination, even the most filthy and poorly equipped feeding center in southern Sudan was considered a "humanitarian showcase." Columnist Jonathan Power wrote that relief officials were "crazy with anger." (A similar situation ensued in late 1987 and early 1988 when actions by the Ethiopian government, the EPLF, and the TPLF prevented food from reaching hungry peasants. Unfortunately, in this case, despite an exemplary human rights record built up during many years, the EPLF's behavior was little better than the SPLA's.)

How many starved to death because of Sudanese intransigence? Who knows? Maybe tens of thousands, maybe more. Or maybe photographer Anthony Suau was right, and the whole thing was blown out of proportion from the start. In a region where a visit to just one lonely outpost could mean a life-threatening situation, who was keeping count? Remember, this was a crisis for the West only. The only crisis for the Sudanese was how to get the relief agencies off Sudanese backs.

None of this escaped the media, which duly recorded the frustrations experienced by the relief community. Network crews had to justify their expenses at the $120-a-night Khartoum Hilton, so they recorded what was not happening rather than what was. The short burst of television coverage that accompanied the nonlift-off of Operation Rainbow in October 1986 constituted the very last mini-event of the great 1980s famine in northeast Africa. By 1987, the famine story had moved south to Mozambique, although by the end of that year, famine again reared its head in Ethiopia, thereby resulting in renewed media attention. In addition to television, some newspapers, particularly the *Washington Post,* provided detailed and colorful coverage of the relief nightmare in southern Sudan. But most of these stories ran on inside pages and, like the television spots, had limited effect because the general public had long before switched its attention to other foreign news stories.

In all this time, the debate in the United States about famine had barely changed. Academic blather about development programs and a Western "commitment" to Africa filled up even more space on newspaper editorial pages in 1987 than had been the case in early 1984. Money and agricultural technology still could solve everything. Fingers still were being pointed at the European Economic Community because of the vast mountains of milk and butter it destroyed rather than ship to more needy areas of the globe. The far greater evil of Africa's own callous and hypocritical attitudes toward its starving millions was much less written about, as if such information were charged and radioactive. Neither U.S. thinking nor that of the African ruling class was all that much affected by the unfolding of events on the ground during those momentous years in the Horn. The actual behavior of African leaders had little impact on the United States, just as U.S. efforts in Africa had little impact on African leaders.

*   *   *

On a late October night in 1986 I said goodbye for the last time to Athanasios Pagoulatos and took a battered taxi to the airport for the 2 A.M. flight to Nairobi. I did not think I would be coming back to Sudan. As the Khartoum dust scoured my eyes, two incidents replayed themselves in my mind that, for me, were emblematic of Africa as I briefly experienced it.

The first incident involved a colleague, Paul Vallely. He wrote a story about it entitled, "Riding the Lifeline Lorry" (*The Times*, July 26, 1985). To my mind, it was the best single feature story I ever read about the famine. It's too bad that the U.S. public never got to see it.

> For weeks the requests had been trickling into the old British garrison post of El Geneina, the furthermost town in the west of Sudan. . . .
>
> These particular requests came from the chief of police at Beida, through the cursive handwriting of the little border town's scribe. At first they were for food. Then last week came a plea for shrouds.
>
> "We have nothing in which to bury our dead, and 15 children died yesterday," said the letter addressed to Peter Verney, the Save the Children (SCF) representative in Geneina.

As Vallely related the story, so little food was coming into Geneina from Khartoum on account of floods and other difficulties that there was not enough to send onward to Beida, about fifty miles south along Sudan's western border with Chad. Those dying of starvation in Beida were all Chadian refugees, and the local Sudanese commissioner Sherife was not cooperating in the release of emergency grain. Finally, however, Verney managed to secure 150 sacks of food and seed. Then the head of the Sudanese haulage firm doubled and tripled the price. Verney did not have enough cash on hand to pay for the lorry and in desperation went to the local army brigadier in Geneina, Ibrahim Muhammad, who told Verney, "This is the situation everywhere. No food is reaching the extremities. It reaches the hands but not the fingers. Of course you can have one of my trucks."

Three hours after leaving Geneina for Beida, the food lorry got caught in a torrential rain. Vallely and the driver whom Verney had rented were stuck for nine hours in the mud; sixty peasants helped to dig the two men out.

It was two days before we reached Beida. . . . We were welcomed by Muhammad Ahmed Bashir, the local chief of police. Over sweet tea on the rafia mat before his office he was effusive in his thanks for the food.

"I will put it straight into the store with the other food." The other food? "Yes, we already have 140 bags in store but we have had no authority from Sherife or his nephew Ali Mansour to distribute it."

Because of Sudanese bureaucracy, Chadians were starving to death with food only a few feet away. The next day, Ali Mansour, the executive officer of the rural council, agreed to distribute the grain. "You will take my photograph," he said to a news agency photographer with Vallely. "This will be good for me."

The distribution caused a riot among the refugees. Sudanese soldiers responded by lashing at the crowd with whips in all directions. The news agency photographer started snapping away, even though editors had become bored with photos of starving Africans. The photographer confided to Vallely that starving people being whipped had novelty value that would result in his pictures gaining wide distribution. Sure enough, the photos of the riot in Beida were picked up in Europe.

*   *   *

I arrived in El Geneina a few weeks after Vallely had, and my first stop was at a feeding center for Chadian refugees fleeing civil war as well as drought. My guide asked if I would like to see a newborn baby. I said certainly. Although the population was growing all the time—and even in good years, food production could not keep pace with the population increase—out here I still could think only of new life in the abstract. In the flesh, it was beyond my comprehension under the present circumstances, with mass death all around.

I was taken to a wattle hut. In the corner stood a little Chadian boy, a broomstick-like figure, who was suffering from marasmus. He looked just like so many of the famine victims the U.S. audience had become used to seeing on television. In place of sorghum, his mother was boiling herbs in a pot. Beside her, concealed under a coarse blanket, lay the newborn baby, a boy, who, when the blanket was pulled back, looked astonishingly healthy. A relief worker explained that the effects of the mother's malnutrition were not visible on the child.

But I couldn't help wondering what was going to happen to that baby. Would he grow up to be as malnourished as his older brother? If, indeed, the baby lived that long. Chad, Sudan, and Ethiopia all were embroiled in civil wars that had helped spark famines. What could be the future of such a child, trapped in the soft, sandy center of a fragmenting world?

selected bibliography

BOOKS

Brzezinski, Zbigniew. *Power and Principle.* New York: Farrar Straus Giroux, 1983.

Canetti, Elias. *Crowds and Power.* London: Victor Gollancz, 1962.

Caputo, Philip. *Horn of Africa.* New York: Dell, 1980.

Carter, Jimmy. *Keeping Faith: Memoirs of a President.* New York: Bantam, 1982.

Clay, Jason W., and Holcomb, Bonnie K. *Politics and the Ethiopian Famine, 1984–1985.* Cambridge, Mass.: Cultural Survival, 1986.

Conquest, Robert. *The Harvest of Sorrow.* New York: Oxford University Press, 1986.

Farer, Tom J. *War Clouds on the Horn of Africa: The Widening Storm.* Washington, D.C.: Carnegie Endowment for International Peace, 1979.

Gill, Peter. *A Year in the Death of Africa.* Boulder, Co.: Paladin, 1986.

Hancock, Graham. *Ethiopia: The Challenge of Hunger.* London: Victor Gollancz, 1985.

Hancock, Graham; Pankhurst, Richard; and Willetts, Duncan. *Under Ethiopian Skies.* London: Editions HL, 1983.

Harris, Myles F. *Breakfast in Hell.* New York: Poseidon Press, 1987.

Hoagland, Edward. *African Calliope: A Journey to the Sudan.* New York: Random House, 1979.

Holt, P. M., and Daly, M. W. *The History of the Sudan.* London: Weidenfeld and Nicolson, 1961.

Hudson, Michael C. *Arab Politics: The Search for Legitimacy.* New Haven, Conn.: Yale University Press, 1977.

Jacobs, Dan. *The Brutality of Nations.* New York: Alfred A. Knopf, 1987.

Jenner, Michael. *Yemen Rediscovered.* London: Longman Group Limited and Yemen Tourism Company, 1983.

Kapuscinski, Ryszard. *The Emperor: Downfall of an Autocrat.* New York: Harcourt Brace Jovanovich, 1983.

Khalid, Mansour. *Nimeiri and the Revolution of Dis-May.* London: KPI Limited, 1985.

Korn, David A. *Ehiopia, The United States and the Soviet Union.* Carbondale: Southern Illinois University Press, 1986.

Lamb, David. *The Africans: Encounters from the Sudan to the Cape.* New York: Random House, 1983.

Lefort, Rene. *Ethiopie: Revolution Heretique.* Paris: Francoise Maspero, 1981.

Levine, Donald N. *Wax and Gold: Tradition and Innovation in Ethiopian Culture.* Chicago: University of Chicago Press, 1965.

Mansfield, Peter. *The Arabs.* London: Allen Lane, 1976.

Mockler, Anthony. *Haile Selassie's War: The Italian-Ethiopian Campaign, 1935–1941.* Oxford: Oxford University Press, 1984.

Moorehead, Alan. *The White Nile.* London: Hamish Hamilton, 1960.

_____. *The Blue Nile.* London: Hamish Hamilton, 1962.

Orwell, George. *The Penguin Essays of George Orwell.* Harmondsworth: Penguin, 1984.

Ottaway, Marina, and Ottaway, David. *Ethiopia: Empire in Revolution.* Africana Publishing Company, 1978.

Parfitt, Tudor. *Operation Moses: The Untold Story of the Exodus of the Falasha Jews from Ethiopia.* London: Weidenfeld and Nicolson, 1985.

Revel, Jean-Francois. *How Democracies Perish.* Garden City, N.Y.: Doubleday, 1983.

Seale, Patrick. *The Shaping of an Arab Statesman: Abd al-Hamid Sharaf and the Modern Arab World.* London: Quartet, 1983.

Selassie, Bereket Habte. *Conflict and Intervention in the Horn of Africa.* New York: Monthly Review Press, 1980.

Selassie, Kiros Habte, and Dina, Mazengia. *Ethiopia: A Short Illustrated History.* Addis Ababa: Ethiopian Ministry of Education and Fine Arts, 1969.

Shawcross, William. *The Quality of Mercy: Cambodia, Holocaust and Modern Conscience.* London: Andre Deutsch, 1984.

Sulzberger, C. L. *A Long Row of Candles: Memoirs & Diaries, 1934–1954.* New York: Macmillan, 1969.

Timberlake, Lloyd. *Africa in Crisis: The Causes, The Cures of Environmental Bankruptcy.* Washington, D.C.: Earthscan, 1985.

Traveller's Guide to Yemen. Sana'a: Yemen Tourist Company, 1983.

Ungar, Sanford J. *Africa: The People and Politics of an Emerging Continent.* New York: Simon and Schuster, 1978, 1985.

Vance, Cyrus. *Hard Choices: Critical Years in America's Foreign Policy.* New York: Simon and Schuster, 1983.

Waugh, Evelyn. *Remote People: A Report from Ethiopia and British Africa, 1930–31.* Harmondsworth: Penguin, 1931, 1985.

World Human Rights Guide, London. London: The Economist, 1986.

Wolfe, Bertram D. *Three Who Made a Revolution.* New York: Dell, 1948.

Worrall, Nick. *Sudan.* London: Quartet, 1980.

LETTERS, REPORTS, AND SUPPLEMENTS

"Briefing Packet: Famine in the Non-Government Held Areas of Eritrea and Ethiopia, and Refugees in Eastern Sudan." Khartoum: Interfam Information Project, August 1985.

"Briefing Packet on Eritrea and Tigre." Khartoum: The Information Desk, March 1985.

Clark, Lance. "Report on Refugee Influx to Northwest Somalia in 1986."

Clay, Jason W. "Refugees in Somalia Flee Ethiopian Collectivization" (1986).

Clay, Jason W. Letters to Robert D. Kaplan about Cultural Survival's research methods, October 1, 1986, November 21, 1986.

Cohen, John M. "Agrarian Reform in Ethiopia: The Situation on the Eve of the Revolution's 10th Anniversary." Cambridge, Mass.: Harvard Institute for International Development, 1984.

Keyes, Alan L. "Ethiopia: The U.N.'s Role." Statement before Subcommittee on African Affairs of the Senate Foreign Relations Committee, Washington, D.C., March 6, 1986. Washington, D.C.: U.S. Department of State, Bureau of Public Affairs, 1986.

Legum, Colin, and Firebrace, James. "Eritrea and Tigre." *Minority Rights Group,* Report no. 5 (1983).

Marxist Leninist League of Tigre. "Declaration of the Founding Congress." Khartoum: Tigre People's Liberation Front, 1985.

Niggli, Peter. "Ethiopia: Deportations and Enforced-Labor Camps." Berliner Missionswerk, May 1985.

Phillips, James A. "Ethiopia's Kremlin Connection." The Heritage Foundation, Report no. 404 (January 17, 1985).

"Power and Famine in Ethiopia." *The East-West Papers,* no. 5 (December 1986).

Smith, J. Edwin. Eight-page supplement on Eritrea, *The Atlanta Journal-Constitution,* June 22, 1986.

U.N. High Commissioner for Refugees. "Briefing Note on Refugees in the Sudan." Khartoum: UNHCR, June 9, 1985.

U.S. Embassy, Khartoum, Office of Refugees Affairs. "Focus on Refugees." (April 1984).

U.S. Senate, Subcommittee on Immigration and Refugee Policy, Committee of the Judiciary. "Ethiopia and Sudan One Year Later: Refugees and Famine Recovery Needs." 99th Cong., 2nd sess. Washington, D.C.: U.S. Government Printing Office, 1986.

Washington Quarterly: Washington Review of Strategic and International Studies. "Horn of Africa." White Paper (May 1978).

NEWSPAPER AND MAGAZINE ARTICLES

Bennett, Jon. "Beyond Banditry." *The New Statesmen,* June 17, 1983.

Blundy, David. "Cover-Up." *The Sunday Times,* November 3, 1985.

Brittain, Victoria. "Sudan's Hidden War Escalates as Ugandans Join the Fray." *The Guardian,* June 13, 1986.

Brooke, James. "Marxist Constitution Takes Effect in Ethiopia." *International Herald Tribune* (New York Times Service), February 24, 1987.

———. "As Ethiopia's Famine Threat Subsides, Western Aid Efforts Shift to Development." *International Herald Tribune* (New York Times Service), March 13, 1987.

Dines, Mary. "The Cancer of Religion: Ethiopia." *Index on Censorship,* no. 5 (1983).

Eshete, Aleme. "Betrayal of the Revolution." *Sudan Times,* October 20, 1986.

Girardet, Edward. "Meet the Pagoulatoses and Their Hotel, the Place to Stay in Khartoum." *The Christian Science Monitor,* July 8, 1985.

Harden, Blaine, "Ethiopian Drive to Villagize Is Forcing Millions to Relocate." *International Herald Tribune* (Washington Post Service), December 18, 1985.

―――. "Resettlement Means Death for Thousands in Ethiopia." *International Herald Tribune* (Washington Post Service), March 11, 1986.

―――. "Ethiopian Rebels Kill 2 in U.S. Aid Program." *International Herald Tribune* (Washington Post Service), March 29–30, 1986.

―――. "Hunger Is a Weapon in Sudan's Civil War." *International Herald Tribune* (Washington Post Service), August 29, 1986.

―――. "Civil War in Sudan Changes Lifestyle of Nomads." *International Herald Tribune* (Washington Post Service), September 10, 1986.

―――. "Sudan Rebel Leader 'Not Repentant' Despite Famine, Downing of Aircraft." *International Herald Tribune* (Washington Post Service), September 19, 1986.

Harrison, Charles. "Ugandans Hold Up Sudan Aid." *The Times,* August 28, 1986.

Hatch, Orrin. "Keep Ethiopia Part of the Reagan Doctrine." *Wall Street Journal,* April 4, 1986.

Henze, Paul B. "The Dilemmas of the Horn." *The National Interest,* no. 2 (Winter 1985/86).

Hertzog, Gilles. "Le scandale de l'aide." *L'Express,* October 3, 1986.

Hirst, David. "How the Eritreans Achieved Sex Equality Under Fire." *The Guardian,* February 19, 1985.

Hoben, Allen. "The Origins of Famine." *The New Republic,* January 21, 1985.

Johnson, Paul. "How Tyrannies Flourish." *The New Republic,* January 21, 1985.

Kaplan, Robert D. "Ethiopian Exodus." *The New Republic,* January 21, 1985.

―――. "How to Make Col. Mengistu Cry 'Uncle' in Eritrea." *Wall Street Journal/Europe,* May 14, 1985.

―――. "Ethiopian Regime Bites the Hand Feeding Its People." *Wall Street Journal/Europe,* July 17, 1985.

―――. "Ethiopia: Africa's Killing Fields." *Wall Street Journal/Europe,* October 1, 1985.

―――. "Sudan: A Microcosm of Africa's Ills." *The Atlantic Monthly* (April 1986).

―――. "The Battle for North Yemen." *Wall Street Journal,* April 15, 1986.

―――. "Behind Ethiopia's Hunger." *The American Spectator* (June 1986).

―――. "Why Sudan Starves on Western Aid." *Wall Street Journal/Europe,* October 29, 1986.

―――. "*The Harvest of Sorrow* by Robert Conquest" (Book Review). *The American Spectator* (April 1987).

―――. "Out of Africa." *The New Republic,* July 6, 1987.

Keating, Robert. "Live Aid: The Terrible Truth." *Spin* (July 1986).

———. "Sympathy for the Devil." *Spin* (September 1986).

Legum, Colin. "Ethiopia: A Regime of Torture." *International Herald Tribune*, May 20, 1986.

Matthews, Christopher J. "The Road to Korem." *The New Republic*, January 21, 1985.

May, Clifford D. "War Rivals Drought in Africa's Hunger Crisis." *New York Times*, September 29, 1985.

Merritt, Giles. "Americans May be Hooked on Africa." *International Herald Tribune*, October 1985.

Owen, Richard. "No Roubles in the Live Aid Fund." *The Times*, July 23, 1985.

Puddington, Arch. "Ethiopia: The Communist Uses of Famine." *Commentary* (April 1986).

Randal, Jonathan C. "Relief Effort Grinds to a Halt on Sudan Railways." *The Manchester Guardian* (Washington Post Service), Summer 1985.

———. "War in Southern Sudan Heightens Food Crisis, Hampers Relief Effort." *International Herald Tribune* (Washington Post Service), July 1, 1986.

Revzin, Philip. "With Famine Easing, Many Ethiopians Flee Collectivizing Farms." *Wall Street Journal/Europe*, May 26, 1986.

Rogg, Margaret L. "Sudan Says Rebels Downed Civilian Plane Carrying 60." *International Herald Tribune* (New York Times Service), August 18, 1986.

Rule, Sheila. "For Ethiopia, New Villages, New Concern." *New York Times*, June 22, 1986.

———. "To Ethiopians Who Flee, Somalis Offer Squalor." *New York Times*, July 12, 1986.

Shepherd, Jack. "Ethiopia: The Use of Food as an Instrument of U.S. Foreign Policy." *Issue* 14 (1985).

Suau, Anthony. "Eritrea: Region in Rebellion." *National Geographic* (September 1985).

Tucker, Jonathan B. "The Politics of Famine in Ethiopia." *The Nation*, January 19, 1985.

Tyler, Patrick E., and Ottaway, David B. "Ethiopian Security Police Seized, Tortured CIA Agent." *Washington Post*, April 25, 1986.

Vallely, Paul. "Famine: Russia and U.S. on Collusion Course." *The Times*, June 4, 1985.

———. "Riding the Lifeline Lorry." *The Times*, July 26, 1985.

Wall Street Journal/Europe. "Today's Holocaust (Editorial)," January 29, 1986.

Wieseltier, Leon. "Brothers and Keepers." *The New Republic*, February 11, 1985.

Wilde, James; Desmond, Edward W.; and Russell, George. "Flight from Fear." *Time*, January 21, 1985.

Wilde, James, and Greenwald, John. "Red Star over the Horn of Africa." *Time*, August 4, 1986.

Wilde, James, and Muller, Henry. "'To Free Ourselves from Backwardness,' Iron-willed and Icy, Mengistu Haile Mariam Defends His Policies." *Time,* August 4, 1986.

Wilkinson, Ray, and Deming, Angus. "Master Plan—Misery." *Newsweek,* May 5, 1986.

Willis, David K. "U.S. Set to Send Food to Rebel-held Provinces." *Christian Science Monitor,* July 20–26, 1985.

index